Modern Critical Interpretations

Modern Critical Interpretations

THE OLD MAN AND THE SEA

Edited and with an introduction by
Harold Bloom
Sterling Professor of the Humanities
Yale University

CHELSEA HOUSE PUBLISHERS
Philadelphia

Bloom's Modern Critical Interpretations: The Old Man and the Sea

© 1999 by Infobase Publishing
Introduction © 1999 by Harold Bloom

Chelsea House
An imprint of Infobase Publishing
132 West 31st Street
New York NY 10001

Library of Congress Cataloging-in-Publication Data
The old man and the sea / edited and with an introduction
by Harold Bloom.
     p.   cm. — (Modern critical interpretations)
  Includes bibliographical references and index.
  ISBN 0-7910-4778-4 (alk. paper)
  1. Hemingway, Ernest, 1899–1961. Old man and the sea.
2. Aged men in literature. I. Bloom, Harold. II. Series.
  PS3515.E370528   1998
  813'.52—dc21   98-24047

You can find Chelsea House on the World Wide Web at
http://www.chelseahouse.com

Printed in the United States of America

Lake 10 9 8 7 6 5 4

This book is printed on acid-free paper.

Contents

Editor's Note

My Introduction meditates upon some of the limitations of Hemingway's late short novel, while granting the continuing popularity of *The Old Man and the Sea*. After a gracious tribute from the novelist William Faulkner, the critical essays begin with Carlos Baker's account of the love between the old man and the boy.

Leo Gurko finds a new kind of heroism in *The Old Man and the Sea*, while Delmore Schwartz sees the book as the extension of the American Dream. For Joseph Waldmeir, the short novel is an exercise in humanistic religion, after which Nemi D'Agostino sees the universe of the book as fundamentally non-religious.

Clinton S. Burhans Jr., is persuaded that Santiago is a tragic hero, while Robert P. Weeks manifests considerably more skepticism. In Bickford Sylvester's view, the book is a triumph of paradox and symbolism, after which we are given Philip Young's study of Hemingway's self-revision.

Claire Rosenfield finds a primitive religious structure, rather than a Christian one, in *The Old Man and the Sea*, while Sheldon Norman Grebstein analyzes Hemingway's writerly craft in the book.

To Linda W. Wagner, imperfect human love is the harmonizing force in Hemingway's narrative, while G.R. Wilson Jr., finds instead images of Christian incarnation and redemption.

James H. Justus investigates the patterns of what he calls "the aesthetics of failure" in the book, after which Gerry Brenner uncovers Oedipal patterns in Santiago.

The contrasts in structure between Faulkner's *The Bear* and Hemingway's short novel are explored by David Timms, after which Bickford Sylvester returns to conclude this volume with a description of *The Old Man and the Sea*'s Cuban background.

Introduction

Hemingway's greatness is in his short stories, which rival any other master of the form, be it Joyce or Chekhov or Isaak Babel. Of his novels, one is constrained to suggest reservations, even of the very best: *The Sun Also Rises*. *The Old Man and the Sea* is the most popular of Hemingway's later works, but this short novel alas is an indeliberate self-parody, though less distressingly so than *Across the River and Into the Trees*, composed just before it. There is a gentleness, a nuanced tenderness, that saves *The Old Man and the Sea* from the self-indulgences of *Across the River and Into the Trees*. In an interview with George Plimpton, Hemingway stated his pride in what he considered to be the aesthetic economy of *The Old Man and the Sea*:

> *The Old Man and the Sea* could have been over a thousand pages long and had every character in the village in it and all the processes of the way they made their living, were born, educated, bore children, etc. That is done excellently and well by other writers. In writing you are limited by what has already been done satisfactorily. So I have tried to learn to do something else. First I have tried to eliminate everything unnecessary to conveying experience to the reader so that after he or she has read something it will become part of his or her experience and seem actually to have happened. This is very hard to do and I've worked at it very hard.
>
> Anyway, to skip how it is done, I had unbelievable luck this time and could convey the experience completely and have it be one that no one had ever conveyed. The luck was that I had a good man and a good boy and lately writers have forgotten there still are such things. Then the ocean is worth writing about just as a man is. So I was lucky there. I've seen the marlin

1

mate and known about that. So I leave that out. I've seen a
school (or pod) of more than fifty sperm whales in that same
stretch of water and once harpooned one nearly sixty feet in
length and lost him. So I left that out. But the knowledge is
what makes the underwater part of the iceberg.

The Old Man and the Sea unfortunately is too long, rather than exquisitely
curtailed, as Hemingway believed. The art of ellipsis, or leaving things out,
indeed is the great virtue of Hemingway's best short stories. But *The Old
Man and the Sea* is tiresomely repetitive, and Santiago the old fisherman is
too clearly an idealization of Hemingway himself, who thinks in the style
of the novelist attempting to land a great work:

> Only I have no luck anymore. But who knows? Maybe today.
> Every day is a new day. It is better to be lucky. But I would
> rather be exact. Then when luck comes you are ready.

Contemplating the big fish, Santiago is even closer to Hemingway
the literary artist, alone with his writerly quest:

> His choice had been to stay in the deep dark water far out
> beyond all snares and traps and treacheries. My choice was to
> go there to find him beyond all people. Beyond all people in the
> world. Now we are joined together and have been since noon.
> And no one to help either one of us.

Santiago's ordeal, first in his struggle with the big fish, and then in
fighting against the sharks, is associated by Hemingway with Christ's agony
and triumph. Since it is so difficult to disentangle Santiago and
Hemingway, this additional identification is rather unfortunate in its
aesthetic consequences, because it can render a reader rather uncomfort-
able. There is a longing or nostalgia for faith in Hemingway, at least from
The Sun Also Rises until the end of his career. But if *The Old Man and the Sea*
is a Christian allegory, then the book carries more intended significance
than it can bear. The big fish is no Moby-Dick or Jobean adversary;
Santiago loves the fish and sees it as his double. What can we do with
Santiago-as-Christ when we attempt to interpret the huge marlin?
William Faulkner praised *The Old Man and the Sea* as being
Hemingway's best work, but then Faulkner also considered Thomas Wolfe
to be the greatest American novelist of the century. The story, far from

Hemingway's best, cannot be both a parable of Christian redemption and of a novelist's triumph, not so much because these are incompatible, but because so repetitive and self-indulgent a narrative cannot bear that double burden. Sentimentality, or emotion in excess of the object, floods *The Old Man and the Sea*. Hemingway himself is so moved by Hemingway that his famous, laconic style yields to uncharacteristic overwriting. We are not shown "grace under pressure," but something closer to Narcissus observing himself in the mirror of the sea.

WILLIAM FAULKNER

Review of The Old Man and the Sea

His best. Time may show it to be the best single piece of any of us, I mean his and my contemporaries. This time, he discovered God, a Creator. Until now, his men and women had made themselves, shaped themselves out of their own clay; their victories and defeats were at the hands of each other, just to prove to themselves or one another how tough they could be. But this time, he wrote about pity: about something somewhere that made them all: the old man who had to catch the fish and then lose it, the fish that had to be caught and then lost, the sharks which had to rob the old man of his fish; made them all and loved them all and pitied them all. It's all right. Praise God that whatever made and loves and pities Hemingway and me kept him from touching it any further.

From *Ernest Hemingway: Six Decades of Criticism.* © 1987 by Linda W. Wagner.

CARLOS BAKER

The Boy and the Lions

The relationship between Santiago and the boy Manolo is of a special and memorable kind. In the light of the experiment in symbolic doubling which Hemingway tried in *Across The River and Into The Trees*, the meaning of this other relationship becomes clear. In one of her aspects, Renata stands for Colonel Cantwell's lost youth. Manolo fulfills a similar purpose, and with greater success in that we do not have to overcome the doubt raised by the difference of sexes between the Colonel and his lady. To claim such a purpose for Manolo is not, of course, to discount his dramatic function, which is to heighten our sympathy with the old fisherman. At the beginning and end of the story, we watch Santiago through the boy's admiring and pitying eyes. From the charitable . . . Martin, owner of The Terrace, Manolo brings Santiago a last supper of black beans and rice, fried bananas, stew, and two bottles of beer. On the morning of the expedition, Manolo arranges for the simple breakfast of coffee in condensed milk cans. He also procures the albacores and sardines which Santiago will use for bait. After helping to launch the skiff, the boy sees Santiago off in the dark with a wish for his luck on this eighty-fifth day. At the close of the story, after the ordeal, Manolo brings coffee and food for the old man's waking, and ointment for his injured hands, commiserating on the loss, and planning for a future when they will work side by side again. The love of Manolo for Santiago is that of a disciple for a

From *Hemingway: The Writer as Artist*. © 1952 by Carlos Baker.

master in the arts of fishing. It is also the love of a son for an adopted father.

But from Santiago's point of view the relationship runs deeper. He has known the boy for years, from the period of childhood up to this later time when Manolo stands, strong and lucky and confident, on the edge of young manhood. Like many other aging men, Santiago finds something reassuring about the overlay of the past upon the present. Through the agency of Manolo he is able to recapture in his imagination, and therefore to a certain degree in fact, the same strength and confidence which distinguished his own young manhood as a fisherman, earning him the title of *El Campéon*.

During the old man's ordeal, the two phrases, "I wish the boy was here," and "I wish I had the boy," play across Santiago's mind often enough to merit special attention. In each instance he means exactly what he says: the presence of the boy would be a help in a time of crisis. But he is also invoking by means of these phrases the strength and courage of his youth. Soon after he has hooked his marlin and knows that he must hang onto the line for some time, Santiago says, "I wish I had the boy." Immediately his resolution tightens. During the first night he says it again. He is just reflecting that "no one should be alone in their old age," though in this case it is unavoidable. Again, and as if the mere mention of the boy were a kind of talisman, he then resolves to eat the tuna he has caught, though the thought of the raw fish sickens him, "in order to keep strong." Later the same night, he says aloud, "I wish the boy was here"—and promptly settles himself against the planks of the bow for another period of endurance. Near dawn he says again, "I wish I had the boy." Then he upbraids himself for wishful thinking. "But you haven't got the boy, he thought. You have only yourself and you had better work back to the last line now . . . and cut it away and hook up the two reserve coils." So he does exactly that.

As he summons the courage to eat the raw tuna for his breakfast on the second day, he links the boy and salt in what amounts to a metaphor: "I wish the boy were here and that I had some salt." Then he proves to himself that he has enough of both in their metaphorical meaning to eat the tuna and renew his waning strength. While he wills to unknot the cramp, he thinks that "if the boy was here" a little massaging would loosen the muscles of the forearm and maybe help the still useless gnarled claw of the hand. Yet when, soon afterwards, his great marlin breaches, Santiago summons the strength he needs to play his fish.

On the next breaching it is the same. While the marlin leaps again and again, unseen in the darkness of the second night, and while the old man and his line are both strained and stretched almost to the breaking-point, he triples the refrain: "If the boy was here he would wet the coils of line . . . Yes. If the boy were here. If the boy were here." Once more the effect of the invocation is nearly magical as if, by means of it, some of the strength of youth flowed in to sustain the limited powers of age. Always, just after he has said the words, Santiago manages to reach down into the well of his courage for one more dipperful. Then he goes on.

From this point onwards, having served its purpose, the refrain vanishes. It is not until the return voyage, while the old man reflects Job-like on the problem of the connection between sin and suffering and while the sharks collect their squadrons unseen in the dark waters, that the boy's image returns again. "Everything kills everything else in some way," he tells himself. "Fishing kills me exactly as it keeps me alive." Then he corrects the misapprehensions that can come from false philosophizing. "The boy keeps me alive . . . I must not deceive myself too much." It is good, at this point, that the old man has the thought of the boy to keep him alive. For the sharks wait, and a very bad time is just ahead.

In the night in which he is preparing for betrayal by the sharks, though he does not yet absolutely know that they will come, Santiago has recourse to yet another sustaining image—a pride of lions he once saw at play on an African beach when he was a young man like Manolo. Hemingway early establishes a clear symbolic connection between the boy and the lions. "When I was your age," Santiago says, "I was before the mast on a square rigged ship that ran to Africa and I have seen lions on the beaches in the evening." Manolo's answer—"I know. You told me."—indicates not only that the reminiscence has arisen before in their conversations, but also that the incident of the lions is a pleasant obsession in Santiago's mind. "There is for every man," writes the poet Yeats, "some one scene, some one adventure, some one picture that is the image of his secret life, and this one image, if he would but brood over it his life long, would lead his soul." Santiago finds such an image in the lions of his youthful experience.

The night before his ordeal, after the boy has left him to sleep, the old man dreams of the lions. "He was asleep in a short time and he dreamed of Africa when he was a boy and the long golden beaches and the white beaches, so white they hurt your eyes, and the high capes and the great brown mountains. He lived along that coast now every night and in his dreams he heard the surf roar and saw the native boats come riding through it. He smelled the tar and oakum of the deck as he slept and he smelled the smell of Africa that the land breeze brought at morning. Usually when he smelled the land breeze he woke up and dressed to go and wake the boy. But tonight the smell of the land breeze came very early and he knew it was too early in his dream and went on dreaming to see the white peaks of the Islands rising from the sea and then he dreamed of the different harbours and roadsteads of the Canary Islands."

Santiago "no longer dreamed of storms, nor of women, nor of great occurrences, nor of great fish, nor fights, nor contests of strength, nor of his wife. He only dreamed of places now and of the lions on the beach. They played like young cats in the dusk and he loved them as he loved the boy."

Early in the afternoon of his second day out, having strengthened his resolution by the saying of the prayers, Santiago thinks again about his lions. The marlin is pulling steadily. "I wish he'd sleep and I could sleep and dream about the lions," thinks Santiago. "Why are the lions the main thing that is left?" Much later the same day, "cramping himself against the line with all his body," and "putting all his weight onto his right hand," the old man manages to sleep. Soon then he begins to dream of the long yellow beach, and in the dream, we are told, "he saw the first of the lions come down onto it in the early dark and then the other lions came and he rested his chin on the wood of the bows where the ship lay anchored with the evening off-shore breeze and he waited to see if there would be more lions and he was happy." In his old age and the time of his suffering, Santiago is supported by the memory of his youth and the strength of his youth. Living so, in the past, he is happy. But there is the further realization that "the child is father to the man." Luckily for this old man, he has also the thought of the strength of the boy Manolo, a young lion of just the age Santiago was when he first sailed to Africa. These together help him to endure.

They help in a very notable way. For the boy and the lions are related to one of the fundamental psychological laws of Santiago's—and indeed of human—nature. This is the constant wave-like operation of bracing and relaxation. The boy braces, the lions relax, as in the systolic-diastolic movement of the human heart. The phenomenon is related to the alternation of sleep and waking through the whole range of physical nature. But it is also a law which fulfills itself on the level of mentality. Its effects can be traced in our reaction to works of literature like this story of the acquisition and loss of the great marlin. The basic rhythms of the novel, in its maritime sections, are essentially those of the groundswell of the sea. Again and again as the action unfolds, the reader may find that he is gradually brought up to a degree of quiet tension which he is barely able to accept, as in the ascent by a small craft of a slow enormous wave. When he has reached the theoretical peak of his resistance, the crest passes and he suddenly relaxes into a trough of rest. The rhythm of the story appears to be built on such a stress-yield, brace-relax alternation. The impression is furthered by the constant tension which Santiago and his fish maintain on the line which joins them. Again and again one finds the old man telling himself that he has stretched the cord to a degree just short of the breaking-point. Then the stress relaxes, and the involved reader relaxes with it. This prolonged tug-of-war involves not only the fisherman and his fish but also the reader and his own emotions.

The planned contiguity of the old man with the double image of the boy and the lions converts the story of Santiago, in one of its meanings, into a parable of youth and age. It may be suggested that Hemingway, who read the whole of Conrad during the days of his writing apprenticeship in Paris and Toronto, has recollected the central strategy of Conrad's long short story, "Youth." For that story is built upon a brilliant contrast between young and old manhood. The ill-fated voyage of the barque *Judea*, out of London bound for Bangkok, shows young Marlow, with all the illusions and prowess of his youth, working side by side with old Captain Beard, the ship's master and a brave man. "He was sixty, if a day," says Marlow of the captain. "And he had blue eyes in that old face of his, which were amazingly like a boy's, with that candid expression some quite common men preserve to the end of their days by a rare internal gift of simplicity of heart and rectitude of soul." Again Marlow says, as the fated ship beats her way through a sea of trouble, that Beard was "immense in the singleness of his idea."

It may of course be a coincidence that these are qualities which Santiago shares. If so, it is a happy one. Two "quite common men" rise to the level of the heroic through simplicity of heart, rectitude of soul, and that immensity which is gained for them through the singleness of their concentration on a particular object. "Do or die" is the motto which adorns in flaking gilt the stern-timbers of the old *Judea*. The same words might with equal justice be carved into the weather-beaten wood of Santiago's skiff.

Conrad's story depends for its effect not only upon the contrast between young Marlow and old Beard but also, since the story is told some twenty years after the event, upon the contrast between the aging Marlow and his remembrance of his own youthful self. Santiago happily recalls the lions on the shore of Africa. Marlow recollects the brown men on the jetty of a Javanese port. This was where the small boats from the wrecked *Judea*, filled with exhausted men, at last reached the land. "I remember my youth," says Marlow, "and the feeling that will never come back any more—the feeling that I could last for ever, outlast the sea, the earth, and all men; the deceitful feeling that lures us on to joys, to perils, to love, to vain effort—to death; the triumphant conviction of strength, the heat of life in the handful of dust, the glow in the heart that with every year grows dim, grows cold, grows small, and expires." This feeling, which William Hazlitt has well described as the feeling of immortality in youth, is closely associated in Marlow's mind with the East—"the mysterious shores, the still water, the lands of the brown nations." As he tells his auditors: "For me, all the East is contained in that vision of my youth. It is all in that moment when I opened my young eyes on it. I came upon it from a tussle with the sea—and I was young—and I saw it looking at me. And this is all that is left of it! Only a moment; a moment of strength, of romance, of glamour—of youth!"

For Santiago it is not the coast of Java but that of Africa, not the faces of the brown men crowding the jetty but the playing lions, which carry the associations of youth, strength, and even immortality. "This is all that is left of it," cries Marlow of his youthful vision. "Why are the lions the main thing that is left?" cries Hemingway's old man in the midst of his ordeal. For both of them, in Marlow's words, it is "the time to remember." Santiago manages to put his vision to work in the great trial of his old age. "I told the boy I was a strange old man," he says. "Now is when I must prove it." And the author adds: "The thousand times that he had proved it meant nothing. Now he was proving it again. Each time was a new time and he never thought about the past when he was doing it." If he does not, at such times, think about the past to brood over it, he periodically calls back what it means to him through the double vision of the boy and the lions. If he can prove his mettle for the thousand-and-first time, there is no reason short of death why he cannot continue to prove it, as long as his vision lasts.

Of how many events in the course of human life may this not be said? It is Marlow once more who reminds us of the way in which one account of one man on one journey can extend outwards in our imaginations until it easily becomes a paradigm of the course of all men's lives. "You fellows know," says Marlow, beginning his account of the *Judea*, "there are those voyages that seem ordered for the illustration of life, that might stand for a symbol of existence. You fight, work, sweat, nearly kill yourself, sometimes do kill yourself, trying to accomplish something—and you can't. Not from any fault of yours." If it is so with the *Judea*, bound for Bangkok, do or die, it is so with Santiago of Havana, bound for home, with the sharks just beginning to smell the blood of his great fish. Do or die. In such works as these we all put to sea. Santiago makes his voyage on what used to be known as the Spanish Main. But it is also, by the process of synecdoche, that more extensive main, or mainstream, where we all drift or sail, with or against the wind, in fair weather or foul, with our prize catches and our predatory sharks, and each of us, perhaps, like the ancient mariner of Coleridge, with some kind of albatross hanging round his neck.

LEO GURKO

The Heroic Impulse in The Old Man and the Sea

Most of Hemingway's novels emphasize what men cannot do, and define the world's limitations, cruelties, or built-in evil. *The Old Man and the Sea* is remarkable for its stress on what men can do and on the world as an arena where heroic deeds are possible. The universe inhabited by Santiago, the old Cuban fisherman, is not free of tragedy and pain but these are transcended, and the affirming tone is in sharp contrast with the pessimism permeating such books as *The Sun Also Rises* and *A Farewell to Arms*.

One aspect of this universe, familiar from the earlier works, is its changelessness. The round of Nature—which includes human nature—is not only eternal but eternally the same. The sun not only rises, it rises always, and sets and rises again without change of rhythm. The relationship of Nature to man proceeds through basic patterns that never vary. Therefore, despite the fact that a story by Hemingway is always full of action, the action takes place inside a world that is fundamentally static.

Moreover, its processes are purely secular in character: Hemingway's figures are often religious but their religion is peripheral rather than central to their lives. In *The Old Man and the Sea*, Santiago, the principal figure, is a primitive Cuban, at once religious and superstitious. Yet neither his religion nor his superstitious beliefs are relevant to his tragic experience with the great marlin; they do not create it or in any way control its meaning. The

From *Twentieth Century Interpretations of The Old Man and the Sea*. © 1955 by the National Council of Teachers of English.

fisherman himself, knowing what it is all about, relies on his own resources and not on God (in whom he devoutly believes, just as Jake Barnes, while calling himself a bad Catholic, is also a devout believer). If he succeeds in catching the fish, he "will say ten Our Fathers and ten Hail Marys . . . and make a pilgrimage to the Virgen de Cobre," but these are rituals that come after the event and have no significant relationship with it.

In this universe, changeless and bare of divinity, everyone has his fixed role to play. Santiago's role is to pursue the great marlin, "That which I was born for," he reflects; the marlin's is to live in the deepest parts of the sea and escape the pursuit of man. The two of them struggle with each other to the death, but without animosity or hatred. On the contrary, the old man feels a deep affection and admiration for the fish. He admires its great strength as it pulls his skiff out to sea, and becomes conscious of its nobility as the two grow closer and closer together, in spirit as well as space, during their long interlude on the Gulf Stream. In the final struggle between them, his hands bleeding, his body racked with fatigue and pain, the old man reflects in his exhaustion:

> You are killing me, fish. . . . But you have a right to. Never have I seen a greater, or more beautiful, or a calmer or a more noble thing than you, brother. Come on and kill me. I do not care who kills who.

On the homeward journey, with the marlin tied to the boat and already under attack from sharks, Santiago establishes his final relationship with the fish, that great phenomenon of Nature:

> You did not kill the fish only to keep alive and to sell for food, he thought. You killed him for pride and because you are a fish-erman. You loved him when he was alive and you loved him after. If you love him, it is not a sin to kill him.

A sense of brotherhood and love, in a world in which everyone is killing or being killed, binds together the creatures of Nature, establishes between them a unity and an emotion which transcends the destructive pattern in which they are caught. In the eternal round, each living thing, man and animal, acts out its destiny according to the drives of its species, and in the process becomes a part of the profound harmony of the natural universe. This harmony, taking into account the hard facts of pursuit, violence, and death but reaching a stage of feeling beyond them, is a primary aspect of Hemingway's view of the world. Even the sharks have their place. They are largely scavengers, but the strongest and most powerful among them, the great Mako shark which makes its way out of the deep part of the sea, shares the grandeur of the marlin. Santiago kills him but feels identified with him as well:

> But you enjoyed killing the *dentuso*, he thought. He lives on the live fish as you do. He is not a scavenger nor just a moving appetite as some sharks are. He is beautiful and noble and knows no fear of anything.

Nature not only has its own harmony and integration but also its degrees of value. In *The Old Man and the Sea* this is contained in the idea of depth. The deeper the sea the more valuable the creatures living there and the more intense the experience deriving from it. On the day that he catches the great marlin, the old man goes much farther out than the other fishermen and casts bait in much deeper water. The marlin itself is a denizen of the profounder depths. Even the Mako shark lives in the deep water and its speed, power, and directness are qualities associated with depth. There are, in fact, two orders in every species: the great marlins and the lesser, the great sharks and the smaller, bad-smelling, purely scavenger sharks who dwell in shallower water and attack with a sly indirectness in demeaning contrast with the bold approach of the Mako. There are also two kinds of men—as there have always been in Hemingway—the greater men and the lesser, heroes and ordinary humans.

To be a hero means to dare more than other men, to expose oneself to greater dangers, and therefore more greatly to risk the possibilities of defeat and death. On the eighty-fifth day after catching his last fish, Santiago rows far beyond the customary fishing grounds; as he drops his lines into water of unplumbed depth he sees the other fishermen, looking very small, strung out in a line far inland between himself and the shore. Because he is out so far, he catches the great fish. But because the fish is so powerful, it pulls his skiff even farther out—so far from shore then that they cannot get back in time to prevent the marlin being chewed to pieces by the sharks.

> "I shouldn't have gone out so far, fish," he said. "Neither for you nor for me. I'm sorry, fish."

The greatness of the experience and the inevitability of the loss are bound up together. Nature provides us with boundless opportunities for the great experience if we have it in us to respond. The experience carries with it its heavy tragic price. No matter. It is worth it. When Santiago at last returns with the marlin still lashed to the skiff but eaten away to the skeleton, he staggers uphill to his hut groaning under the weight of the mast. He falls asleep exhausted and dreams of the African lions he had seen in his younger days at sea. The next morning the other fishermen gaze in awe at the size of the skeleton, measure it to see by how much it is recordbreaking, while the reverential feeling of the boy, Manolin, for the fisherman is strongly re-enforced. Everyone has somehow been uplifted by the experience. Even on the lowest, most ignorant level, it creates a sensation. The tourists in the last scene of the story mistake the marlin for a shark but they too are struck by a sense of the extraordinary.

The world not only contains the possibilities of heroic adventure and emotion to which everyone, on whatever level, can respond, but it also has continuity. Santiago is very old and has not much time left. But he has been training Manolin to pick up where he leaves off. The boy has been removed by his parents from the old man's boat because of his bad luck, but this in no way diminishes the boy's eagerness to be like Santiago. The master-pupil relationship between them suggests that the heroic impulse is part of a tradi-tional process handed down from one generation to another, that the world is a continuous skein of possibility and affirmation. This affirming note, subdued in Hemingway's earlier fiction, is sounded here with unambiguous and unrestricted clarity.

Indeed, Santiago is the clearest representation of the hero because he is the only major character in Hemingway who has not been permanently wounded or disillusioned. His heroic side is suggested throughout. Once, in Casablanca, he defeated a huge Negro from Cienfuegos at the hand game and was referred to thereafter as *El Campéon*. Now in his old age, he is hero-worshipped by Manolin who wants always to fish with him, or, when he cannot, at least to help him even with his most menial chores. At sea Santiago, sharing the Cuban craze for baseball, thinks frequently of Joe DiMaggio, the greatest ballplayer of his generation, and wonders whether DiMaggio, suffering from a bone spur in his heel, ever endured the pain which the marlin is now subjecting him to. And at night, when he sleeps, he dreams of lions playing on the beaches of Africa. The constant association with the king of ballplayers and the king of beasts adds to the old man's heroic proportions. He is heroic even in his bad luck. The story opens with the announcement that he has gone eighty-four days without taking a fish—ordinary men are seldom afflicted with disaster so outsized.

Heightening and intensifying these already magnified effects is the extraordinary beauty of Nature which cozens and bemuses us with its sensuous intoxications. The account of the sea coming to life at dawn is one of the most moving passages in the story, supplemented later at rhapsodic intervals by the drama of the great pursuit. This comes to its visual climax with the first great jump of the marlin when, for the first time, Santiago sees the gigantic size of his prey. Hemingway pays very close attention to the rippling and fluting of the water, to wind currents, the movements of turtles, fish, and birds, the rising of sun and stars. One is filled not simply with a sense of Nature's vastness, but of her enchantment. This enchantment adds an aesthetic dimension to Santiago's adventure, an adventure whose heroism invests it with moral meaning and whose invocation of comradeship and identity supply it with emotional grandeur.

Within this universe, where there is no limit to the depth of experience, learning how to function is of the greatest importance. It is not enough to have will; one must also have technique. If will is what enables one to live, technique is what enables one to live successfully. Santiago is not a journeyman fisherman, but a superb craftsman who knows his business thoroughly and always practices it with great skill. He keeps his lines straight where others allow them to drift with the current. "It is better to be lucky," he thinks. "But I would rather be exact. Then when luck comes you are ready." To be ready—with all one's professional as well as psychological resources—that is the imperative. One reason that Hemingway's stories are so crammed with technical details about fishing, hunting, bull-fighting, boxing, and war—so much so that they often read like manuals on these subjects—is his belief that professional technique is the quickest and surest way of understanding the physical processes of Nature, of getting into the thing itself. Men should study the world in which they are born as the most serious of all subjects; they can live in it only as they succeed in handling themselves with skill. Life is more than an endurance contest. It is also an art, with rules, rituals, and methods that, once learned, lead on to mastery.

Furthermore, when the great trial comes, one must be alone. The pressure and the agony cannot be shared or sloughed off on others, but must be endured alone. Santiago, his hands chafed and bleeding from the pull of the marlin, his face cut, in a state of virtual prostration from his struggle, several times wishes the boy were with him to ease the strain, but it is essential that he go unaccompanied, that in the end he rely on his own resources and endure his trial unaided. At the bottom of this necessity for solitariness, there is the incurable reliance on the individual which makes Hemingway the great contemporary inheritor of the romantic tradition. The stripping down of existence to the struggle between individual man and the natural world, during the course of which he rises to the highest levels of himself, has an early echo in Keats's line "Then on the shore of the wide world I stand alone. . . ." In modern fiction it is Melville and Conrad who give this theme its most significant shape. The mysterious, inscrutable, dramatic

Nature into which their heroes plunge themselves in search of their own self-realization supplies Hemingway with the scaffolding for *The Old Man and the Sea*. Like Captain Ahab, like Lord Jim, Santiago is pitched into the dangerous ocean; for only there, and with only himself to fall back on, can he work out his destiny and come to final terms with life.

The concept of the hero whose triumph consists of stretching his own powers to their absolute limits regardless of the physical results gives *The Old Man and the Sea* a special place among its author's works. It confronts us with a man who is not only capable of making the ultimate effort, but makes it successfully and continuously. This theme of affirmation, that had begun to be struck in *Across the River and into the Trees*, is present here much more convincingly. Colonel Cantwell of the immediately preceding novel is forever talking about his heroism; Santiago acts his out. Cantwell reminisces on past triumphs; the old fisherman demonstrates them before our eyes. The strain of boastful exhibitionism that causes some readers to regard Hemingway as an adolescent Byron spoiled Cantwell's story. It is almost totally absent from Santiago's.

Here we have entered a world which has to some degree recovered from the gaping wounds that made it so frightening a place in the early stories. The world which injured Jake Barnes so cruelly, pointlessly deprived Lieutenant Henry of his one love, destroyed Harry Morgan at the height of his powers, and robbed Robert Jordan of his political idealism has now begun to regain its balance. It is no longer the bleak trap within which man is doomed to struggle, suffer, and die as bravely as he can, but a meaningful, integrated structure that challenges our resources, holds forth rich emotional rewards for those who live in it daringly and boldly though continuing to exact heavy payment from them in direct proportion to how far they reach out. There is no less tragedy than before, but this has lost its bleakness and accidentality, and become purposive. It is this sense of purposiveness that makes its first appearance in Hemingway's philosophy, and sets off *The Old Man and the Sea* from his other fiction.

After the first World War the traditional hero disappeared from Western literature, to be replaced in one form or another by Kafka's Mr. K. Hemingway's protagonists, from Nick Adams on, were hemmed in like Mr. K. by a bewildering cosmos which held them in a tight vise. The huge complicated mushrooming of politics, society, and the factory age began to smother freedom of action on the individual's part. In his own life Hemingway tended to avoid the industrialized countries including his own, and was drawn from the start to the primitive places of Spain, Africa, and Cuba. For there, the ancient struggle and harmony between man and Nature still existed, and the heroic possibilities so attractive to Hemingway's temperament had freer play. At last, in the drama of Santiago, a drama entirely outside the framework of modern society and its institutions, he was able to bring these possibilities to their first full fruition, and re-discover, in however specialized a context, the hero lost in the twentieth century.

Thus *The Old Man and the Sea* is the culmination of Hemingway's long search for disengagement from the social world and total entry into the natural. This emerges in clearer focus than ever before as one of the major themes in his career both as writer and man. Jake and Bill are happy only in the remote countryside outside Burguete, away from the machinery of postwar Europe. It is when Lieutenant Henry signs his separate peace, deserts from the Italian army, and retires with his love to the high Swiss mountains far removed from the man-made butchery of the war that he enjoys his brief moment of unclouded bliss. The defeated writer in "The Snows of Kilimanjaro," as he lies dying, laments his inability to free himself from the complicated temptations of money, fashion, the life of sophisticated dilettantism, and thinks of his lost talent as resting unspoiled on the remote virginal snows cresting the summit of an African mountain (height on land is plainly the moral equivalent in Hemingway to depth in the sea). Robert Jordan must first disengage himself from the political machinery of Spain before the act of sacrificing his life for his comrades can acquire its note of pure spiritual exaltation.

The movement to get out of society and its artifices is not motivated by the desire to escape but by the desire for liberation. Hemingway seeks to immerse himself totally in Nature not to "evade his responsibilities" but to free his moral and emotional self. Since life in society is necessarily stunting and artificial, cowardice consists not of breaking out of it but of continuing in it. To be true to oneself makes a return to the lost world of Nature categorically imperative. And that lost world, as *The Old Man and the Sea* reveals, has its own responsibilities, disciplines, moralities, and all-embracing meaning quite the equivalent of anything present in society and of much greater value because it makes possible a total response to the demands upon the self. Santiago is the first of the main figures in Hemingway who is not an American, and who is altogether free of the entanglements of modern life. It is toward the creation of such a figure that Hemingway has been moving, however obscurely, from the beginning. His ability to get inside this type of character without the fatal self-consciousness that mars so much literary "primitivism" is a measure of how far he has succeeded, in imagination at least, in freeing himself from the familiar restraints of convention.

In this movement from the confinements of society to the challenges of Nature, Hemingway is most closely linked to Conrad. Conrad thrust his Europeans into the pressures of the Malayan archipelago and darkest Africa because he was convinced that only when removed from the comforts and protective mechanisms of civilization could they be put to the test. In his one London novel, *The Secret Agent*, Conrad demonstrated that suffering and tragedy were as possible in Brixton and Camberwell as off the Java coast; heroism, however, was not, and *The Secret Agent* stands as his one major work that remained hero-less. This embracing of Nature has nothing of Rousseau in it; it is not a revulsion against the corruption and iniquity of urban life. It is, instead, a flight from safety and the atrophying of the spirit produced by safety. It is for the sake of the liberation of the human spirit rather than the purification of social institutions that Conrad and Hemingway play out their lonely dramas in the bosom of Nature.

Because *The Old Man and the Sea* records this drama in its most successful form, it gives off in atmosphere and tone a buoyant sense of release that is new in Hemingway. The story, then, may well be less a capstone of Hemingway's extraordinary career to date than a fresh emotional point of departure for the work to come.

DELMORE SCHWARTZ

The Old Man and the Sea *and the American Dream*

*T*he *Old Man and the Sea*, Hemingway's most recent novel (1952), is not so
much a masterpiece in itself as a virtuoso performance, a new demonstration
of the novelist's gifts far more than a new development of them. The experience of literature is always comparative; Hemingway's sixth novel has almost
the same theme as *The Undefeated*, a story written twenty-five years before,
and the old fisherman who has not made a catch for eighty-four days is in the
same human situation as the aging matador of that story. Compared with that
and other stories, and with the best episodes in Hemingway's previous
novels, there is a certain thinness of characterization and situation.

Yet *The Old Man and the Sea* does give a new definition and meaning to
Hemingway's work as a whole. It gives the reader an intensified awareness of
how, for Hemingway, the kingdom of Heaven, which is within us, is moral
stamina alone, and experience, stripped of illusion, is inexhaustible threat. It
is completely clear in this novel, as it is not when his characters are expatriates in Europe, that Hemingway's primary sense of existence is the essential
condition of the pioneer. It is above all the terror and isolation of the pioneer
in the forest that Hemingway seeks in his prize fighters, matadors, soldiers,
and expatriate sportsmen. The old man's solitude is also meaningful: apart
from the brief appearance of the young boy who is devoted to him, sorry for
him, and has been told to avoid him, Santiago is the only human being in a

From *Perspectives USA* 13 (Autumn 1955): 82–88. © 1955 by Intercultural Publications, Inc.

narrative more than one hundred pages in length! The giant marlin is a sympathetic character for whom the old man develops a certain fondness and the sharks who destroy all but the marlin's skeleton are villains whom he detests: the astonishing fact remains that one human being is enough to make a genuine narrative. Moreover the old man is not only alone physically, but since he is old he will always be alone, cut off from youth, hope, friendship, love, and all the other relationships which sustain human beings. Hence, as the old man struggles with the sea—with time, nature, and death—he possesses a singular purity of will and emotion. The completeness of his solitude does much to relate the novel to all of Hemingway's work, making one more aware of how some form of solitude isolated every other leading character, giving a new clarity to Jake Barnes' mutilation, Frederick Henry's "separate peace," the solitude which the shell-shocked Nick Adams seeks on a fishing trip in *Big Two-Hearted River*, and the monologue of the dying writer in *The Snows of Kilimanjaro*. Thus, in a way, the old fisherman is the quintessential hero of Hemingway's fiction. Other human beings are simply absent now, and only the sharks are present to interfere with the naked confrontation of man and nature. It is the solitude which requires absolute courage and complete self-reliance.

With the old fisherman the pattern of Hemingway's fiction has come full circle. The hero as an old man stands in clear relation to the hero as a young boy and Nick Adams as a child in *Indian Camp*, the first story of Hemingway's first book. In that story Nick goes with his father, a doctor, to witness the mystery of birth: but he witnesses the horror of death also. The young Indian woman his father has come to help has been in labor for two days. "Daddy, can't you give her something to stop the screaming?" Nick asks his father. The doctor tells his son that despite her outcry the woman wants to be in labor and pain because she wants to have the baby and the baby too wants to be born. Then Dr. Adams performs a Caesarean using a jackknife. Dr. Adams feels exalted as he goes to tell the woman's husband the operation was successful—and finds him dead. His wife's screaming has made the Indian kill himself. This is hardly the initiation Dr. Adams had intended for his son. Yet, as father and son row home across the lake, Nick's reassurance grows as his father replies to his questions about suffering and death. As the sun rises over the lake Nick feels "sure that he would never die." This sentence illustrates the extreme illusion about existence which is native to the Hemingway hero and which makes disillusion, when it occurs, so astonishing and disastrous.

Just as the birth of a child causes the death of a man in *Indian Camp*, so in the last chapter of *A Farewell to Arms*, not only does the birth of a child cause the heroine's death, but before her death when she cries out in her agony, she speaks exactly like Nick Adams: "Can't they give me something?" and Frederick Henry says to himself: "She can't die," just as Nick was sure that he would not die. When the heroine dies, the burden of the hero's experience of birth, love, and death is a characterization of the nature of existence:

> So now they got her in the end. You never got away with anything . . . You did not know what it was about. They threw you in and told you the rules and the first time they caught you off base they killed you . . . They killed you in the end . . . You could count on that. Stay around and they would kill you.

The first illusion is that one will not die. The essential disillusion is death. Hence without exception every Hemingway hero suffers serious physical wounds, often as an initiation to the disillusion of reality and the ultimate wound of death.

The exact parallel of detail which links *Indian Camp* and the last chapter of *A Farewell to Arms* ought not to conceal an emotional difference which is quite important. Nick's primary illusion about existence in the first story, though it is shaken by his direct encounter with the reality of the agony of birth and suicide, is quickly restored: he concludes, as he began, with the same illusion that he will never die. Frederick Henry in *A Farewell to Arms* concludes in disillusion and despair. He has made a separate peace not only with war and love, but with life itself. Santiago in *The Old Man and the Sea* surpasses both prior characters. He suffers neither from illusion nor disillusion: he lives, as he says, by hope: "It is silly not to hope," he tells himself, and "besides, it is a sin." His kind of hope is clearly very different from Nick's return to illusion and Frederick Henry's surrender to disillusion. The passage from illusion through various phases of disillusion to the conclusion of sober hope represents the novelist's profound spiritual and emotional progress during the thirty years of his career.

The Capital of the World (1936) is perhaps one of Hemingway's most illuminating stories. The hero, a young waiter, gets killed in a pointless accident while practicing "the great media-veronica" of the matador. This is the author's comment and conclusion:

> He [the young waiter] died, as the Spanish phrase has it, full of illusions. He had not had any time in his life to lose any one of them, nor even, at the end, to complete an act of contrition . . . . he had not even had time to be disappointed in the Garbo film which disappointed all Madrid for a week . . . The audience disliked the Garbo picture thoroughly . . . they were intensely

disappointed to see the great star in miserable and low surround-
ings when they had been accustomed to her surrounded by great
luxury and brilliance.

This is the most complete description of illusion in Hemingway and at the
same time the most extreme statement of despair. Since the loss of illusion
can only be prevented by early death, the only available anesthetic is the
opium of death. This is as far as it is possible to travel from the belief that
one will never die without believing in suicide. And it is a further indication
of the immense experience of suffering which Hemingway's fiction encom-
passes. The vision of experience as pain, the imagination of suffering of every
kind, requires a quality of compassion and sympathy on the author's part
which seldom has been recognized.

Despair can only be known after the disappointment of hope; disillusion
can only occur after the experience of illusion. The primary illusion in *The
Capital of the World*—and the same illusion in all Hemingway's fiction—is illus-
trated by the reference to Greta Garbo in a Hollywood film. But the primary
illusion and hope existed long before Hollywood, and it has often been called
the American Dream. Hollywood has popularized and vulgarized the American Dream so widely, that its true character and dignity has become somewhat
obscured. It is formulated in the American Constitution as every human
being's inalienable right to life, liberty, and the pursuit of happiness.

The American Dream is believed by many human beings who, like
Hemingway's disillusioned characters, are unaware of their belief or
convinced that they have awakened from it. The fact, which must be
pointed out once more, that disillusion is inseparable from illusion and
despair from hope, is disregarded. The right to happiness as the law of the
land is the belief by which Hemingway's most desperate and unhappy characters live when they drink, travel, and play games. Like many more
sanguine human beings, they have converted the legal right to life, liberty,
and happiness into attitudes, emotions, an organized way of life which
believes not only in the pursuit but the certainty of happiness. The American Dream converts the pursuit of happiness into the guarantee of a happy
ending. For some this is promised by the nature of reality; for far more, it
is supported by the nature of America as the New World where all are
equal. And the American Dream is so primary and so important as a source
of illusion and hope that the dream becomes insomnia when it is not
fulfilled, or in a like way, courage is needed solely to cope with the unbear-
able pain of disappointment. Hemingway's fiction bears the same witness as
the essential substance and avowed faith in the writings of Emerson,
Thoreau, Whitman, and Melville.

The Hemingway hero's attitude toward himself and toward existence depends immediately upon the American Dream. Thus the first onset of disillusion is one in which the hero as a young man persuades the heroine to have an abortion: "We can have everything," the heroine says, "if we get married." "No, we can't," the hero answers, "it isn't ours anymore . . . Once they have taken it away, you never get it back." And when he adds this brief description of himself, "You know how I get when I worry," the heroine agrees to the abortion, thus: "If I do it you won't ever worry?" because never to worry is part of the dream. And when disillusion becomes despair, when the stock market crash begins a depression which seems unending, Hemingway, as his own hero, hunting big game in Africa feels that he is through with America since the American Dream has ended:

> A continent ages quickly once we come . . . The earth gets tired of being exploited . . . *A country was made to be as we found it*. Our people went to America because that was the place to go then. It had been a good country and we had made a bloody mess of it and I would go, now, somewhere else as *we always had the right to go somewhere else*. Let others come to America who did not know that it was too late . . . I knew a good country when I saw one. Here there was *game, plenty of birds* . . . *Here I could hunt and fish*.

Hemingway's sentences have been italicized to demonstrate that the pioneer and the immigrant and the hunter and fisherman are identical in the Hemingway hero whenever he thinks of how to regain the dream, and now how like Huck Finn he can always "light out for the frontier."

When the American Dream seems to have collapsed once and for all, the Hemingway hero (in *To Have and Have Not*) loses an arm smuggling to keep his family off the relief rolls, and decides that the heroic individual no longer has a chance by himself. And although the Hemingway hero has made a separate peace and said a farewell to arms years back, he goes to fight for the Loyalists in Spain because, as he says, he believes in life, liberty, and the pursuit of happiness, thus identifying the Spanish Civil War and the American Revolution: one man alone has a chance, after all, to save humanity and hence the hero, Robert Jordan, blows up a bridge as a way of firing a shot which will be heard around the world. Robert Jordan's father has killed himself because of the Wall Street stock market crash, just as Nick Adams' father has committed suicide because, being a sentimental man, he was always being betrayed. And every American of Hemingway's generation has known the most exalted expectations and the most desperate disasters. Living through the First World War, the great era of prosperity, the crash, the long depression, the Second World War, and a new era of prosperity, he has been subjected to the American Dream's giddy, unpredictable, magical, tragic, and fabulous juggernaut. It is thus natural enough that the Hemingway hero should always feel threatened, always in danger, always subject to what the sociologists call "status panic." A society committed to the American Dream is one which creates perpetual social mobility but also one in which the individual must suffer perpetual insecurity of status as the price of being free of fixed status. Hence the Hemingway hero is always afraid of failure, no matter how often he has succeeded, which is precisely what the old fisherman says: "'I will show him what a man is and what he endures' . . . The thousand times that he had proved it meant nothing. Now he was proving it again. Each time was a new time." This is the reason that the Hemingway hero must continually assert his masculinity: he may always lose it, as he may always lose his strength, his youth, his health, his skill, his success, and thus his sense of self-hood.

Of all modern novelists it is Hemingway who has written the most complete moral history of the American Dream in the twentieth century: the greatest of human dreams is the beginning of heartbreaking hope and despair; its promise is the cause of overwhelming ambition and over-whelming anxiety: the anxiety and the hope make courage an obsession and an endless necessity in the face of endless fear and insecurity: but the dream, the hope, the anxiety, and the courage began with the discovery of America.

JOSEPH WALDMEIR

Confiteor Hominem: Ernest Hemingway's Religion of Man

In recent years, critics have become increasingly suspicious that it is necessary to read Ernest Hemingway's work on the symbolic as well as on the story
level in order to gain a full appreciation of its art. Since the publication of
The Old Man and the Sea, the suspicion has become first an awareness, then a
certainty. Of all Hemingway's work, this one demands most to be read on
both levels; and the story, its details, its method of presentation, are sufficiently similar to the balance of his work as to suggest strongly the possibility
of a similar reading and perhaps a similar interpretation.

   The Old Man and the Sea is, as story, very good Hemingway. It is swiftly
and smoothly told; the conflict is resolved into a struggle between a man and
a force which he scarcely comprehends, but which he knows that he must
continue to strive against, though knowing too that the struggle must end in
defeat. The defeat is only apparent, however, for, as in "The Undefeated," it
becomes increasingly clear throughout the story that it is not victory or
defeat that matters but the struggle itself. Furthermore, *The Old Man and the
Sea*, while reasserting the set of values, the philosophy which permeates all
of Hemingway, is built upon the great abstractions—love and truth and
honor and loyalty and pride and humility—and again speaks of the proper
method of attaining and retaining these virtues, and of the spiritual satisfaction inevitably bestowed upon their holder.

From *PMASAL* XLII (1956): 277–81. © The University of Michigan Press.

The Christian religious symbols running through the story, which are so closely interwoven with the story in fact as to suggest an allegorical intention on Hemingway's part, are so obvious as to require little more than a listing of them here. The Old Man is a fisherman, and he is also a teacher, one who has taught the boy not only how to fish—that is, how to make a living—but how to behave as well, giving him the pride and humility necessary to a good life. During the trials with the great fish and with the sharks his hands pain him terribly, his back is lashed by the line, he gets an eyepiercing headache, and his chest constricts and he spits blood. He hooks the fish at noon, and at noon of the third day he kills it by driving his harpoon into its heart. As he sees the second and third sharks attacking, the Old Man calls aloud "'Ay,'" and Hemingway comments: "There is no translation for this word and perhaps it is just such a noise as a man might make, involuntarily, feeling the nail go through his hand and into the wood." On landing, the Old Man shoulders his mast and goes upward from the sea toward his hut; he is forced to rest several times on his journey up the hill, and when he reaches the hut he lies on the bed "with his arms out straight and the palms of his hands up."

The Christian symbolism so evident here shifts from man to fish—a legitimate symbol for Christ since the beginning of Christianity, as it was a legitimate religious symbol before Christianity—and back to man throughout the story. This apparent confusion is consistent not only within the Hemingway philosophy as an example of the sacrificer-sacrificed phenomenon (a point which I will discuss later in this paper) but within formal Christianity as well, if the doctrine of the Trinity be accepted. Furthermore, the phenomenon itself closely parallels the Roman Catholic sacrifice of the Mass, wherein a fusion of the priest-man with Christ takes place at the moment of Transubstantiation.

Along with the Christ symbols, reinforcing them, but depending on them for its importance, is a rather intricate numerology. It is not formalized—neither is the numerology of Christianity—but it is carefully set forth.

Three, seven, and forty are key numbers in the Old and New Testaments, and in the religion, and Hemingway makes a judicious use of them. The Old Man, as the story opens, has fished alone for forty-four famine days and with the boy for forty more. The Old Man's trial with the great fish lasts exactly three days; the fish is landed on the seventh attempt; seven sharks are killed; and, although Christ fell only three times under the Cross, whereas the Old Man has to rest from the weight of the mast seven times, there is a consistency in the equal importance of the numbers themselves.

But, once it has been established that *The Old Man and the Sea* may be read on the symbolic as well as on the story level, a new problem presents itself, a problem which grows out of the nature of the symbolic level and out of the disturbing realization that the two levels exist harmoniously in the work. I think that the problem may best be expressed by two questions which the discerning reader must have asked himself as he put *The Old Man and the Sea* down: Is the story, as it appears at first glance to be, a Christian allegory? Has the old master tough guy decided, in the words of Colonel Cantwell, "to run as a Christian"? If neither of these questions can be answered with an unqualified affirmative—and I submit that they cannot—then a further question must be asked: Just what is the book's message?

The answer assumes a third level on which *The Old Man and the Sea* must be read—as a sort of allegorical commentary by the author on all his previous work, by means of which it may be established that the religious overtones of *The Old Man and the Sea* are not peculiar to that book among Hemingway's works, and that Hemingway has finally taken the decisive step in elevating what might be called his philosophy of Manhood to the level of a religion.

Two aspects of the total work, including *The Old Man and the Sea*, must be considered at this point in order to clarify the above conclusion on the one hand, and to answer the questions concerning Hemingway's Christianity on the other.

The first of these aspects is Hemingway's concern with man as man, with man in his relation to things of this world almost exclusively. The other world, God, does not often enter into the thoughts, plans, or emotions of a Hemingway character. God exists—most of the characters are willing to admit His existence, or at least, unwilling to deny it—but not as an immanent Being, not ever benevolent or malevolent.

God is sometimes prayed to by the Hemingway hero at moments of crisis, but His aid or succor are never depended upon, never really expected. Thus we have Jake Barnes in the Cathedral at Pamplona, on the eve of his great trial, praying for everybody he can think of, for good bullfights and good fishing; and as he becomes aware of himself kneeling, head bent, he

> was a little ashamed, and regretted that I was such a rotten Catholic, but realized that there was nothing I could do about it, at least for awhile, and maybe never, but that anyway it was a grand religion, and I only wished I felt religious and maybe I would the next time. . . .

And thus, too, we have the Old Man, who, after twenty-four hours of his monumental struggle have passed, prays for heavenly assistance mechanically, automatically, thinking, "I am not religious," and "Hail Marys are easier to say than Our Fathers." And after forty-five hours, he says:

"Now that I have him coming so beautifully, God help me to endure. I'll say a hundred Our Fathers and a hundred Hail Marys. But I cannot say them now."

Consider them said, he thought, I'll say them later.

But when the struggle is ended and the full ironic impact of his "victory" is clear, he asks himself what it was that beat him, and answers, "Nothing . . . I went out too far."

He who depends too heavily on prayer, or for that matter on any external aids when faced with a crisis, is not very admirable to Hemingway. In *Death in the Afternoon*, when he wants to describe the unmanliness of a "cowardly bull-fighter" girding himself for action, Hemingway places him in church

> in his bullfighting clothes to pray before the fight, sweating under the armpits, praying that the bull will embiste, that is, charge frankly and follow the cloth well; oh blessed Virgin that thou wilt give me a bull that will embiste well, blessed Virgin, give me that bull, blessed Virgin, that I should touch this bull in Madrid to-day on a day without wind; promising something of value or a pilgrimage, praying for luck, frightened sick. . . .

A man must depend upon himself alone in order to assert his manhood, and the assertion of his manhood, in the face of insuperable obstacles, is the complete end and justification of his existence for a Hemingway hero. The Old Man *must* endure his useless struggle with the sharks; Manuel, in "The Undefeated," *must*, in spite of his broken wrist and a terrible goring, go in on the bull six times and accept the horn at last; Jake *must* continue to live as "well" and "truly" and "honestly" as he is able in spite of his overwhelming frustration. And each must face his struggle alone, with no recourse to other-worldly help, for only as solitary individuals can they assert their manhood.

And significantly they must go it alone without regard to otherworldly blame. As far as sin is concerned, Jake would probably say along with the Old Man, "Do not think about sin. It is much too late for that and there are people who are paid to do it. Let them think about it." And Manuel would probably nod agreement.

However, in spite of such obvious rejections of otherworldly Christianity in his affirmation of Manhood, Hemingway has formulated as rigid a set of rules for living and for the attainment of Manhood as can be found in any religion. These rules, along with the detailed procedure for their application, constitute the second aspect of Hemingway's total work to be considered in this paper.

The rules are built upon the great abstractions mentioned above. They are so bound up with the procedure for their application that the procedure itself might be considered to be a rule—or better, that neither rules nor procedure exist without one another. Hemingway's philosophy of Manhood is a philosophy of action; a man is honest when he acts honestly, he is humble when he acts humbly, he loves when he is loving or being loved. Thus, taking an awareness of the rules as he has taken an awareness of the abstractions for granted, Hemingway concerns himself primarily with the presentation of procedure. The procedure is carefully outlined; it is meticulously detailed. If no part of it is overlooked or sloughed off, it must result in a satisfying experience almost in and of itself.

This procedure, this ritual—for such is what the procedure actually amounts to—is most clearly evident in Hemingway's treatment of the bullfight. *Death in the Afternoon* is devoted to an evaluation of the manhood of various bullfighters on the basis of their ability to abide by the rules, and to a description of the ritual by means of which they prove possession and communicate the satisfaction to be gained from a proper performance of function to the spectator. War, the prize ring, fishing, hunting, and making love are some of the other celebrations by means of which Hemingway's religio-philosophy of Man is conveyed. But the bullfight is the greatest because, besides possessing, as the others do also, a procedure inviolate, intimately related to the great abstractions, it always ends in death. It assumes the stature of a religious sacrifice by means of which a man can place himself in harmony with the universe, can satisfy the spiritual as well as the physical side of his nature, can atone for the grievous omissions and commissions of his past, can purify and elevate himself in much the same way that he can in any sacrificial religion. The difference between Hemingway's religion of man and formal religion is simply—yet profoundly—that in the former the elevation does not extend beyond the limits of this world, and in the latter, Christianity for example, the ultimate elevation is totally otherworldly.

The bullfighter is in a sense a priest, performing the sacrifice for the sake of the spectator as well as for his own sake, giving each that "feeling of life and death and mortality and immortality" which Hemingway described in *Death in the Afternoon*, and, as does the Roman Catholic priest on the ideal level, the bullfighter actually places his own life in jeopardy. This curious phenomenon of the sacrificer gambling on becoming the sacrificed serves to clarify the terms of Hemingway's system, rather than, as at first glance it might seem, to confuse them. The bullfighter recognizes the possibility and immanence of death when he steps into the ring, and he must face it bravely. He must perform the sacrifice cleanly, with one true stroke, preserving both his honor and the bull's dignity. If he kills out of malice or out of fear his actions will show it, and the spectator will be distracted from concentration upon the sacrifice to awareness of the man, and no satisfaction will result.

There must be a cognizance of death both from the standpoint of killing and from that of being killed; there must be more than a cognizance actually; there must be an acceptance. Knowledge of death's inevitability so that he does not react to its immediacy, coupled with unconcern for the possibilities of life after death, are necessary attributes of the ideal bullfighter. His aim can extend no further than the great abstractions themselves, how he earns them and how he communicates them. He must realize that it is not *that* one dies but *how* one dies that is important. And equally important, that it is not *that* one kills but *how* one kills.

It is not only in his treatment of the bullfight that this second aspect of Hemingway's total work is evident, though there it may be most immediately apparent. The abstractions, the rules, the ritual, the sacrifice dominate the details of *The Old Man and the Sea* as they dominate those of "The Undefeated" and *The Sun Also Rises*. We are told carefully, painstakingly, how the Old Man performs his function as fisherman; how he prepares for the hoped-for struggle:

> Before it was really light he had his baits out and was drifting with the current. One bait was down forty fathoms. The second was at seventy-five and the third and fourth were down in the blue water at one hundred and one hundred and twenty-five fathoms. Each bait hung head down with the shank of the hook inside the bait fish, tied and sewed solid and all the projecting part of the hook, the curve and the point, was covered with fresh sardines. Each sardine was hooked through both eyes so that they made a half-garland on the projecting steel.
>
> . . . Each line, as thick around as a big pencil, was looped onto a green-sapped stick so that any pull or touch on the bait would make the stick dip and each line had two forty-fathom coils which could be made fast to the other spare coils so that, if it were necessary, a fish could take out over three hundred fathoms of line.

We are told how he hooks the fish and secures the line, waiting suspensefully for the fish to turn and swallow the bait, then waiting again until it has eaten it well, then striking, "with all the strength of his arms and the pivoted weight of his body," three times, setting the hook; then placing the line across his back and shoulders so that there will be something to give when the fish lunges, and the line will not break. We are told specifically, in terms reminiscent of such descriptions of the bullfight, how the kill is made:

The old man dropped the line and put his foot on it and lifted the harpoon as high as he could and drove it down with all his strength, and more strength he had just summoned, into the fish's side just behind the great chest fin that rose high in the air to the altitude of a man's chest. He felt the iron go in and he leaned on it and drove it further and then pushed all his weight after it.

The immanence of death for the sacrificer as well as for the sacrificed, and his total disregard of its possibility, are made clear at the climax of the struggle when the Old Man thinks: "You are killing me, fish . . . Come on and kill me, I do not care who kills who."

It is at this point I think that the questions asked earlier in this paper can be answered. Has Hemingway decided to "run as a Christian"? I think not; the evidence in *The Old Man and the Sea*, with the exception of the Christian symbolism, indicates that he is no more Christian now than he was when he wrote *The Sun Also Rises*. But the Christian symbolism *is* in the book, and it *does* appear to constitute a Christian religious allegory. Yes, but on a superficial level. The religious allegory, attached to the two aspects of the total body of Hemingway's work as they appear in *The Old Man and the Sea*, which have been the subject of most of my discussion thus far, actually constitute a third level on which *The Old Man and the Sea* must be read—as the allegorical interpretation of the total body of the work.

I said above that Hemingway is no more Christian now than he was thirty years ago; it has been my intention in this paper to show that he was *no less religious* thirty years ago than he is now. The evidence which I have presented adds up to something more than a philosophy or an ethic, the two terms which have most often been used to describe Hemingway's world view; it adds up to what I would call a Religion of Man. Hemingway did not turn religious to write *The Old Man and the Sea*. He has always been religious, though his religion is not of the orthodox, organized variety. He celebrates, he has always celebrated, the Religion of Man; *The Old Man and the Sea* merely celebrates it more forcefully and convincingly than any previous Hemingway work. It is the final step in the celebration. It is the book which, on the one hand, elevates the philosophy to a religion by the use of allegory, and on the other, by being an allegory of the total body of his work, enables us to see that work finally from the point of view of religion.

NEMI D'AGOSTINO

The Later Hemingway

The impulse toward autobiography, which Hemingway had hitherto so wisely restrained, thrusts itself to the fore at the beginning of the Thirties, at the time of his great wave of popularity and the journalistic build-up of the Hemingway legend. The inner lyricism of works like *A Farewell to Arms* gives way to a manifest regression into sensationalism and melodrama in the two biographical books on bullfighting and African big-game hunting. The clear-cut presentation becomes blurred by the impulse to confession and exhibitionism, is marred by rhetoric and sentimentality, and dimmed by a new sophisticated attitude. Under the absurd Byronic pose which Hemingway could strike so effectively, a crisis was taking place. It was a crisis in his fundamental romanticism, which the very nature of his talent and his cultural background forced toward an accentuated aestheticism. He had been the poet of a complex of emotions which had sprung from the atmosphere of war. But within the violent frame of that world Hemingway had emerged as the upholder of the only humanism which seemed possible at the time. His art, penetrated by a tragic sense of loss, seemed to represent the dilemma of all contemporary humanity. Now the world which had been so desperately lost to his heroes, suddenly appeared to be well lost to him. From extreme disillusion and distrust of all values he swung round to the exaltation of daring, of the beauty of violence and of the beauty of death; and in adopting

From *The Sewanee Review* LXVIII (Summer 1960): 482–93. © 1960 by The University of the South.

himself the code of behavior which was so convincing and humane in his heroes, he turned it into a preposterous and unironical search for excitement for its own sake. While his youthful rebellion sprang from a vivid consciousness of the collapse of a moral order in a precise historical moment, now he seemed to want to cut himself off from historical development, taking refuge in irresponsible and self-complacent isolation. Tied up to his lost generation, he was now beginning to live in a time whose issues he was no more able to grasp.

Death in the Afternoon, the "treatise" in which he collected in 1932 his experiences as a lover of Spain and *aficionado* of the bull ring, was striking in its implicit (and certainly unconscious) denial of that fundamental postulate of his art, the search for the "exact sequence," the real thing, the inflexible fidelity to the dry and concrete evidence of the senses. It was really surprising that the Hemingway who had looked at the war with such a disillusioned eye should now be taken in to such an extent by the tragic masquerade of the bullfight. In an exhibition of that kind, a frame-up playing on the bravado of danger, exploiting the cruelty and the brutality of the crowd, there is certainly nothing that can be called art, any more than in the risks run by the acrobat or the lion tamer. And of course these activities, whose end is the exhibition of their own technique, lack the ethical and intellectual basis of art. The limitation of Hemingway's "spiritual diary" lies in his sentimental conception of Spain, a literary interpretation utterly lacking in Manzoni's demand for reality, so that he can see in that violent display a form of tragic poetry and a ritual symbolizing a profound conception of human destiny.

This passion for the bull ring, this over-subtle primitivism, this craving for sensation which finds vent in moments of morbid and bloodthirsty ecstasy, actually springs from a cultured and detached pleasure in the primitive and the barbaric. As Geismar and other critics have suggested, the Hemingway who gazes in fascination at the sight of the indescribable whiteness of bone in the bullfighter's torn thigh, and who describes the disembowelling of the horse as the comic scene in the tragedy, is at heart an intellectual driven to a renunciation of culture and of that conquest essential to human progress, the suppression of the blood instinct. Hemingway, in the belief that he is getting at the very heart of Spain, and communing in spirit with its people, is merely exalting his own decadence into a canon of refinement: a "philosophy" we can only see as an abdication from maturity.

Behind the stylized killing that links the two strange "lovers" of the "tragedy," the hunter and its victim, some critics have described the real hero of the book, Death. But what we find in the "treatise" is not the

emotion of death as the profound, inspiring, and infinitely human phenomenon that it is, but only the celebration of that sordid postprandial
slaughter, with its cruel and mannered ritual. The whole book is debased by
the incomprehension implied in this impoverished idea of death. The style is
verbose, crammed with wedges of rhetoric and fake lyricism, becoming the
vehicle now of polemic, now of petulance, and now of private grudges. It is
decked out in the trappings of magic, but unable to transform into the true
substance of poetry its basic concepts, which are easily shown up for
commonplaces and sentimental frippery. The most genuine passages are the
objective accounts of the lives of bullfighters, which bring us back to the
mournful poetry of the "unvanquished," the commentaries to the
photographs: here a coolly tragic camera has picked out the squalid corners
of the arenas, the livid faces of the gladiators, the heavy and desperate
shadow of the beasts, or certain anguished faces of the dead among indifferent onlookers—and here at last it seems to us that we catch the solid and
painful reality which belies Hemingway's whole literary travesty of Spain.

But after all, the book on bullfighting shoud be seen as one of those
unpleasant but useful outlets which sometimes serve to purify an author's
talent. From *Death in the Afternoon* to *Green Hills of Africa*, another book
which, as Aldridge says, was written not by Hemingway but by his legend,
the pursuit of excitement becomes less convinced, nearer to the point of
crisis. The second is certainly the least important and most untidy of
Hemingway's books. But from amongst the medley of shots and oaths, irrelevant details and purple passages, emotions which leave us cold and irrational
outbursts of happiness, we can already catch the obscure dissatisfaction
which in the same year finds vent in "The Short Happy Life of Francis
Macomber" and "The Snows of Kilimanjaro," and which was to lead up to
the tentative change in Hemingway's attitude reflected in his abortive novel
of 1937, *To Have and Have Not*.

In the meanwhile, the world of "Macomber" had a dramatic immediacy
and a living rhythm not to be found in the real world of *Green Hills*. The
characters were once again felt and objectified, violent figures from out of
the young world without hope of the early novels and tales, that world in
which the relation between man and woman is torture and a *safari* is only
another drug for the conscience, a costly anaesthetic. It is a pity that in the
second of the two stories, where the crisis of the intellectual hero is still more
intense, the desire for renovation should find a fictitious outlet in a sentimental sublimation, which breaks up and dilutes the crisp language into
confused lyricism and technical virtuosity in a mannered "metaphysical"
style and in pursuit of rather banal effects. In spite of the sincerity of its
motives and the skilful plot, "The Snows of Kilimanjaro" is spoiled by

rhetoric, and more than "Macomber" it remains one of Hemingway's most static and literary stories.

The crisis which was to break down some at least of the pales of Hemingway's aestheticism and its "poetics" (set out in a well-known passage of *Green Hills*), coincided with the development in America, in the years after the Slump, of a rather naïve and doctrinaire Marxist culture, and with the establishment of Fascism in Europe, leading up to its try-out in the Spanish Civil War. For a time the liberal and democratic propensities in Hemingway had the upper hand and pushed him towards a socialist position, even though cautious and wary. Although in his article on Tolstoy in *Men at War* he declared that he wished to remain true to his nature as a narrator of effects and not of causes, his new novel shows a programmatic intention, a thesis as ill-defined and as full of anger. His short, intense, and angry book *To Have and Have Not* was actually the outcome of the imperfect piecing together of two stories of derangement and violence (written in 1933 and 1936) and of a third part dashed off out of a sense of social duty to the sound of the first guns of the Spanish war. Hemingway had certainly neither the talent nor the training necessary to create a work of art *engagé* in the deepest sense, to write the epic of ideological and social conflicts in a tragic epoch. The result was perforce a novel in which his old individualistic postulate and the new social urge met and clashed without fusing. His fierce and tormented hero, Harry Morgan, was but a vacuous intensification of his standard protagonist, the solitary heir of the Frontier spirit, and Hemingway's fresh burst of rage only swelled his character of Giaour and romantic rebel to the limits of parody and grotesque. Nor did Hemingway succeed in welding into a moral and artistic whole the aspects of violence, corruption and social disintegration against which Morgan should be seen as struggling. The meanness and turpitude of the middle-class world form in the background a heap of meaningless horrors, and are set out in a series of unrelated scenes, which the thread of the main plot links together only externally, and which are filled with figures that are more or less abstractions; while the alternation of various narrative techniques, mostly borrowed and alien to Hemingway's genius, is more the fruit of critical calculation than of inner necessity. Even in the most authentic passages the language seems to be in an acute stage of crisis: at the one end, through an exaggerated desire to "express," it falls into documentary naturalism, at the other it scales heights of a lucid intensity, but it does not succeed in creating a continuous and pregnant rhythm for a new grasp of reality, or in giving full expression to the sense of pity, bitterness, and indignation from which the novel sprang.

II

It has been said that Morgan's last words ("a man alone ain't got no bloody chance") open a new period in Hemingway's art, that now should be seen as imbued with a fresh faith in the social destinies of man, with that fervid sense of the human community reflected in the Donnean epigraph of *For Whom the Bell Tolls*. In the midst of the rage and suffering of a new war this novel was the product of a tumult of experience and emotions: the over-throw of the author's non-political attitude in the face of a pressing need for action, the hate of Fascism and sympathy for the Loyalist Republic, a romantic love of old Spain, and the enthusiasm and anxiety for the future of the world which flung many artists into the international brigades as if to fight a decisive crusade for human liberty. All these feelings surge through the book, in the very urgency and compactness of its structure, in the fervor of its language which now accepts and sweeps into its ardent eloquence the reasoning, the meditations, the search for explanations and causes of which Hemingway had been so impatient in the past. It was unquestionably subject matter which had been almost religiously felt by the author, and the book was written with a brusque tenderness and compassion which touches the heart, and which assured it the sympathetic reception it deserved.

On the other hand, the critics were right to point out that the novel had certain basic weaknesses. Its language was intended to be in part the intimate expression of the intellectual protagonist, and in part to shape itself around the simple heroes of the guerilla, and to throw an epic light on the events. It is instead dim and turgid in the long meditations of the hero; and in the passages of dialogue, where Hemingway tried to create a Platonic language composed of the Spanish idiom, the Bible, and the Elizabethans, it is overloaded with dialectal quotations (which is a critical transfer and not an artistic solution), weighed down with overmuch local color, and often forced into melodramatic effects. The element of melodrama found its way also into the tension of the plot, into the structure of the various "scenes" (including the improbable expedient of Pilar's long story), and into the confused and ill-defined character of the hero himself.

In spite of all this *For Whom the Bell Tolls* is in many respects a very interesting work. It is, first of all, a work in which Hemingway's story-telling broke free from its aesthetic *impasse* of the Thirties and re-entered a zone of deeply human feeling, even though the experience represented was no longer new. What we find in the book is another lost young man, another individual failure, a solitary drama that is symbolic of all the individual dramas of all times and places. The only difference is that now the individual failure is overtly seen as part of a collective failure, a common drama in which the new ideals and hopes one by one prove fruitless, and in the end the only thing which remains is the unbroken chain of pessimism and despair. As Kazin rightly noted, the novel was written in the same spirit as the fine short story "Old Man at the Bridge" of 1938: it was born out of pity for the hopeless drama of each single man; it was again a picture of a fatalistic world, centering round the drama of the individual. Not an epic of the war, nor even the story of Robert Jordan's education in the war, but almost an elegy sung in praise of the lonely rebel, serving in a foreign country with a foreign army, though now with the illusion of a "cause": a lost man whom the war overwhelms without changing him. In the face of this central feeling of the impossibility of belief, the Marxist ideal, like every other ideal, can only be the opium of the people, an austere façade hiding deceit. Actually each new faith frightens and unsettles the writer, and Jordan-Hemingway is the old tormented individualist divided between his need for the community and the scorn and fear it excites in him. And the novel is not so much imbued with history as impregnated by the confused attitude of that no-man's party to which Hemingway belongs.

An elegy of a dying man, a symphonic study of suffering and dissolution, a triumph of death: here lies the true feeling which shapes the book. It has been rightly pointed out that it opens with the theme of awaited death (the image of the man lying full length which is one of its leitmotivs, and with which it also closes), and immediately introduces the theme of fatalism (the hopeless and ironic fatalism of the frequent interjection: *Qué va!*), while the theme of dissolution is interwoven with that of destruction in the very structure of the four *movements*, and the whole, in the end, is only an interval stretching between two supine postures. The utter uselessness of the attempt on the bridge, upon which the future of the human race might depend, is made clear from the start, as is the uselessness of the pathetic heroism of that group of solitary eccentrics which Hemingway selects as his chief characters. The sky overhanging the sierra is without depth and beyond the mountains there is no crusade but only the confused movements of heterogeneous crowds, a massacre in a betrayed land. Jordan is a new Frederic Henry, who finds a code of behavior by which to endure life in the exact fulfilment of his mission, and in the end is driven to "sacrifice" more by desperation than by any certainty. Even his improbable sentimental idyl (and those scenes of love in the face of death are among Hemingway's most inadequate, naturalistic, and yet abstract writing) only serves to emphasize the self-centeredness and irresponsibility of his character. His drama is too oppressive and restricted to reflect the so much wider and more complex tragedy of Spain.

Nevertheless we are moved as we reread this novel, born out of a new and bitterer disenchantment—a melodrama perhaps, but ennobled, in its naïve solemnity, by the breath of poetry. Hemingway has attempted a freer and broader narrative rhythm, which is not always successful, but which touches at times moments of true intensity and genuine dramatic power: the wiping out of El Sordo's band, Andrés' journey behind the republican lines and the moving close of that episode. And he has tried to create varied and trenchant characters, succeeding in setting beside the somewhat inadequate protagonist and the conventionally picturesque portraits of Pilar and Maria such fierce and poetic figures as El Sordo, Joaquin and Anselmo.

Hemingway had to wait for another war, and live in it through another of his eccentric adventures, before writing another book, which turned out to be the most autobiographical and weakest of all his novels. His standard hero, grown old in a world torn by constant war, and more lonesome and tormented than ever, goes in *Across the River and Into the Trees* toward the death beautiful, indulging for the last time in his favorite occupations: hunting, love-making, and the pursuit of precious sensations. And for once fortune favors him: in the exquisite and slightly decayed beauty of Venice in the wintertime, surrounded alike by the affection of aristocrats and of the people, and loved by his dream-princess, he can finally indulge his weakness for self-confession and his longing to arouse admiration and pity. Hemingway wanted to transfigure his eternal hero, making him a pathetic and solemn figure, a creature of bitter passions and childish goodness, whose solitary experience has brought wisdom, nobility, and peace. But the character he actually portrays is that of an embittered and bad-tempered old man, querulous and self-conceited to the point of parody, full of boring and depressing boasts. Indeed, there had never been such a striking contrast between Hemingway's intention and his results. Tied still to his world of desperate young men, he has only been able to fall back on his old type, in a mannered and senile version. Linked to the brittle and laconic language of his vanquished heroes, he has been unable to create an idiom of the upper classes and aristocracy: the characters of *Across the River* speak in a conventional and literary style frozen into tired Alexandrine cadences, spun out by a flow of repetitions. His youthful gift for intensity has failed him.

"I want you to die with the grace of a happy death," Renata, the unconvincing character who is both mistress and nurse, tells the hero. But the good death fails to find poetic fulfilment. From beneath the golden and musical idyl that Hemingway has built up to lead his hero into a safe port, the old desperation breaks through. What the writer really felt was the anguish of Cantwell's lonely march towards extinction: the despair behind the kisses, the funereal thoughts at the moment of love-making, the cold wind blowing over worn and decaying things, the death of all certainty, the turning of his thoughts in "a movement without hope," like the neck of the wounded mallard drake in the jaws of the dog.

Certainly the exotic and primitive setting of the tropics in *The Old Man and the Sea* is better suited to Hemingway's aged hero than is the new Europe. The main theme of the story is absolute failure in life and the irrational sublimation of the defeat. The saintly Santiago goes back in the end to his dreams, his head almost encircled with the halo of holiness. The old man is certainly not the brother of the great realistic heroes of Tolstoy or Verga, nor is he, on the other hand, a fully convincing character in the tradition of symbolism. The story leaves the realistic level as soon as Hemingway tries to make it something more than an immediate objective reality, the moment the strange old man begins to accompany the action with a lyrical commentary, using a refined oratorical language, emphasizing its symbolical substratum, its nature as a projection of the poet's consciousness. As soon, that is, as the chase itself stands revealed as an exploit springing from *un élan d'infini, un amour de l'impossible*. The fable contains a subtle analogy, which unfortunately is more imposed from without than an intrinsic part of it. Whatever the old man is intended to symbolize (and he seems to be a biblical and Melvillean version of the usual Hemingway hero) he simply does not come poetically true; the symbolism remains a fictitious disguise, and the religious or mystical implications are forced in so far as they want to be more than the religion and morality of aestheticism.

Actually the rhythm and idiom of the tale are a clue to its essential emotion. The rhythm is the cadence of the lyrical paragraph, which proceeds with a sumptuous and solemn fall. The language is rich in suggestive and exotic words, in rich and sensuous imagery, in highly literary expressions, in bright and exquisite touches, and is consciously regulated by a love of verbal magic. It is, in short, the rhythm and language of a decadent *poème en prose*, which, however suggestive and intense, must always remain an artificial and minor form, incapable of full historical and moral significance. Within these limits *The Old Man* is certainly a refined work, with its admirable linear development and its brilliant "imagistic" style. A late work by a tired writer who believes more than ever in the religion of beauty, its subtly mannered idiom, its elegant and frozen rhythms, are separated by the space of a whole lifetime from the lucid movement, the fresh and crystalline clarity, the poignancy and the shock-power of the language of the young Hemingway.

III

In spite of all his brave restlessness, Hemingway's basic attitude to reality remained unchanged from *In Our Time* to *The Old Man and the Sea*. Life is a solitary struggle, a desperate fever of action, conscious of having no sense or reason beyond itself. Nothing in it that can be justified, bettered or saved, no problem that can really be set and solved. In this fundamentally non-religious world man can rage and die—and the writer, the defender of humanity, looks sadly and impotently on over the fence. For he too must cling to his own rigid code, in cultivating his small golden garden. Art, as Goethe said in another context and in another time, is the attempt of the individual to save himself from the destructive power of the All.

Hemingway is not of course an easy writer. In his personality are concealed romantic, puritanical, irrationalistic elements. He felt the crisis of romantic individualism in all its complexity, and his characters are also engaged in living out the deep and tormenting problem of liberty of which Mann speaks in *Meine Zeit*. It is true that only the characters in his youthful works are fully symbolic of their own time, while his later heroes are figures in a myth which grows more and more rigid, artificial and poetically ineffective.

It is also true, although Hemingway's effort toward the ideal of the great European novel yielded noble results, so that even his failures are not devoid of dignity and interest, his true genius tended to express itself in an elementary narrative form, in the limpidity of a lyrical and subjective "imagism," which apparently simplifies the context of life, but in effect contrives to include, in the sort of essential emotion it presents, a wide range of connotations. He is at his best in *A Farewell to Arms*, in *The Sun also Rises* and in his early short stories. These works, springing from the climate of war and its aftermath, will certainly continue to hold a very important place in American literature. The vast influence they had until the Forties on the young novelists both of America and Europe has many negative and ephemeral aspects, but has also been seriously constructive: in helping for instance young European writers to break away from narrow literary zones, to seek rejuvenation in greater closeness to present life, to revitalize their language, and also to turn back to certain forgotten lessons of the past.

CLINTON S. BURHANS JR.

The Old Man and the Sea:
Hemingway's Tragic Vision of Man

In *Death in the Afternoon*, Hemingway uses an effective metaphor to describe the kind of prose he is trying to write: he explains that "if a writer of prose knows enough about what he is writing about he may omit things that he knows and the reader, if the writer is writing truly enough, will have a feeling of those things as strongly as though the writer had stated them. The dignity of movement of an iceberg is due to only one-eighth of it being above water."

Among all the works of Hemingway which illustrate this metaphor, none, I think, does so more consistently or more thoroughly than the saga of Santiago. Indeed, the critical reception of the novel has emphasized this aspect of it: in particular, Philip Young, Leo Gurko, and Carlos Baker have stressed the qualities of *The Old Man and the Sea* as allegory and parable. Each of these critics is especially concerned with two qualities in Santiago—his epic individualism and the love he feels for the creatures who share with him a world of inescapable violence—though in the main each views these qualities from a different point of the literary compass. Young regards the novel as essentially classical in nature; Gurko sees it as reflecting Hemingway's romanticism; and to Baker, the novel is Christian in context, and the old fisherman is suggestive of Christ.

From *American Literature* XXXI (January 1960): 446–55. © 1960 by Duke University Press.

Such interpretations of *The Old Man and the Sea* are not, of course, contradictory; in fact, they are parallel at many points. All are true, and together they point to both the breadth and depth of the novel's enduring significance and also to its central greatness: like all great works of art it is a mirror wherein every man perceives a personal likeness. Such viewpoints, then, differ only in emphasis and reflect generally similar conclusions—that Santiago represents a noble and tragic individualism revealing what man can do in an indifferent universe which defeats him, and the love he can feel for such a universe and his humility before it.

True as this is, there yet remains, I think, a deeper level of significance, a deeper level upon which the ultimate beauty and the dignity of movement of this brilliant structure fundamentally rest. On this level of significance, Santiago is Harry Morgan alive again and grown old; for what comes to Morgan in a sudden and unexpected revelation as he lies dying is the matrix of the old fisherman's climactic experience. Since 1937, Hemingway has been increasingly concerned with the relationship between individualism and interdependence; and *The Old Man and the Sea* is the culminating expression of this concern in its reflection of Hemingway's mature view of the tragic irony of man's fate: that no abstraction can bring man an awareness and understanding of the solidarity and interdependence without which life is impossible; he must learn it, as it has always been truly learned, through the agony of active and isolated individualism in a universe which dooms such individualism.

II

Throughout *The Old Man and the Sea*, Santiago is given heroic proportions. He is "a strange old man," still powerful and still wise in all the ways of his trade. After he hooks the great marlin, he fights him with epic skill and endurance, showing "what a man can do and what a man endures." And when the sharks come, he is determined to " 'fight them until I die,'" because he knows that "'man is not made for defeat. . . . A man can be destroyed but not defeated.'"

In searching for and in catching his big fish, Santiago gains a deepened insight into himself and into his relationship to the rest of created life—an insight as pervasive and implicit in the old fisherman's experience as it is sudden and explicit in Harry Morgan's. As he sails far out on the sea, Santiago thinks of it "as feminine and as something that gave or withheld great favours, and if she did wild or wicked things it was because she could not help them." For the bird who rests on his line and for other creatures who share with him such a capricious and violent life, the old man feels friendship and love. And when he sees a flight of wild ducks go over, the old man knows "no man was ever alone on the sea."

Santiago comes to feel his deepest love for the creature that he himself hunts and kills, the great fish which he must catch not alone for physical need but even more for his pride and his profession. The great marlin is unlike the other fish which the old man catches; he is a spiritual more than a physical necessity. He is unlike the other fish, too, in that he is a worthy antagonist for the old man, and during his long ordeal, Santiago comes to pity the marlin and then to respect and to love him. In the end he senses that there can be no victory for either in the equal struggle between them, that the conditions which have brought them together have made them one. And so, though he kills the great fish, the old man has come to love him as his equal and his brother; sharing a life which is a capricious mixture of incredible beauty and deadly violence and in which all creatures are both hunter and hunted, they are bound together in its most primal relationship.

Beyond the heroic individualism of Santiago's struggle with the great fish and his fight against the sharks, however, and beyond the love and the brotherhood which he comes to feel for the noble creature he must kill, there is a further dimension in the old man's experience which gives to these their ultimate significance. For in killing the great marlin and in losing him to the sharks, the old man learns the sin into which men inevitably fall by going far out beyond their depth, beyond their true place in life. In the first night of his struggle with the great fish, the old man begins to feel a loneliness and a sense almost of guilt for the way in which he has caught him; and after he has killed the marlin, he feels no pride of accomplishment, no sense of victory. Rather, he seems to feel almost as though he has betrayed the great fish; "I am only better than him through trickery," he thinks, "and he meant me no harm."

Thus, when the sharks come, it is almost as a thing expected, almost as a punishment which the old man brings upon himself in going far out "beyond all people. Beyond all people in the world" and there hooking and killing the great fish. For the coming of the sharks is not a matter of chance nor a stroke of bad luck; "the shark was not an accident." They are the direct result of the old man's action in killing the fish. He has driven his harpoon deep into the marlin's heart, and the blood of the great fish, welling from his heart, leaves a trail of scent which the first shark follows. He tears huge pieces from the marlin's body, causing more blood to seep into the sea and thus attract other sharks; and in killing the first shark, the old man loses his principal weapon, his harpoon. Thus, in winning his struggle with the marlin and in killing him, the old man sets in motion the sequence of events which take from him the great fish whom he has come to love and with whom he identifies himself completely. And the old man senses an inevitability in the coming of the sharks, a feeling of guilt which deepens into remorse and regret. "I am sorry that I killed the fish . . . ," he thinks, and he tells himself that "You did not kill the fish only to keep alive and to sell for food. . . . You killed him for pride and because you are a fisherman."

Earlier, before he had killed the marlin, Santiago had been "'glad we do not have to try to kill the stars.'" It is enough, he had felt, to have to kill our fellow creatures. Now, with the inevitable sharks attacking, the old man senses that in going far out he has in effect tried "to kill the sun or the moon or the stars." For him it has not been "enough to live on the sea and kill our true brothers"; in his individualism and his need and his pride, he has gone far out "beyond all people," beyond his true place in a capricious and indifferent world, and has thereby brought not only on himself but also on the great fish the forces of violence and destruction. "'I shouldn't have gone out so far, fish . . . ,'" he declares. "'Neither for you nor for me. I'm sorry, fish.'" And when the sharks have torn away half of the great marlin, Santiago speaks again to his brother in the sea: "'Half-fish,' he said. 'Fish that you were. I am sorry that I went too far out. I ruined us both.'"

The old man's realization of what he has done is reflected in his apologies to the fish, and this realization and its implications are emphasized symbolically throughout the novel. From beginning to end the theme of solidarity and interdependence pervades the action and provides the structural framework within which the old man's heroic individualism and his love for his fellow creatures appear and function and which gives them their ultimate significance. Having gone eighty-four days without a catch, Santiago has become dependent upon the young boy, Manolin, and upon his other friends in his village. The boy keeps up his confidence and hope, brings him clothes and such necessities as water and soap, and sees that he has fresh bait for his fishing. Martin, the restaurant owner, sends the old man food, and Perico, the wineshop owner, gives him newspapers so that he can read about baseball. All of this the old man accepts gratefully and without shame, knowing that such help is not demeaning. "He was too simple to wonder when he had attained humility. But he knew he had attained it and he knew it was not disgraceful and it carried no loss of true pride."

Santiago refuses the young boy's offer to leave the boat his parents have made him go in and return to his, but soon after he hooks the great marlin he wishes increasingly and often that the boy were with him. And after the sharks come and he wonders if it had been a sin to kill the great fish, the old man thinks that, after all, "everything kills everything else in some way. Fishing kills me exactly as it keeps me alive." But then he remembers that it is not fishing but the love and care of another human being that keeps him alive now; "the boy keeps me alive, he thought. I must not deceive myself too much."

As the sharks tear from him more and more of the great fish and as the boat gets closer to his home, the old man's sense of his relationship to his friends and to the boy deepens: "I cannot be too far out now, he thought. I hope no one has been too worried. There is only the boy to worry, of course. But I am sure he would have confidence. Many of the older fishermen will worry. Many others too, he thought. I live in a good town." In the end, when he awakens in his shack and talks with the boy, he notices "how pleasant it was to have someone to talk to instead of speaking only to himself and to the sea." This time he accepts without any real opposition the boy's insistence on returning to his boat, and he says no more about going far out alone.

This theme of human solidarity and interdependence is reinforced by several symbols. Baseball, which the old man knows well and loves and which he thinks and talks about constantly, is, of course, a highly developed team sport and one that contrasts importantly in this respect with the relatively far more individualistic bullfighting, hunting, and fishing usually found in Hemingway's stories. Although he tells himself that "now is no time to think of baseball", the game is in Santiago's thoughts throughout his ordeal, and he wonders about each day's results in the *Gran Ligas*.

Even more significant is the old man's hero-worship of Joe DiMaggio, the great Yankee outfielder. DiMaggio, like Santiago, was a champion, a master of his craft, and in baseball terms an old one, playing out the last years of his glorious career severely handicapped by the pain of a bone spur in his heel. The image of DiMaggio is a constant source of inspiration to Santiago; in his strained back and his cut and cramped left hand he, too, is an old champion who must endure the handicap of pain; and he tells himself that he "must have confidence and . . . be worthy of the great DiMaggio who does all things perfectly even with the pain of the bone spur in his heel."

But DiMaggio had qualities at least as vital to the Yankees as his courage and individual brilliance. Even during his own time and since then, many men with expert knowledge of baseball have considered other contemporary outfielders—especially Ted Williams of the Boston Red Sox—to be DiMaggio's equal or superior in terms of individual ability and achievement. But few men have ever earned the affection and the renown which DiMaggio received as a "team player"—one who always displayed his individual greatness as part of his team, one to whom the team was always more important than himself. It used to be said of DiMaggio's value as a "team player" that with him in the line-up, even when he was handicapped by the pain in his heel, the Yankees were two runs ahead when they came out on the field.

From Santiago's love of baseball and his evident knowledge of it, it is clear that he would be aware of these qualities in DiMaggio. And when Manolin remarks that there are other men on the New York team, the old man replies: "'Naturally. But he makes the difference.'"

The lions which Santiago dreams about and his description in terms of Christ symbols further suggest solidarity and love and humility as opposed to isolated individualism and pride. So evocative and lovely a symbol is the dream of the lions that it would be foolish if not impossible to attempt its literal definition. Yet it seems significant that the old man dreams not of a single lion, a "king of the beasts," a lion proud and powerful and alone, like the one from which Francis Macomber runs in terror, but of several young lions who come down to a beach in the evening to play together. "He only dreamed of places now and of the lions on the beach. They played like young cats in the dusk and he loved them as he loved the boy." It seems also significant that the old man "no longer dreamed of storms, nor of women, nor of great occurrences, nor of great fish, nor fights, nor contests of strength nor of his wife,"—that is that he no longer dreams of great individualistic deeds like the one which brings violence and destruction on him and on the marlin. Instead, the lions are "the main thing that is left," and they evoke the solidarity and love and peace to which the old man returns after hunting and killing and losing his great fish.

These qualities are further emphasized by the symbolic value of the old fisherman as he carries the mast crosslike up the hill to his shack and as he lies exhausted on his bed. His hands have been terribly wounded in catching the great marlin and in fighting the sharks, and as he lies sleeping "face down on the newspapers with his arms out straight and the palms of his hands up," his figure is Christlike and suggests that if the old man has been crucified by the forces of a capricious and violent universe, the meaning of his experience is the humility and love of Christ and the interdependence which they imply.

Such, then, are the qualities which define man's true place in a world of violence and death indifferent to him, and they are the context which gives the experience of the old fisherman its ultimate significance as the reflection of Hemingway's culminating concept of the human condition—his tragic vision of man. For in his understanding that "it is enough to live on the sea and kill our true brothers," the fellow creatures who share life with us and whom he loves, the old man is expressing Hemingway's conviction that despite the tragic necessity of such a condition, man has a place in the world. And in his realization that in going alone and too far out, "beyond all people in the world," he has ruined both himself and also the great fish, the old man reflects Hemingway's feeling that in his individualism and his pride and his need, man inevitably goes beyond his true place in the world and thereby brings violence and destruction on himself and on others. Yet in going out too far and alone, Santiago has found his greatest strength and courage and dignity and nobility and love, and in this he expresses Hemingway's view of the ultimate tragic irony of man's fate: that only through the isolated individualism and the pride which drive him beyond his true place in life does man develop the qualities and the wisdom which teach him the sin of such individualism and pride and which bring him the deepest understanding of himself and of his place in the world. Thus, in accepting his world for what it is and in learning to live in it, Hemingway has achieved a tragic but ennobling vision of man which is in the tradition of Sophocles, Christ, Melville, and Conrad.

III

It is not enough, then, to point out, as Robert P. Weeks does, that "from the first eight words of *The Old Man and the Sea* . . . we are squarely confronted with a world in which man's isolation is the most insistent truth." True as this is, it is truth which is at the same time paradox, for Santiago is profoundly aware that "no man was ever alone on the sea." Nor is the novel solely what Leo Gurko feels it is—"the culmination of Hemingway's long search for disengagement from the social world and total entry into the natural." If the old man leaves society to go "far out" and "beyond all people in the world," the consciousness of society and of his relationship to it are never for long out of his thoughts; and in the end, of course, he returns to his "good town," where he finds it pleasant "to have someone to talk to instead of speaking only to himself and to the sea." To go no further than Santiago's isolation, therefore, or to treat it, as Weeks does, as a theme in opposition to Hemingway's concern with society is to miss the deepest level of significance both in this novel and in Hemingway's writing generally.

For, surely, as Edgar Johnson has shown, the true direction of Hemingway's thought and art from the beginning and especially since 1937 has been a return to society—not in terms of any particular social or political doctrine, but in the broad sense of human solidarity and interdependence. If he began by making "a separate peace" and by going, like Santiago, "far out" beyond society, like the old man, too, he has come back, through Harry Morgan's "'no man alone,'" Philip Rawlings's and Robert Jordan's "no man is an island," and Santiago's "no man is ever alone on the sea," with a deepened insight into its nature and values and a profound awareness of his relationship to it as an individual.

In the process, strangely enough—or perhaps it is not strange at all—

he has come back from Frederic Henry's rejection of all abstract values to a reiteration for our time of mankind's oldest and noblest moral principles. As James B. Colvert points out, Hemingway is a moralist: heir, like his world, to the destruction by science and empiricism of nineteenth-century value assumptions, he rejects equally these assumptions and the principle under-lying them—that intellectual moral abstractions possess independent super-sensual existence. Turning from the resulting nihilism, he goes to experience in the actual world of hostility, violence, and destruction to find in the world which destroyed the old values a basis for new ones—and it is precisely here. Colvert suggests, in reflecting the central moral problem of his world, that Hemingway is a significant moralist.

But out of this concern with action and conduct in a naturalistic universe, Hemingway has not evolved new moral values; rather, he has reaf-firmed man's oldest ones—courage, love, humility, solidarity, and interde-pendence. It is their basis which is new—a basis not in supernaturalism or abstraction but hard-won through actual experience in a naturalistic universe which is at best indifferent to man and his values. Hemingway tells us, as E. M. Halliday observes, that "we are part of a universe offering no assurance beyond the grave, and we are to make what we can of life by a pragmatic ethic spun bravely out of man himself in full and steady cognizance that the end is darkness."

Through perfectly realized symbolism and irony, then, Hemingway has beautifully and movingly spun out of an old fisherman's great trial just such a pragmatic ethic and its basis in an essentially tragic vision of man; and in this reaffirmation of man's most cherished values and their reaffirmation in the terms of our time rests the deepest and the enduring significance of *The Old Man and the Sea*.

ROBERT P. WEEKS

Fakery in The Old Man and the Sea

From the vignettes and stories of his first book, *In Our Time*, to his last, *The Old Man and the Sea*, Ernest Hemingway repeatedly made skillful use of animals to epitomize the subjective state or the situation of his characters. Nick Adams' trout holding itself steady against the cold current of the Big Two-Hearted River, Francis Macomber's gut-shot lion standing off death in the tall grass, the huge, filthy vultures keeping a death-watch on Harry on the plains at the foot of Kilimanjaro—objectively and precisely epitomize the crisis confronting the protagonist in each of these stories.

Yet these animals, and the others Hemingway uses to perform the same function, are nonetheless marvelously real. They possess in abundance what James called solidity of specification: they move, sound, and look like real animals.

The difference, however, in the effectiveness with which Hemingway employs this characteristic device in his best work and in *The Old Man and the Sea* is illuminating. The work of fiction in which Hemingway devoted the most attention to natural objects, *The Old Man and the Sea*, is pieced out with an extraordinary quantity of fakery, extraordinary because one would expect to find no inexactness, no romanticizing of natural objects in a writer who loathed W. H. Hudson, could not read Thoreau, deplored Melville's rhetoric in *Moby Dick*, and who was himself criticized by other

---

From *College English* 24 (1962): 182–92. © 1962 by the National Council of Teachers of English.

writers, notably Faulkner, for his devotion to the facts and his unwillingness to "invent."

Santiago, the only human being in the story, is himself depicted as a natural phenomenon, a strange old man whose heart beats like a turtle's, whose "feet and hands are like theirs," whose eyes are "the same color as the sea" and with which he could once "see quite well in the dark. Not in the absolute dark. But almost as a cat sees." But even these natural affinities do not prepare us for what this strange old man can do. As he sits in his skiff with more than six hundred feet of heavy line—the thickness of a pencil—slanting steeply down into the darkness of the stream, Santiago feels a fish nibble at the bait.

> He felt no strain nor weight and he held the line lightly. Then it came again. This time it was a tentative pull, not solid or heavy, and he knew exactly what it was. One hundred fathoms down a marlin was eating the sardines that covered the point and the shank of the hook where the hand-forged hook projected from the head of the small tuna.

This is not fishing skill; it's clairvoyance. The signals that can be transmitted over a pencil-thick line dangling more than six hundred feet into the ocean are relatively gross. Moreover, as Hemingway himself points out in his essay "Marlin Off Cuba," in *American Big Game Fishing*, published in an elegant limited edition of 906 copies by the Derrydale Press in 1935, one cannot tell whether the fish taking his bait is a marlin or a broadbill for they "take the bait in much the same manner, first, perhaps picking off a few of the sardines with which the point of the hook is covered, then seizing the whole fish used as bait between their jaws to crush it a moment before swallowing it."

This hint that Hemingway may be padding his characterization of Santiago by means of fakery is abundantly confirmed by the action that follows. His combat with the fish is an ordeal that would do in even a vigorous young man. He is at sea nearly four full days, almost all of that time without sleep and during much of it hanging onto a 1,500-pound fish that steadily tows him and his boat for miles, most of it *against* the current of the Gulf Stream. At noon on the third day, the giant fish circles the boat and the old man harpoons it, lashes it to the boat, and sets sail for home. Almost at once the sharks attack the fish, and the old man attacks the sharks. He battles them for more than twelve hours, quitting only when he runs out of weapons. Then, competently—and evidently without sleeping—he sails his little skiff for his home port, arriving shortly before dawn.

The extent to which this is an incredible performance is made clear when we turn to Hemingway himself for some notion of how an actual old Cuban fisherman behaved under similar circumstances. In "On the Blue Water," an essay that appeared in *Esquire* in 1936, Hemingway wrote:

> Another time an old man fishing alone in a skiff out of Cabanas hooked a giant marlin that, on the nearby sashcord handline, pulled the skiff far out to sea. Two days later the old man was picked up by fishermen sixty miles to the eastward, the head and forward part of the marlin lashed alongside. . . . He was crying in the boat when the fishermen picked him up, half crazy from his loss, and the sharks were still circling the boat.

It is hardly surprising that Santiago's clairvoyancy also enables him to be an uncanny meteorologist. While he is being towed by his fish, he looks at the sky, then soliloquizes: "If there is a hurricane you always see signs of it in the sky for days ahead, if you are at sea. They do not see it ashore because they do not know what to look for." Scientists on land, sea, and in the air equipped with delicate pressure-sensing devices and radar cannot duplicate the powers that Hemingway off-handedly—and unconvincingly—gives to Santiago. According to the Chief District Meteorologist of the United States Weather Bureau in Miami, Florida, Gordon E. Dunn, "It is usually impossible to see signs of a tropical storm for more than two days in advance and on occasion it is difficult to tell for sure that there is a tropical storm in the vicinity for even a day in advance."

But it is when Santiago's fish makes its first appearance that the fakery truly begins to flow. For example, the old man perceives at once that it is a male. Hemingway heroes almost always measure themselves against male animals, whether they are kudu, lions, bear, bulls, or fish. The tragedy enacted in the bull ring becomes a farce if you replace the bull with a cow. The hunter, the torero, the fisherman prove that *they* have *cojones* by engaging another creature that has them beyond dispute. Santiago's marlin is both huge and possessed of incredible endurance. He tows man and boat for nearly three days.

But the marlin presents problems. Its *cojones* are internal. "The sexes are not recognizable in these animals except by internal dissection," according to Gilbert Voss, an icthyologist with the University of Miami Marine Laboratory. Confronted by this dilemma—by the need to pit his hero against a male fish on the one hand, but a fish whose sex he won't be able to determine by dissection before the sharks devour all the evidence, on the other—Hemingway resorts to the fakery of having Santiago identify him at once as a male. In an effort, perhaps, to make this bit of fakery more believable, Hemingway has Santiago recall an experience with marlin in which he was able to distinguish the male from the female.

> He remembered the time he had hooked one of a pair of marlin. The male fish always let the female fish feed first and the hooked fish, the female, made a wild, panicstricken, despairing fight that soon exhausted her, and all the time the male had stayed with her, crossing the line and circling with her on the surface. He had stayed so close that the old man was afraid he would cut the line with his tail which was sharp as a scythe. . . . When the old man had gaffed her and clubbed her, . . . and then, . . . hoisted her aboard, the male fish had stayed by the side of the boat. Then while the old man was clearing the lines and preparing the harpoon, the male fish jumped high into the air beside the boat to see where the female was and then went down deep . . . He was beautiful, the old man remembered, and he had stayed.

Santiago's story of the devoted male marlin actually creates more problems than it solves. It is a preposterous piece of natural history, combining sentimentality and inexact observation. The Associate Curator of Fishes of the American Museum of Natural History, who was also a friend of Hemingway's, Francesca LaMonte, noticed an interesting parallel between Santiago's story and one Hemingway recounts in his marlin essay in *American Big Game Fishing*:

> Another time . . . my wife caught a 74-pound white marlin which was followed by three other marlin all through the fight. These three refused bait but stayed with the female fish until she was gaffed and brought aboard. Then they went down.

Miss LaMonte comments on this story that "You will note that the sex of the other fishes is not stated." Hemingway has Santiago incredibly enough identify the uncaught fish as males but in his essay he is more realistic.

Santiago and his fish are yoked by Hemingway's method of using the animal to epitomize some aspect of the man. The result, as Carlos Baker admiringly puts it, is "gallantry against gallantry." It is in fact more nearly fakery against fakery: a make-believe super-fish duelling a make-believe superfisherman.

It must be conceded that leaving aside these two formidable adversaries, there are brilliant flashes of Hemingway realism in *The Old Man and the Sea*. The sharks, for example, are depicted with remarkable vividness as they rush the dead marlin and savagely tear it apart. The shovel-nosed sharks with their "wide, flattened, shovel-pointed heads . . . and their slitted yellow cat-like eyes" are made "good and true enough" so that they are convincing as sharks *and* as embodiments of pure evil.

With the mako shark, however, Hemingway has not wholly resisted the impulse to fake. He has claimed for the mako that he can swim "as fast as the fastest fish in the sea" and equipped him with eight rows of teeth "shaped like a man's fingers when they are crisped like claws. They were nearly as long as . . . fingers . . . and they had razor-sharp cutting edges on both sides." E. M. Schroeder, of the Harvard Museum of Comparative Zoology, an authority on the sharks of the Atlantic, and other shark experts seriously doubt that the mako is as fast as the fastest fish. And they find support from Hemingway who in an article in *Game Fish of the World* says that the mako can "run faster than most," and in another article mentions the tuna and wahoo as "the fastest fish in the sea."

To describe the mako as having eight rows of teeth, as Hemingway does, is a great deal like saying that a five-year-old child has forty or so teeth. Only two rows of the shark's teeth are functional; the others are replacements which become functional as the forward teeth are lost or destroyed. Also, according to Professor Voss, only the main teeth in the mid part of the shark's jaw are as long, slender, and sharp as Hemingway describes *all* the teeth as being. Just as Santiago and his fish are given extraordinary powers they could not in fact possess, the biggest and most dangerous of the sharks, the mako, is made more menacing than he actually is.

II

Why are these inaccuracies of any consequence? No one thinks less of Keat's sonnet "On First Looking into Chapman's Homer" because in it Keats confused "stout Cortez" with Balboa as the discoverer of the Pacific; nor have the numerous anachronisms in Shakespeare's plays diminished his reputation or our enjoyment of his plays. Don't we read imaginative literature with an entirely different attitude toward fact from the one with which we consult an encyclopedia? The answer must be yes, but a qualified yes. We do not read either Keats or Shakespeare with the same expectations or assumptions as those we have when we read Hemingway. Hemingway is above all a realist; his aim had always been to communicate the facts exactly; and his reputation rests squarely on his success in doing so. As we read a Hemingway story or novel, his preoccupation with factual detail is immediately apparent. It is nowhere more apparent than in his heroes' respect for accuracy and a firm grip on the facts. Frederic Henry speaks for Hemingway, too, in what is probably the best known passage in *A Farewell to Arms* when he says: "Abstract words such as glory, honor, courage, or hallow were obscene beside the concrete names of villages, the number of roads, the names of rivers, the numbers of regiments and the dates." In short, the facts. And, likewise, those characters whom Hemingway places in contrast to his heroes are most readily distinguished not by their lack of honor, their insensitivity, or their political allegiances but by their sloppy handling of the facts. There is no clearer example of this than the tourist couple at the end of *The Old Man and the Sea* who look down into the water from the Terrace, see the skeleton of Santiago's great marlin, and ignorantly mistake it for a shark.

And Hemingway saw himself as a realist, too. His task in *The Old Man and the Sea*, as he saw it, was to give us a *real* old man, a *real* fish, and a *real* sea that would, if he had made them truly and well, mean many things. This is a reasonable definition of the goal of any realistic writer and provides us with a useful gauge of Hemingway's achievement. However, many critics have turned Hemingway's gauge upside down and upon discovering that the story of the old Cuban fisherman's ordeal can mean many things have praised it without troubling themselves to discover if the old man, the fish, and the sea are indeed "real," if they are indeed made "good and true."

The realism of Hemingway's first published stories is not an arbitrarily selected technique: it is an inevitable part of his world view. Confronted by the violence and meaninglessness of the world he saw as a boy in upper Michigan, as an 18-year-old police reporter on the *Kansas City Star*, and as a young man on the Italian front in World War I, in the Greco-Turkish War, and in the cities of Europe in the 1920's, he cultivated a bare, stoical, tight-lipped style that was an ideal instrument for exploring that God-abandoned world. The bullfighters, expatriates, soldiers, boxers, and guerillas were rendered vividly but truly and objectively. And their stance, if they were among the initiated, was much like the style that depicted them, one of tense control, like Nick Adams' trout holding itself steady against the current of the Big Two-Hearted River.

But the style has gone soft in *The Old Man and the Sea* because the view of the world has gone soft. Santiago's universe is not the chaotic universe in which Nick Adams, Frederic Henry, Jake Barnes, and Robert Jordan encountered meaningless violence and evil. It is more nearly a cozy universe in which fish have nobility and loyalty and other virtues no one since St. Francis of Assisi—and least of all Ernest Hemingway—would have suspected them of. It is a universe so chummy that the hero calls various birds his brothers. The sharks introduce a semblance of evil into this warm universe, but it tends to be a stagey, melodramatic evil almost too villainous to be believable. The same is true of the big Portuguese man-of-war trailing its poisonous tentacles as it sails by Santiago's skiff fully six months before an animal this size would normally appear in Cuban waters.

The soft, fuzzy tone of *The Old Man and the Sea* reaches its nadir in that scene shortly after sunset when the incredible old man, still being towed by his incredible fish, looks into the heavens and sees the first star of this universe shining out. Hemingway comments: "He did not know the name of Rigel but he saw it and knew soon they would all be out and he would have all his distant friends." This cosmic camaraderie is patently false and forced. This is not the violent, chaotic world that young Hemingway discovered and explored with a style whittled from a walnut stick. In that world the stars were cold and remote—as stars really are. In the world of *The Old Man and the Sea*, they are "friends" whom the author in a patronizing intrusion identifies for us—incorrectly. Rigel does not appear in Cuban skies at sunset in September but some five hours after Santiago sees it. It is, perhaps, a trifling error, which, even if we happen to be aware of it, does not surprise us in a novel in which so much else is inexactly observed or tricked out in an effort to extort more feeling than a reasonable person would find there.

The honest, disciplined quest for "the way it was" finally ran down. *The Old Man and the Sea* stands as an end point of that quest. Yet it is not without greatness. To call it an inferior Hemingway novel still leaves it standing well above most other novels of our time. But some of its greatness is that of a monument serving to remind us of earlier glories.

The test of any book is how much good stuff you can throw away. I try to write on the principle of the iceberg: seven-eighths of it is underwater. The Old Man and the Sea could have been a thousand pages long. But I had a good man and a good boy, and of course the ocean is worth writing about just as the man is. So I was lucky. I've seen the marlin mate and know about that. So I could leave that out. I've seen a school of more than fifty sperm whales and once harpooned one nearly sixty feet in length, then lost him. So I could leave that out. All the stories I heard from the fishing village I left out. But the knowledge was there— and it was what made up the underwater part of my iceberg.

ERNEST HEMINGWAY

BICKFORD SYLVESTER

Hemingway's Extended Vision:
The Old Man and the Sea

Cleanth Brooks wrote recently that the early story, "Fifty Grand," "presents Hemingway's basic theme quite as well as *The Old Man and the Sea.*" "Nor do I think," he continued, "that Hemingway in his most recent story now finds the world any more meaningful than he once found it." For once Mr. Brooks was following rather than initiating opinion. Ever since *The Old Man and the Sea* was published, critics have admitted that in its effect upon the reader the book is somehow different from Hemingway's earlier work. Those who like the difference and those who do not have tried to account for it in many ways, most of them familiar to readers of the early reviews and of the surprisingly few later readings of the story. But to a man commentators have assumed that whatever the story's new impact—whatever the nature of that affirmative power most readers have felt—it reflects no essential change in Hemingway's view of an inscrutable natural order in which, ultimately, man can play no part. I want to suggest, on the contrary, that *The Old Man and the Sea* reveals Hemingway's successful achievement at last of a coherent metaphysical scheme—of a philosophical naturalism which, although largely mechanistic in principle, embraces the realm of human affairs and gives transcendent meaning to the harsh inevitabilities Hemingway has always insisted upon recording.

I think it is precisely the failure to recognize the presence of this informing scheme that has hampered the most searching students of the

From *PMLA* 81 (1966): 130–38. © 1966 by Modern Language Association.

story. And what is equally important, I think this oversight largely accounts for several recent interpretative extremes. On the one hand we have Clinton S. Burhans with his well-intentioned portrayal of the aging Hemingway as an apologist for conventional views of human solidarity, and on the other hand we have Robert P. Weeks supporting the *Encounter* critics by insisting that because the style and attitude of *The Old Man and the Sea* is different from that in Hemingway's earlier work, the book is a fuzzy-minded failure, inferior to the first short stories.

Therefore, let me work into my analysis of the story by at least attempting to answer Mr. Burhans, whose article has been reprinted by Carlos Baker and is often discussed in the classroom. In referring to Santiago's apology for having "gone out so far," Burhans argues that the old man's sin is specifically that of "isolated individualism in a universe which dooms such individualism." But Santiago's has been a necessary transgression, says Burhans, because in the story "only through the isolated individualism and the pride which drive him beyond his true place in life does man develop the qualities and the wisdom which teach him the sin of such individualism and pride." Like Hemingway himself, Burhans thinks, Santiago has had wrongfully to withdraw from the social community in order finally to appreciate the old values of "human solidarity and interdependence." But rather than the homogeneously interdependent community Burhans posits, in which individualism must be viewed ironically, there are the passive dependents and the active, tested individuals, as always before in Hemingway's works. Indeed, the distinction in the story between those who break the way for themselves and those who depend upon others has been clearly identified by Leo Gurko. As Gurko points out, among all the living creatures in the story, including the men, those who are fearless and aggressive are conspicuously portrayed as clean, beautiful, and aesthetically satisfying in their behavior. On the other hand, the "hateful," "bad smelling" scavengers are uniformly disgusting, dishonest, and awkward. Now the guilt for which Santiago apologizes cannot be that of individualism if individualism is the only mode of behavior sympathetically portrayed. Nor, conversely, can interdependence be the positive norm if it is also evil and dirty.

Then there is a second fundamental error in Burhans' thesis. He insists that "the theme of solidarity and interdependence pervades the action and provides the structural framework within which the old man's heroic individualism and his love for his fellow creatures appear and function." Yet according to most readings—all of which are true, Burhans allows—the basic structural principle of the story is that of natural parallels to man's experience. Thus no framework essentially human in focus, as is Burhans', can include the deepest origins of the story's meaning. We are presented, then, not with a pragmatic ethic spun "out of man himself," as Burhans remarks, quoting E. M. Halliday, but specifically out of man's experience of the rest of nature.

The community element should therefore be considered as a motif somehow ancillary to the theme of natural precedence which accounts for the rich complexity of the story. Burhan's primary assumption, of course, is that Hemingway has increasingly turned from his earlier concern with the universals of nature to concentrate upon the relations between men, and he cites *For Whom the Bell Tolls* as indicative. Still convinced of the inscrutability of the universe, Burhans thinks, Hemingway has settled, finally, for the warmth that men can derive from each other. If an objective appraisal of *all* of *The Old Man and the Sea* establishes anything, however, it is that this particular direction in Hemingway's thought and art has reversed since *For Whom the Bell Tolls*. If the theme of the novel is that "no man is an island," the theme of the story is that man*kind* is not an island. The idea can be found in the Old Testament sermon from which Hemingway took the title of his first novel: "For that which befalleth the sons of men befalleth/beasts; even one thing befalleth them; as the one/dieth so dieth the other; yea, they have all one/breath; so that man hath no pre-eminence above a/beast (Ecclesiastes iii.19). Long ago Hemingway declared of social concerns in general: "Let those who want to save the world if you can get to see it clear and as a whole." And I think that the serenity which readers find new in *The Old Man and the Sea* springs from Hemingway's discovery at last of a quintessential natural truth which gives meaning to all struggles, including man's.

What is this essential perception, then, and how does it reconcile Santiago's individualism with the passivity of the shallow water fisherman? There is indeed in *The Old Man and the Sea* a greater tolerance shown toward the total community than ever before in Hemingway's work. Burhans, like many reviewers, is right in perceiving this much. But rather than interdependence, there is implied the dependence of the many upon the one, of the passive community upon a potent individual redeemer who, in his dependence upon a principle basic to universal order, is independent of all men. This is the implication of the Calvary allusions and it is, furthermore, consistent with the individualism stressed by the system of natural parallels throughout the story. Without going into extensive illustration, I want to outline what I mean.

A careful study of the behavior of the creatures Santiago encounters at sea reveals an affirmation of the values of strength, total immersion in activity, and the exploitation of adversity. Several species include exceptional individual members whose aggression and desire for intensity of experience lead them to oppose natural manifestations. Thus the great marlin turns against the Gulf Stream as soon as he is hooked, and refuses to yield to the current until the moment of his death. Yet his blue stripes, the color of the sea, reveal that in his paradoxical opposition to the sea he is closer to her than are the brown surface fish who always swim with the current.

Accordingly, the other champions of the story, who each bear the color of the sea, also inherit a defiance of their mother's whims. The blue-eyed Santiago, who has only his hands between himself and the sea (no buoys or machines), only the food the sea proffers, and whose very sun cancer is significantly benign, also demonstrates that the sea bestows her greatest favors upon those who make their own conditions. Like the marlin, the blue-backed Mako shark who "would do exactly what he wished", and the golden dolphin who shows purple stripes when he is "truly hungry" enough to take any risk, Santiago opposes the sea when her vagaries conflict with his purpose. He crowds the current, and he gladly risks the dangerous hurricane months in which, significantly, the biggest fish are to be had.

Indeed, by a chain of associations pervading the texture of the story, opposition to nature is paradoxically revealed as necessary to vitality in the natural field upon which the action takes place. Both the marlin and the "September" fisherman are old, oriented away from that phase of the life cycle when the natural sources of energy flow freely. But the greater concentration thus required of them yields the greater intensity which is an indication of life itself. All implications accrue, eventually, to expose a fundamental natural principle of harmonious opposition. Hence flow subsidiary motifs which can also best be stated as oxymorons: compassionate violence, comfortable pain, life in death, aged strength, and victorious defeat. These provide the structure of the story.

Each of the exceptional individuals of the various species has something "strange" about his eyes which suggests his perception of the paradoxical logic of nature. Acting accordingly, each adopts a mode of behavior which leads ultimately to his death in an intense contest with a champion from another species. But upon this contact, which always leads to impossible odds for one, depends the vital interplay of nature, as I shall explain presently. "I killed the shark that hit my fish," says Santiago, suggesting the vital round. And Santiago, because of this acceptance of the terrible odds, is able to become "the towering bitt", the essential link, between humanity and the natural world. Christlike, he must "cushion the pull of the line" with his body. Like the marlin, and the Mako who is also part of the scheme, he bears in calm solitude the terrible brunt of the only genuine communion with nature, and thus in his agony he redeems the unextended ones, the shallow water fishermen who make up most of the human race. The parasitical surface fish and the scavenger sharks, of course, fill out the rest of the other two species involved in the circular scheme.

Very subtly, then, the rationale emerges in which Hemingway is at last able to see some transcendent purpose in the stringent individualism he has hitherto regarded, bleakly, as an end in itself. It is a rationale, I think, in which the exceptional performer's position is secure enough to permit his serene acceptance of his fellows. The majority was not born to be like him and yet, dependent upon him, it has its place in the world. Thus, I suggest, we can account for Santiago's compassionate understanding of the shallow water fishermen, without forcing ourselves to ignore the positive emphasis upon exceptional achievement pervasive in the story.

Indeed, it is entirely wrong to regard Santiago's individual experience as valuable only as a lesson in the folly of isolated activity, and to suggest, therefore, that Santiago's reward comes at the end of his journey as he rejoins the community. For Santiago's reward comes, not on land but at the farthest point in his circular voyage, at the moment of his greatest isolation from other men. It comes when he plunges his lance into his quarry.

As Santiago concludes his awesome chase, the fish leaps high out of the water and dies. The marlin seems at the summit of his death leap "to hang in the air" above his slayer. Surely this is another of the moments of cessation occurring at the high points in the circular experiences of all Hemingway's major heroes, and serving to define the achievement of transcendent experience. Yet the point has not been commented upon. Frederic I. Carpenter, in a discussion of intensified experience in Hemingway's work generally, has noted that Santiago's realistic performance of the "ritual techniques of his trade," and his subsequent identification of "the intensity of his own suffering with that of the fish," contribute to an "occasional mysticism" in the story. Some attention to the moment of the marlin's death, however, would have given greater point to Carpenter's thesis. For as the fish seems to Santiago to hang "motionless in the sky" before it falls, the old man is (like Robert Jordan when he feels the "earth move out and away" from him and Maria) undergoing a sensation of timelessness in time—an ecstatic perception of what Carpenter calls the "eternal now." Santiago "was sure there was some great strangeness and he could not believe it." The contest in which Santiago has been engaged is presented as a pattern of action in time so exactly in accord with what has always happened everywhere that there is no discrepancy between the immediate enactment and the eternal act. As the "now" and the perpetual become fused, relativity ceases; thus for the participants in the action all sensation of motion disappears. Santiago's reward for his struggle is, therefore, not in the nature of a lesson at all. It is that Lear-like perception of the eternal which the very rare creature can wrest from the round of existence, the one boon that cannot be reclaimed by the sea which has provided it.

But what is of greater importance is that Santiago's moment of "strangeness" marks the first time in Hemingway's major fiction in which the experience of ultimate participation culminates a hero's main endeavor. There are Jake Barnes' peaceful fishing trip above Burguete, and Lieutenant Henry's idyllic winter interlude away from the war; and Robert Jordan's ecstasy occurs, of course, during a lull in his preparation for the bridge. Thus each earlier case clearly suggests that the rest of the universe operates only according to the frictionless concord implicit in moments of ideal love—as a Shelleyan cosmos, actually—and that man's manifest dedication to violence must leave him ultimately cut off from consonance with all that is universal and abiding, merely tantalized and diminished by what he has glimpsed. But Santiago's vision culminates his commitment to worldly struggle. Thus the compassionate violence implicit in his slaying of the marlin he loves is revealed as the key to a universal harmony in which man may partake. Hemingway has at last been able to employ the central paradox of the bull-fight and the hunt so as successfully to reconcile the forces of love and violence which have hitherto remained ironically separated in his major works of fiction.

His achievement is partly foreshadowed by two incidents in *For Whom the Bell Tolls*. As Jordan sets up a machine gun, soon after his experience of sexual transport with Maria, she begs him to tell her that he loves her and at the same time to let her help him shoot. But Jordan still lives in the world of all Hemingway's earlier heroes, a world in which there can be no meeting ground for love and killing:

> "Dejamos. Get thee back. One does not do that and love all at the same moment."
> "I want to hold the legs of the gun and while it speaks love thee all in the same moment."
> "Thou art crazy. Get thee back now."

Only in the last chapter of the novel, just before he crosses the fatal road, does Jordan learn better.

> He had never thought that you could know that there was a woman if there was battle; nor that if there was a woman that she should have breasts small, round and tight against you through a shirt; *nor that they, the breasts, could know about the two of them in battle*. But it was true and he thought, good. That's good. (italics mine)

It is good because it means that under certain conditions violence and love turn on the same axis, that the course of Jordan's return to worldly entanglement does not lead away from the meaningful continuity of the universe, but is only another part of its endless flux. Jordan's thoughts at this point mark a major advance in Hemingway's work, I think, for they express the insight which is modified and developed in *The Old Man and the Sea*. Jordan seems to realize as he lies alone at the end of the novel that by killing "to prevent something worse from happening to other people" he is, in effect, committing an act of love. And as he presses himself against the forest floor, his eyes fixed on the white clouds, there is the suggestion that he is once again caught up in natural order as he had been when making love to Maria.

Yet his violent delaying action against the fascists is to be, after all, not in itself an act of love, but an act in the service of love. Clearly Jordan's second feeling of consonance with nature is but a reward for his championship of the blissful ideal which informs the love scene. His experience is emphatically more intense in the earlier scene than in the later one. It is not until *The Old Man and the Sea*, therefore, when Hemingway shifts his focus from human affairs to the vital contact between species—and between the creatures and the rest of nature—that he manages to compress the bases for Jordan's separate mystical experiences into a single culminative moment.

Now the fact that Hemingway is able at last to see the world "clear and as a whole" only by perceiving that love and violence may be simultaneously expressed—and that in order to do so he has had to replace the protective aspect of Jordan's love by Santiago's sense of identification with a respected adversary—leaves his new conception obviously vulnerable to all sorts of value judgments. His vision of something rather like a cosmic bull ring invites us to question whether there are not metaphysical, social, and even biological complexities which cannot be crowded into such an arena. But I am concerned here with the specific way in which Hemingway extends *his* view of reality so as to discover a harmony between human and natural affairs as he sees them. And there is evidence beyond his published work that Hemingway was preoccupied during the last of his productive period with employing the paradoxical fusion of affection and violence more centrally in his fiction than he ever had earlier. In 1951 Professor Harry Burns of the University of Washington read manuscripts of *The Old Man and the Sea* and of the novella now tentatively entitled *The Sea Chase*, one of the series of works that we have heard Hemingway originally intended to publish with *The Old Man and the Sea*. Professor Burns has given me permission to report that Hemingway had been working back and forth between these other units and *The Old Man and the Sea* intermittently for ten years. He had indeed thought of publishing the whole group together. And *The Sea Chase*, the other unit most nearly in finished form in 1951, dealt with an anti-submarine captain in the Caribbean whose animosity toward an enemy submarine commander developed into grudging admiration and finally into love, even as he intensified a deadly pursuit of his unseen undersea victim. The thematic parallel to *The Old Man and the Sea* is striking, of course.

But to return to *The Old Man and the Sea* itself, Santiago's epiphany is not our only indication that in their tense struggles the champions in the story act in accord with natural order. The marlin's fight lasts exactly forty-eight hours; it is seventy-two hours, from morning to morning, between Santiago's departure and his resurgence of vitality at the story's end; and another great primitive up against invincible odds, the "Great negro from Cienfuegos" whom Santiago defeats in "the hand game," struggles just twenty-four hours even—from dawn to dawn. Thus the champions' ordeals achieve temporal synchronization with the larger units of natural order. Furthermore, the marlin's "strange" death occurs at noon. He dies at the crest of a leap as the sun is at its apex. And we are reminded that for the sun, too, the moment of defeat is also one of supreme victory. The sun also falls, but like the marlin, the Negro, and the fisherman, it has lasted all the way around. Nor can we forget the shape of Santiago's entire sea-journey, far out to the moment of brief stasis in which victory and defeat are in fleeting balance—and then the return to port. This temporal and spatial coincidence between the journey of the sun and the various rounds of combat implies consonance with an order which is supra-animate—which is universal in the observable physical world.

Moreover, the emphasis upon temporal completion suggests specifically that nature sanctions the champions' intuitive maintenance of a precise degree of intensity—the source of that good pain, "the pain of life," which comes to Santiago *"easily* and *smoothly"* (italics mine). The marlin's aggressive reaction to the current is tempered by his calmness. He does not seek brief balance, but a prolonged approximate balance. Rather than run himself out in a futile flurry as do lesser fish, or break the line and immediately free himself, Hemingway makes clear, he seems to accept his inevitable sacrifice and, like Santiago against the sharks, seek rather to endure than to prevail— to last a certain amount of time while fighting all the way. It is this ideal degree of force—not great enough to end the tension, and yet enough to keep up as much tension as possible—which earns him his harmony with the sun, and which emerges as the final dynamic principle of natural perpetuity. (The fishing line, stretched just under the breaking-point throughout the chase, is a suggestive symbol.) The fish has left just enough strength for his great leap as he dies, and Hemingway remarks, "Then the fish came *alive,* with his *death* in him" (italics mine). The marlin has found the most intense life in this kind of death—in having lasted all the way around while retaining enough strength to meet the final thrust of the harpoon with the same resolute aggression he has shown toward the stream and the weight of the boat.

And the sharks are to the man what the man and current have been to the fish. Led by the champion shark, they are the final overwhelming natural odds against which a champion must pit himself. As they do their work Santiago's material gain and his strength are eaten away as had been the marlin's heading against the Gulf Stream, so that the reader feels a parallel between the old man's continued struggle after his marketable take is gone and the marlin's stubborn resistance even when he is turned "almost east" with the current. But like the fish the man has paced himself. He fights the sharks until "something" in his chest is broken (just as the fish's heart had been pierced by the harpoon) and he notices the "coppery" taste of his blood in his mouth. Yet even at the end of the story, as he tells the boy of his broken chest, he undergoes a resurgence of life and plans another trip. He, too, comes alive "with his death in him." He will die. That is why the boy is "crying again" as he leaves the old man sleeping. Death is the final concomitant of life in a champion's combat with nature. And the only reason Santiago's death is not portrayed within the story is that his heart, like that of the great turtle he loves, will continue to beat "for hours after he has been cut up and butchered."

But what matters is that as a champion he has contributed to the order of the universe: that like the great creatures he has opposed he possesses innate qualities which have permitted him to bring his struggle to cyclical completion without relaxing the tension of life even though he has felt his death in him. I doubt that Hemingway could have found a more felicitous representation of this orderly opposition of forces than the twenty-four-hour hand-game which ends the great Negro's competitive career. As we have observed at length, the mechanistic principle of life objectified in that scene reverberates throughout the story. It insinuates itself kinesthetically into our nerves and muscles as we read. And this is what accounts, I suggest, for much of that extraordinary artistic impact which has for so long intrigued interpreters and eluded definition.

Clearly, then, the value of the rare act is found in the act itself, not in a reaction against it, as Burhans' thesis demands, nor even primarily in its power to inspire others in the community or yield satisfaction for its participants, as Earl Rovit has suggested. Such an act—such a life—on the part of its exceptional creatures is valuable as the only means whereby each species is permitted its contribution to the systematic tension of the universe. And this contribution is the object of that mythic quest which Rovit quite rightly perceives in Santiago's journey.

The sin for which Santiago apologizes, therefore, is not that of having left his "true place in the world," as Burhans claims. Yet contrary to Rovit's feeling, there is an element of tragic sin in the story. There is the suggestion that Santiago's slaying of the marlin and his responsibility for its mutilation are sins, and that they are tragic precisely because they are a necessary result of his behavior as a champion of his species. In Hemingway's work, generally, the destruction of beauty is a sin. We are reminded of the rhetorical question in *Death in the Afternoon*: "Do you know the sin it would be to ruffle the arrangement of the feathers on a hawk's neck if they could never be replaced?" And within the context of *The Old Man and the Sea* Santiago's sin is even greater. For he has destroyed the huge fish's power of opposition, his spiritual as well as his physical beauty. Santiago does not want to look at the fish after the sharks have started their attack because, "drained of blood and awash he looked the colour of the silver backing of a mirror and his stripes still showed." The association with a mirror, which reflects whatever is before it, suggests complete passivity; and the stripes still show to remind Santiago that this champion once was predominantly blue, bright with the color of opposition. At the end of the story the lifeless tail of the great fish who has so resolutely battled the powerful current lifts and swings "with the tide," and his stripped skeleton waits "to go out with the tide." Santiago has rendered his respected adversary devoid of autonomy in a world where autonomy is the supreme virtue.

Indeed, the old man's human consciousness of his guilt, his awareness that in order to be right he must also be wrong, is the most formidable obstacle to resolution which he encounters during his voyage. Perhaps this uniquely human handicap is the hampering "bone spur" Santiago ponders as he thinks of DiMaggio: "Maybe we have them without knowing of it," he reflects. At any rate, it is the one valid element of humanism in the story. In overcoming it Santiago demonstrates the one thing "that a man can do" that is not duplicated by the other natural aristocrats. In this limited sense the story can be seen as profoundly humanistic, as a modern parable of man's fallen state in which the universe requires man to overcome more in order to achieve what is necessary for all creatures. But no reading should ignore the fundamental emphasis upon natural aristocracy which alone gives the book its value as a commentary upon man.

It is therefore unfortunate that Burhans, who is the only critic to direct sufficient attention to the concept of necessary sin in *The Old Man and the Sea*, is led astray by his need to make Hemingway into something he is not. Burhans' approach may please those who are resigned to the absence of supernaturalism in great contemporary works, but who will not accept the pragmatic ethic they find in such works unless it happens to support the

traditions of western humanism. Hemingway suffers as much from the ratio-
nalizations of such critics as he does from those of the Marxists. For although
man may be in the foreground he is not the measure of Hemingway's final
world, and uniquely human qualities do not provide the norms of that world.

That is why Hemingway remained primarily fascinated by those
rare men whose talents spring from their natural superiority rather than
from their methodical application of experience. In the last published work
of his lifetime, his magazine account of the contest between the matadors
Dominguin and Antonio Ordoñez, Hemingway demonstrated his new-
found tolerance and made a statement which might seem to bear out the
contention that he had indeed abandoned his exclusivism. Contemplating a
foolish chauffeur who once tried to make the sign of the cross a substitute for
skill, Hemingway recalled: "Then I thought again and remembering . . . the
need for solidarity in this passing world I repeated his gesture." But the
whole account of the contest itself turns upon a qualitative distinction
between Dominguin, a skilled and intellectual performer, and Ordoñez, who
is "a natural." Hemingway is first escorted to Ordoñez by a very successful
matador: "Jesus Cordoba is an excellent boy and a good and intelligent
matador and I enjoyed talking with him. *He left me at the door of Antonio's
room*." With characteristic understatement, of course, Hemingway was
suggesting the almost mystical reverence with which he observed a separation between the intelligent man and the natural rarity. Then, precisely
echoing his description of another great man—and a marlin and a shark—he
said, "I noticed the eyes first . . . those strange eyes." Hemingway had
mellowed, but he had abandoned nothing. He had simply moved forward.

What is new in *The Old Man and the Sea*, let me repeat, is
Hemingway's discovery that the need for extended effort in the face of
inevitable darkness is not merely a man-made hypothesis, not a masochistic
sop to the unmoored human ego, but the reflection of a natural law man is
permitted to follow. The idea of an immanent order based upon the tension
between opposed forces is in one formulation or another a familiar one, of
course. We think of Heraclitus, and Hegel, as well as of more recent philoso-
phers. But the idea has perhaps never been so consummately concretized in
a work of art as it is in *The Old Man and the Sea*, where its presence is in all
likelihood almost entirely a product of Hemingway's life-long observation of
man and nature. The order with which Santiago achieves consonance is
indeed limited to the natural world. But within the observable physical
universe of this story man is seen to play his part in a way which has not yet
been sufficiently articulated by any critic.

We can see a way, then, in which Mr. Weeks is wrong to be
disturbed by the several errors in factual observation in the story.

Hemingway is working here partly with new artistic means to match his new vision. Formerly, convinced of the absence of a perceptible order in the world, Hemingway made a fetish of presenting objects exactly as they appeared, so that any latent meaning could shine through them without distortion. But here, convinced of the principle behind the facts, he can occasionally take poetic license and present objects for any kind of associational value they may have. Mr. Weeks thinks it merely a lazy error on Hemingway's part, for example, that Rigel, the first star Santiago sees one night, actually appears close to midnight in the Caribbean. But Rigel, after all, is a first-magnitude star in the constellation of Orion, the hunter. And it is entirely appropriate, symbolically, to call attention to Santiago's attunement with the stars in this way. Hemingway is in this story at last attempting to pull the world together, rather than to reveal its ironic division. Thus "the way it was" need no longer be his sole guide as an artist.

It we are accurately to assess Hemingway's total achievement—and it is now our responsibility to begin that task—we must recognize that he was a writer who neither abandoned nor helplessly parodied his essential vision, but who significantly extended it, finding in paradox and symbolism the artistic means to do so. However we may evaluate his advance, we must severely qualify our tendency to regard him as the champion of mindlessness in literature. For we have evidence in the last great published work of his lifetime that either consciously or unconsciously he eventually became as concerned with perfecting what he had to say as he had always been with polishing his way of saying it.

PHILIP YOUNG

The Old Man and the Sea: *Vision/Revision*

This book has many roots in the rest of Hemingway's work. Much of it goes back to an essay, "On the Blue Water (A Gulf Stream Letter)," which the author published in *Esquire*, in April of 1936. In this piece he tried to explain what there is about deep-sea fishing in the Stream that makes it exciting—the mysteries of that largely unexplored place, the indescribable strangeness, wildness, speed, power and beauty of the enormous marlin which inhabit it, and the struggle while their strength is bound to a man's, his thick line "taut as a banjo string and little drops coming from it." He also included a paragraph of more specific interest:

> Another time an old man fishing alone in a skiff out of Cabañas hooked a great marlin that, on the heavy sashcord hand-line, pulled the skiff far out to sea. Two days later the old man was picked up by fishermen sixty miles to the eastward, the head and forward part of the marlin lashed alongside. What was left of this fish, less than half, weighed eight hundred pounds. The old man had stayed with him a day, a night, a day and another night while the fish swam deep and pulled the boat. When he had come up the old man had pulled the boat up on him and harpooned him. Lashed alongside the sharks had hit him and the old man

From *Ernest Hemingway: A Reconsideration*. © 1966 by Philip Young.

had fought them out alone in the Gulf Stream in a skiff, clubbing them, stabbing at them, lunging at them with an oar until he was exhausted and the sharks had eaten all that they could hold. He was crying in the boat when the fishermen picked him up, half crazy from his loss, and the sharks were still circling the boat.

Here, of course, is the germ of the novel. And the old man himself, Santiago, is also an outgrowth of past performances. Just as Col. Cantwell presented the Hemingway hero aged for the first time beyond his young manhood, so Santiago is the first of the code heroes to have grown old. Particularly he is related to men like Jack, the prizefighter, and Manuel Garcia, "The Undefeated" bullfighter, who lose in one way but win in another. Like Manuel, Santiago is a fighter whose best days are behind him, who is too old for what his profession demands of him and, worse, is wholly down on his luck. But he still dares, and sticks to the rules, and will not quit when he is licked. He is undefeated, he endures, and his loss therefore, in the manner of it, is itself a victory.

"A man can be destroyed but not defeated," is how Hemingway put it this time. And so the theme—"What a man can do and what a man endures" ("plenty," as Santiago admits of his suffering)—is also familiar. So are other things—Hemingway's concern with fishing as a deeply meaningful occupation, for instance, and his awareness of death, expertly delivered and received, as the source of much of life's intensity. In a way we have even known the boy before, for in providing that sentimental adulation which is his need for love and pity the other hero once required, Manolin has taken over some of the functions hitherto performed by the heroine.

There is little that is new, either, in the technique. The action is swift, tight, exact; the construction is perfect, and the story is exciting. There is the same old zest for the right details. And there is the extraordinary vividness of the background—the sea, which is very personal to Santiago, whose knowledge of it, and feeling for it, bring it brilliantly and lovingly close. Again there is the foreign speech translated—realistic, fresh and poetic all at once. In short, *The Old Man and the Sea*, in manner and meaning, is unmistakable Hemingway. But where characteristic methods and attitudes have on rare occasion failed him in the past, or have been only partly successful, this short novel is beyond any question a triumph.

This is the first time, in all of Hemingway's work, that the code hero and the Hemingway hero have not been wholly distinct. Wilson the guide, Cayetano the gambler, Morgan the smuggler—all embodied ideals of behavior the Hemingway hero could not sustain. They balanced his deficiencies; they corrected his stance. Of course Santiago is not Hemingway, and is not the Hemingway hero; he is the code hero, based on the experience of an unfictional Cuban fisherman. But now the relation of the author and the code hero is very close. Though Hemingway was thought with the phrase to be acknowledging his eccentricity, whereas Santiago makes it clear that he means he is formidable, both figures were given to remarking "I am a strange old man." And both men were preoccupied with their "luck"—a kind of magic which people have in them, or do not. Indeed it is the only flaw in the book, beyond our involuntary recollections of the heroine, that there are times when the old fisherman sounds a little like Col. Cantwell: "Do not think about sin," Santiago tells himself with uncharacteristic sarcasm. "There are people who are paid to do it."

What this means, among other things, is that Hemingway was narrowing the gap that had always existed between him and his code heroes. Actually he narrowed it to the point where it is possible to show that on one level *The Old Man and the Sea* was wholly personal: as he seemed obscurely to acknowledge his demotion in *Across the River* by removing the stars from Cantwell's shoulders, so here Hemingway seemed, but more obviously, to promote himself back. Harry, dying in "The Snows of Kilimanjaro," was himself a writer, and the Hemingway hero, but not even that story contained a more transparent or confident discussion by the author of those constantly absorbing problems of his professional past, present and future. *The Old Man and the Sea* is, from one angle, an account of Hemingway's personal struggle, grim, resolute and eternal, to write his best. With his seriousness, his precision and his perfectionism, Hemingway saw his craft exactly as Santiago sees his. The fishing and the fishermen turn out to be metaphors so apt that they need almost no translation: Santiago is a master who sets his lines with more care than his colleagues, but he has no luck any more. It would be better to be lucky, he thinks, but he will be skillfully exact instead; then when the luck comes he will be ready for it. Once he was very strong. "The Champion" they called him, and he had beaten many rivals in fair fights. The boy agrees: "There are many good fishermen and some great ones. But there is only you." Still there are many who do not know this, and the whole reputation is gravely imperilled by a streak of bad luck. And so the ex-champion musters his confidence: "I may not be as strong as I think. . . . But I know many tricks and I have resolution."

Santiago needs these things, for he is still out for the really big fish. He has assured the boy he is a strange old man; "Now is when I must prove it." (The times that he has proved it before "meant nothing. Now he was proving it again.") And he does prove it. The sharks may eat his fish, and spoil everything, as they always try to do. But even a young fisherman in the prime of his strength would have done well to land this marlin, and so at the end

Santiago is secure in bed, dreaming happily of the lions. (As for these lions, they play like cats on beaches "so white they hurt your eyes"—as white, we might think, as the "unbelievably white" top of Kilimanjaro that Harry dreamed of, the magical goal of the artist, where the leopard froze. And so we could say here, as Hemingway said of Harry, that Santiago is happy in the end because he knows that "there was where he was going.")

But this time it is the public and not the private parable—the generalized meanings which underlie and impregnate the action—that matters most. On this level there is no allegory in the book and, strictly speaking, no symbols. The marlin Santiago catches, the sharks that eat it away and the lions he dreams of are not so much symbolic of other things as broadly suggestive of them. To pin them down by naming equivalents they do not have would be to limit and decrease, vulgarly and gratuitously, the power of what Hemingway had written. On the public level the lions, for instance, are only so vague as the "poetry" in Santiago, and perhaps the sign of his nostalgia for his youth. The marlin is not even anything so general as "nature"—which would justify the most obvious trap, a man-vs.-nature allegory—for as brothers in this world and life, inextricably joined by the necessity of killing and being killed, Santiago and the fish are tightly bound up in the same thing. If we ask ourselves what *The Old Man and the Sea* is "about" on a public and figurative level, we can only answer "life," which is the finest and most ambitious thing for a parable to be about. Hemingway has written about life: a struggle against the impossible odds of unconquerably natural forces in which—given such a fact as that of death—a man can only lose, but which he can dominate in such a way that his loss has dignity, itself the victory.

The stories of all the best parables are sufficient to themselves, and many will prefer to leave the meanings of this one unverbalized. Such a reading, however, would comprehend less than Hemingway clearly intended. By stripping his book—as only this novelist can—of all but the essentials, and Santiago himself of all but the last things he needs for his survival (the old man owns almost nothing, and hardly even eats), and by the simplicity of the characterization and the style, Hemingway has gently but powerfully urged a metaphor which stands for what life can be. And it is an epic metaphor, a contest where even the problem of moral right and wrong seems paltry if not irrelevant—as in ancient epics, exactly—before the great thing that is this struggle.

If all this sounds a little "classical," it is because this tale of courage, endurance, pride, humility and death is remarkably so. It is classical not only technically, in its narrow confines, its reduction to fundamentals, the purity of its design, and even in the fatal flaw of pride (for Santiago exceeded his limits and went out too far). It is also classical in spirit, in its mature acceptance, and even praise, of things as they are. It is much in the spirit of the Greek tragedies in which men fight against great odds and win moral victories, losing only such tangible rewards—however desirable the prizes and heartbreaking the losses—as will dissipate anyway. It is especially like Greek tragedy in that as the hero fails and falls, one gets an unforgettable glimpse of what stature a man may have.

The story has affiliations, too, with Christian lore. These are not so much this time in its spirit, despite the virtues of pity, humility and charity with which it is invested. They are in its several allusions to Christian symbolism, particularly of the crucifixion. This orientation was not entirely new to Hemingway. Nearly forty years ago he published a little play, "Today Is Friday," in which a Roman soldier who was present at Calvary kept saying of Jesus: "He was pretty good in there today." In *Across the River and Into the Trees* the Colonel, whose heart goes out to anyone who has been hit hard, "as every man will be if he stays," has a twice-wounded and misshapen hand, which he is very conscious of. Renata, running her fingers lightly over the scars, tells him she has stangely dreamed it is "the hand of Our Lord." Now it is Santiago's hands, and the noise that comes from him when he sees the sharks ("a noise such as a man might make, involuntarily, feeling the nail go through his hands and into the wood"), which first relate his ordeal to an ancient one. Then when at the end he carries his mast uphill to his cabin, and falls, exhausted, but finally makes it, and collapses on his cot, "face down . . . with his arms out straight and the palms of his hands up," the allusion is unmistakable.

All this does not indicate that Hemingway was embracing, or even necessarily approaching, the Christian faith. Such passages as the one on the possible nonexistence of sin explicitly disavow it, as does the running insistence on the story as a wholly natural parable, confined to the realms of this world and what we know by experience. Instead Hemingway is implying another metaphor, and seems to say here, as in *Across the River*: the world not only breaks, it crucifies, everyone, and afterwards many are scarred in the hands. But now he has gone further, to add that when it comes, and they nail you up, the important thing is to be pretty good in there like Santiago.

One of the virtues of this short novel is that its meanings emerge from the action with all the self-contained power of the marlin breaking the surface of the ocean. Hemingway did not drag up anything, and one of the means whereby he kept the parable from obtruding is the baseball—that force in Santiago's life which, beside the lions, is all the life he has beyond his calling. Baseball stars are the heroes of this simple man; their exploits are the incidents, and their pennant races the plots, of his mythology. Baseball works a charm on the pages of this book. The talk about it is vastly real, it gives a

little play to the line when unrelieved tension would be dangerous, and the
sober conversations about it, which Santiago conducts with himself and with
the boy, are delicious in their own right:

> "The Yankees cannot lose."
> "But I fear the Indians of Cleveland."
> "Have faith in the Yankees my son. Think of the great
> DiMaggio."
> "I fear both the Tigers of Detroit and the Indians of Cleveland."
> "Be careful or you will fear even the Reds of Cincinnati and
> the White Sox of Chicago."

Nowhere in the book is there the slightest touch of condescension in
the humor of this childlike preoccupation. Hemingway gave it without irony,
without patronizing his characters, without unkindness. This is because he
profoundly respected his characters, and wrote his book with a tenderness
that was new to him and to his work. And that is an important perception,
because it leads to the heart of the book's power.

"I love more than any son of the great bitch alive," said the Colonel in
Across the River, and although he said it "not aloud" it sounded foolish
anyway. But it sounds a little less silly now: *The Old Man and the Sea* is a
powerful book, and a large part of its power is the power of love.

Santiago's respect for his foe, the marlin, which is love, actually, as for
a brother, is surpassed by Hemingway's respect for both that fish and
Santiago himself, and for the whole of life which this battle epitomizes, and
the world that contains it. An extraordinary thing had happened, for
somehow or other a reverence for life's struggle, which this contest dramatizes, and for mankind, for which Santiago stands as a possibility, had
descended on Hemingway like the gift of grace on the religious. This vener-
ation for humanity, for what can be done and endured, and this grasp of
man's kinship with the other creatures of the world, and with the world itself,
is itself a victory of substantial proportions. It is the knowledge that a simple
man is capable of such decency, dignity, and even heroism, and that his
struggle can be seen in heroic terms, that largely distinguishes this book. For
the knowledge that man can be great, and his life great, might be in itself an
approach to greatness. To have had the skill, then, to convince others that
this is a valid vision is Hemingway's achievement.

This is to say, among other less abstract things, that Hemingway had
reached the point where he was able to affirm without forcing, or even
apparent effort, certain things about brotherhood, man, and life which he
had tried and crucially failed to affirm in *For Whom the Bell Tolls*. Indeed,

since Santiago is a man alone and without the boy—for, after all, a man faces certain final things alone—and since the old man catches his fish, Hemingway had sharply qualified the pronouncement of *To Have and Have Not*, which was even more forced. *The Old Man and the Sea* is pregnant with implications about the contestants and the contest, but this time there is no need to say anything about them outright. It seems you never have to say it if you really mean it.

It is the heartening vision of this story, then, and the deep sense one has of a writer who is at long last completely at home in this life and world, which chiefly account for the power of the book. The rest of its force is the result of its remarkable surface virtues. And it may be that the action—so taut that beads of water seem to jump off the lines, all in a world miraculously alive and lasting—will seem one day the greatest thing after all. Hemingway's hope for his short novel, that "all the things that are in it do not show, but only are with you after you have read it," is mostly fulfilled; and, in the end, vicarious experience is the finest gift literature has to offer. It is the genius of Hemingway that our response is intense, rich, and deep. Without that, the vision and the meanings would count for nothing.

"It's as though I had gotten finally what I had been working for all my life," Hemingway also said, and there are many ways in which it would seem that he had. One of the more subtle ways lies in the fact of Santiago's survival: all the rest of the characters Hemingway projected himself deeply into have, if they struggled and attained the code, died in the process; at the end of this story Santiago is confident, happy, and ready for more. In addition, though *The Old Man and the Sea* is not necessarily Hemingway's greatest book, it is the one in which he said the finest single thing he ever had to say as well as he could ever hope to say it.

And so the question occurred to the faithless: then what was left for this one to do? To ask such a question was to reckon without the personal triumph Santiago represented and to forget what the old man said when the boy asked if he was strong enough then for a truly big fish: "I think so. And there are many tricks." Besides, this was indeed a strange old man.

II

If one were rewriting instead of revising this book, one thing he would greatly tone down is his praise for *The Old Man and the Sea*, with which he went farther out than Santiago. (One critic, Marvin Mudrick, wrote recently that I treated it as if it were one of Beethoven's last quartettes.) The feeling is now that although the tale is here and there exciting it is itself drawn out

a little far. Even the title seems an affectation of simplicity, and the realization that Hemingway was now trading on and no longer inventing the style
that made him famous came just too late. Redolent of self-admiration,
Manolin's boyish worship of the old man is harder than ever to take. The boy
himself once seemed a "substitute heroine," but the book by brother
Leicester Hemingway supplied a better insight:

> Ernest was never very content with life unless he had a spiritual
> kid brother nearby . . . someone he could show off to as well as
> teach. He needed uncritical admiration. . . . A little worshipful
> awe was a distinct aid. . . . I made a good kid brother when I was
> around.

Heroine or kid brother, this need was almost always part of the trouble
when Hemingway was around in the novels; self-praise is always most
embarrassing. And, this time, identifying with his "code hero" brought on
confusion as well. Thick as a "pencil," and set out with more care than the
opposition's, Hemingway was thinking more of his own lines than Santiago's;
allegory overwhelms reality when we are told that the young boy carries this
fishing line—three-quarters of a mile of it—plus a harpoon and the gaff to
the boat. (A gaffe indeed, unless, as we are not told, the lad was actually a
giant.) Similarly it does not make very much sense to say that *Santiago* "went
out too far": he did after all boat his fish out there, and the sharks that took
it away from him are not confined to waters distant from land. It is not so
much that Santiago was a fisherman in whom the writer saw himself; rather
that Hemingway was a writer who thought he could disguise himself as
Santiago. The autobiographical element unfortunately triumphs again: is
wasn't Into the Caribbean but *Across the River* where somebody felt he went
out too far. Hemingway, taking a view of that failed novel which occasionally
overrode his concern for his sea story, went way out and hooked his great
prize, a book to keep a man all winter, but then the critics ate away at it until
there was nothing left. Not as strong as he had been once, he felt that he was
still the master of many tricks and still up to bringing in the big one—which,
in his opinion, may have been the same small book that was the allegory of
his vicissitudes.

CLAIRE ROSENFIELD

New World, Old Myths

Criticism has accustomed us to recognize the "American myth" in William Faulkner's "The Bear" and in Ernest Hemingway's *The Old Man and the Sea*. Whether that myth exploited the confrontation between man—the innocent, the child-like, the "American Adam"—and "wild nature"—the huge animal, the monstrous fish—or simply emphasized the "distinctly American" flavor of exaggeration in "tall tales" that paraded animals of extraordinary size or endurance, we eagerly nationalized it first and only then did we analyze it. But any study of the folk tale—products not only of peasant or rustic (or prairie) societies but also of primitive or tribal societies—would reveal the same motif, the same confrontation between the hero and a large indigenous animal he both fears and admires. Perhaps more interesting is why the American writer persistently chooses this almost universal motif, this subject that some would consider a regression to folk materials, this pattern that has led Leslie Fiedler rightly to point out that the American hero is in fact or in spirit a child. Nor is it a question of American civilization developing "by means of a return to wild nature," for it had never really been there in its expressive works. Its culture began *in medias res* with a literature essentially European, often deeply sophisticated and urbane in tone, subject, and style. Once the literature of the New World freed itself from its Puritan emphasis upon sermons, spiritual autobiography, and moral tracts, once its

From *Twentieth Century Interpretations of The Old Man and the Sea*. © 1968 by Claire Rosenfield.

81

novels divorced themselves from the sentimental tradition that hounded books like *Charlotte Temple* and from the Gothic tradition that pervaded Charles Brockden Brown's *Ormond*—and, indeed, all those lesser works in which the terror *was* of Germany and *not* of the soul—then our literature began as near the beginning, as near oral conventions, as a literate culture is now allowed to go. It exploited folk materials which it often placed in a local—hence prairie—setting. Some of its greatest and most representative novels absorbed a very conventional content that only seemed American because the European literary experience in which the early colonists continued to immerse themselves had been so long estranged from its roots, from its awareness of folk patterns. And because these patterns seemed so genuinely American (when, in actuality, they are primarily human), they persisted both in extremely intricate form like "The Bear" and in highly stylized prose like *The Old Man and the Sea*. What is American, then, is the persistence of the folk motif, not the motif itself. Moreover, that it endured for the wrong reason—because of its emotional value rather than its human validity—is also distinctly American.

If completely at odds in style and structure, the two short novels under discussion are more than superficially alike in content. Both are stories which deal with situations of crisis in the lives of the protagonists, crises which are marked by rites of passage, threshold events that bridge the gulf from one state of physical, social, and intellectual being into another. In both, a much older man—simple, intuitive, wise in the life of Nature—acts as a mentor for an innocent "apprentice" upon whose ability to learn and whose devotion to craft his own personal immortality in part depends. Each novel explores a totemic relationship, an association between a man and an object in nature. And in each the totemic relationship provides a stage upon which religious and/or social meanings dramatize themselves. At once game and rite, each hunt exerts a symbolic meaning beyond the physical destruction of a remarkable wild creature.

The Old Man and the Sea begins eighty-four days after the old fisherman's last catch. The boy Manolin, the apprentice whom he has long regarded "with confident loving eyes," who had shared the first forty barren days, has been forced by his parents to "another boat which caught three good fish the first week." In their mutual reminiscences concerning the past the reader discovers that Manolin first accompanied the old man Santiago when the former was five years old, that the boy is lovingly described as "already a man" in his knowledge of things of the sea, that the pupil claims to remember everything "from when . . . [they] first went together." During the intensity of the old man's ordeal, when for three days he tries to land the largest marlin ever seen in that area, he longs again and again for the boy's presence, as much for companionship as for assistance. Now he has only himself and the sea to talk to. Every new crisis recalls Manolin's worth. When his hand is cramped by the coil of rope, he wishes the boy were there to rub it or, later, to wet the abrasive hemp. As he approaches port with the "half-fish," the catch partially consumed by sharks, he meditates upon the others' response to his absence. "There is only the boy to worry, of course. But I am sure he would have confidence."

The imagery of spiritual kinship makes it possible for the reader to see causal relationship in apparently illogical juxtapositions. "'I wish the boy were here and that I had some salt'" not only marks his need and love for the boy and the necessity for making palatable the raw tuna he must eat to preserve his strength but also indicates the connection between the eater and the eaten, the fisherman who must fish to eat and eat to fish, the nourisher of the body and that of the spirit. He wishes that he could "feed the fish" he has hooked because he is his brother. Denied his teacher because his hostile parents regard that teacher as "unlucky," the boy asserts his bond by bringing food for the old man to eat and some sardines for the catch. At first the food he provides substitutes for that which the old man cannot provide for himself; in the end, it marks the boy's assumption of the responsibility for nourishing the man who had long fostered his spirit Fishing, exactly that process by which the man has established communion with the boy, who does bring him food, is part of the cycle that unites all things in nature; it both feeds and destroys. "Fishing kills me exactly as it keeps me alive."

No critic would debate the spiritual kinship between man and boy; the latter inherits not the blood but the knowledge of the former. Nor would anyone longer deny that the fish is a totem animal. As A. R. Radcliffe-Brown posited in 1929, the totem animal of a group is often the one upon which one's subsistence depends. Both man and boy regard their numerous prey as part of the same order of created beings, part of the same human society. Having once hooked the female of a pair of marlins, they pity the reaction of the distraught male. "That was the saddest thing I ever saw with them. . . . The boy was sad too and we begged her pardon and butchered her promptly." To the fish he has just hooked after eighty-four "unlucky" days Santiago says "'I love you and respect you very much. But I will kill you dead before this day ends.'" He calls the fish both "friend" and "brother" and regrets that he must "live on the sea and kill [his] true brothers." How demeaning that those who will feed upon him will not be worthy of him. "There is no one worthy of eating him from the manner of his behaviour and his great dignity." Not simply a "great fish," his captor assigns to the marlin the quality of human thought: he is "following his own plan" as he circles; the old man must "convince" his prey; the marlin may "decide to stay another night." The very desire to prove worthy of this creature's admiration provides additional strength to Santiago's weakening body. "Let him think I am more man than I am and I will be so." The same fish once dead and lashed to his boat is no less dignified, no less a part of communal life. "With his mouth shut and his tail straight up and down we sail like brothers." When the gallant opponent is first mutilated by the sharks, Santiago thinks "it was as though he himself were hit." And when these "bad smelling" sharks, these "scavengers as well as killers," devour the marlin, Santiago can only murmur "'I'm sorry, fish.'" If the totem animal of a group also reflects the society in some way, then this noble marlin reflects the qualities Santiago possesses, admires, and wishes to hand on to the boy: nobility, "greatness," and "glory," endurance, dignity, beauty.

And in his defeat, in his desecration by scavengers, he symbolizes Santiago, who is ridiculed by younger fishermen, who is regarded as "strange" and "unlucky," whose final triumph is destroyed by sharks, and who, broken in body and spirit, a skeleton of his former self, can only sleep and dream of the lions of his youth.

The development of his story through time has little to do with the greater complexity of William Faulkner's emphasis upon initiation and totemism. What determines the complexity is not that we see the relationship between Ike and Sam Fathers progress for seven fall and six spring hunts and that of Manolin and Santiago for two short spaces of less than twelve hours each, but rather that Faulkner consciously exploits what Hemingway only peripherally understands. Ike senses that he is entering in a new life when his day to enter the woods comes; it "seemed to him that he was witnessing his own birth." In order to hunt Old Ben, the bear, he must serve "his apprenticeship in the woods which would prove him worthy to be a hunter . . ." He enters "his novitiate to the true wilderness with Sam beside him as he had begun his apprenticeship in miniature to manhood after the rabbits and such with Sam beside him." Half Indian chief, half Negro slave, Sam Fathers knows intuitively how each step in Ike's initiation must take shape and conveys that knowledge often without words. From Sam he learns that, although Old Ben has been to camp to see him, he cannot see the bear until he has relinquished his gun in order that "all ancient rules and balances of hunter and hunted had been abrogated." By submitting completely to the wilderness, the pathless, ageless wall of trees, by leaving behind the mechanical aids of civilization, his watch and compass, by proceeding "as Sam had coached and drilled him"—only then does he see the bear and partake of its secret life. Moreover, Sam's mysterious affinity to Nature anticipates each step before its explanation in action: he knows why the boy doesn't shoot the bear when he confronts it squarely; he knows the dead colt was not killed by

Old Ben but by the dog that will eventually corner the bear; he senses that his own life and Old Ben's are tied in a mystic unity and will snap together. With no true familial ties, *"no children, no people, none of his blood anywhere above earth that he would ever meet again,"* he bequeathes his knowledge to the boy. Ike, who hardly knew his own father, first manifests his loyalty by disobeying his guardian and cousin, "his kinsman, his father almost," McCaslin Edmonds, in order to stay with the dying Sam. Later he protects Boon when his cousin Cass fails to understand the necessary continuity in Sam's death. Finally, he gives up his birthright to assume Sam's role in the diminishing woods. Spiritual kinship has superseded real ties, has filled the vacuum left both by death and by ancestral depravity.

Old Ben is the symbol both of the bigness of the woods and of its destruction. And, as such, he acquires a more than human status.

> It loomed and towered in his dreams before he ever saw the unaxed woods where it left its crooked print, shaggy, tremendous, red-eyed, not malevolent but just big . . . ; too big for the very country which was its constricting scope. It was as if the boy had already divined what his senses and intellect had not encompassed yet: that doomed wilderness whose edges were being constantly and punily gnawed at by men with plows and axes . . . , men myriad and nameless even to one another in the land where the old bear had earned a name, and through which ran not even a mortal beast but an anachronism indomitable and invincible out of an old death time, a phantom, epitome and apotheosis of the old wild life which the little puny humans swarmed and hacked at in a fury of abhorrence and fear, like pygmies about the ankles of a drowsing elephant . . .

His very name is a mark of hunter's respect; he has "earned" it, "a definite designation like a living man." Like Santiago's reverence for the fish, Sam attributes to Old Ben human curiosity and ability: the desire to survey the camp to see "'who's here, who's new in camp this year.'" He's "'the head bear. . . . the man.'" All congregate "as if they were meeting an appointment with another human being." Even Major de Spain, the Southern gentleman and hunter who believes erroneously that Old Ben has killed his colt, recognizes the bear's superior powers. "'I'm disappointed in him. He has broken the rules. . . . I didn't think he would have done that. He has killed mine and McCaslin's dogs, but that was all right. We gambled the dogs against him; we gave each other warning. But now he has come into my house and destroyed my property, out of season too. He broke the rules.'" To him, Old Ben has purposely ignored the temporal and spatial limitations placed upon him by the rules of the game-hunt.

In the juxtaposition of Old Ben's sacrifice, Lion's mutilation, and Sam's collapse and death we must recognize an artistic chain defining totemic causality. Sam "lay there—the copper-brown, almost hairless body, the old man's body, the old man, the wild man not even one generation from the woods, childless, kinless, peopleless—motionless, his eyes open but no longer looking at any of them." Old Ben in death lay "with his eyes open too." Like Sam, denied his chief's role because his land has been sold and his blood diluted with the blood of slaves, Old Ben belonged to the past aristocrats of the diminishing wilderness. Like Sam, he was old and alone: "widowered, childless, and absolved of mortality—old Priam reft of his old wife and outlived all his sons." Both participate in a mutual life, contingent upon a past grandeur within the timeless woods. Neither can survive the degradation imposed by a different culture.

Thus the totemic animal in "The Bear" is chosen less because he is "eatable" than because, as writers on totemism point out, his situation and his world have an intimate connection with the functioning society. The very existence of two hunts proclaims a hierarchy of birth joined to that of skill. During the fall hunt, the game is deer or bear; the participants, the proven hunters of Southern white landed families. In the spring, they celebrate at one session the widely disparate birthdays of Major de Spain and General Compson. ". . . Boon and the Negroes (and the boy too now) fished and shot squirrels and ran the coons and cats, because the proven hunters, not only Major de Spain and old General Compson . . . but even McCaslin and Walter Ewell who were still young enough, scorned such, other than shooting the wild gobblers with pistols for wagers or to test their marksmanship." As "the man" among animals Old Ben deserves their special attention; the last day of the autumn period is devoted to him. Because of his stature only the "best" are allowed to participate. But the best are those whose superiority is based in a social structure that flourished on slavery, whose wealth is derived from the ownership of land "bought" or stolen from the Indians and from the cultivation of that same land by human chattel. So in its pattern of participation the fall hunt mirrors the hierarchial society. It is also a ritual reenactment of the rape of the land, which the vanishing wilderness recalls.

We see, however, that Ike's ancestors who determined his hereditary role in holding the land, could not provide him with models for emulation or respect. His own grandfather had fathered a child by a slave girl who was both his property and his daughter. In repudiating his land, which he claims should be held by all men in common, Ike in effect separates himself from his personal history. That grandfather's immorality is but the final act of deterioration which telescopes several sins: the mythic disobedience of Adam, the historical crime of slavery, the national crime of private property. For Ike to make Sam Fathers the progenitor of a spiritual patrimony is to deny the real one. Those "proven hunters," who caused Sam, the chief's son to be "peopleless" and "landless," whose sport pursues Old Ben—"Priam reft of his old wife and outlived all his sons"—these men themselves leave no sons to inherit the fruits of their crimes.

The failure of Ike's marriage, his future celibacy, is predictable not simply because he rejects his fathers, not simply because he adopts a deeper tie, but also because his intimate connection with nature demands it. Like his mentor he must be "childless, kinless, peopleless"; like the totem animal, whose woods are annihilated by a mechanical civilization, he must be "landless"; like both he must reflect, not Christian, but primitive values. The image of the crawling serpent is used once to describe the small train inaugurated by the lumber company that eventually denudes the land; as such, its corruption is implied. On his last trip to camp before the timber is cut, Ike sees a hissing snake, a creature that his culture invests with all the connotations of evil because of its role in seducing Eve. At first he recognizes it as "ancient and accursed about the earth, fatal and solitary," its smell "evocative of all knowledge and an old weariness and of pariah-hood and of death." But then he imagines it in its supposed prelapsarian shape, an erect creature moving as if human and on two legs.

> The elevation of the head did not change as it began to glide away from him, moving erect yet off the perpendicular as if the head and that elevated third were complete and all: an entity walking on two feet and free of all laws of mass and balance, and should have been because even now he could not quite believe that all that shift and flow of shadow behind that walking head could have been one snake: going and then gone . . . .

That is, he gradually sees it not as a symbol of Adam's fall, crawling on its belly, but as tradition assigned it before its great offense. He has removed the negative value that his culture insists upon. In hailing it with raised hand, he follows the earlier form and the strange language he learned from Sam Fathers: "'Chief' he said: 'Grandfather.'" This greeting is not the ironic recognition of Ike that his own religious and social tradition is damned. Rather, his change in vision indicates that he now accepts Sam at once as a teacher and guide in matters of the hunt and as an ancestor in a primitive religious tradition, a tradition older and more meaningful than the salvation-oriented one into which he was born. He soon clings to this tradition

because, in uniting all men and animals as brothers, it is without taint of hierarchy, ownership, and innate depravity.

Especially in Faulkner's ability to pursue all the ramifications of
totemism to the larger social and religious community we can mark his superiority to Hemingway. Both present primitive religions, a single and harmonious cosmos in which the self seeks no independent identity apart from its
environment. So when Santiago's left hand is cut and cramps, he addresses it
dispassionately as if it had no special link to his body, were no part of a
human whole that is separate and unique within a physical environment. In
fact, whereas the fish is a "brother," worthy of respect, his left hand is a
"traitor," "something worthless." Nor do I mean to imply anything pejora-
tive when I emphasize the "primitive." Rather, these characters possess a
world view very like that attributed to an early stage in the evolutionary
cycle, a stage that can and does remain a part of the most highly developed
religion. If, as Robert Bellah theorizes, "primitive *religious* action is charac-
terized not . . . by worship, nor, as we shall see, by sacrifice, but by identification, 'participation,' acting-out," then Hemingway's old man is intently
engaged in such action. To address the fish as "friend" and "brother," to identify himself with it indicates that for him, as for the primitive, the "distance
between man and mythical being disappears altogether in the moment of
ritual." The catch has all the external manifestations of ritual: action follows
certain forms; it is isolated from the ordinary world temporally and spatially;
it is calculated to provide its participant with some strange power (i.e., the
power of the marlin). In its final stage the catch takes the form of a circle
which gradually diminishes in size and in depth. "But the circles were much
shorter now and from the way the line slanted he could tell the fish had risen
steadily while he swam." Though he often reiterates his own suffering, he
does not neglect to remind us as readers of the same suffering endured by the
fish. The "no-time" of ritual is approximated when the intensity of that
suffering causes him to become light-headed, to lose the sense of continuity
and reality; his experience seems to be a dream. Having lost his fish to the
sharks, he endures whatever limitations his exhaustion, his age, his aloneness,
his few weapons—all the conditions, in fact, of his existence—impose. He
becomes transformed insofar as he is now able to accept his failure; like the
initiates involved in a ritual, he has come to terms symbolically with ". . . the
'immemorial misdirection of human life.'"

Unfortunately Ernest Hemingway does not perceive the variety that
life forces upon man's expression of religious behavior nor the abundant
permutations even the simplest faith may take. For him the dogma of Christianity and its enactment in ritual define the word; and its verbal forms are
charged with an emotion largely inflated, meaningless, bombastic. So the

author, whose American expatriates usually recognize the validity of tradition within the societies through which they aimlessly ramble, pays some lip service to the old man's nominal Christianity. Though Santiago is "not religious," he promises to make a pilgrimage to the Virgin of Cobre should he catch the marlin, a pilgrimage to that Virgin whose picture in his hut is a reminder of his long-dead wife rather than the image of a transcendent power. He prays not for his own salvation, as a Christian would, but for "the death of this fish. Wonderful though he is."

It is when the author's indiscriminate love of masculine games merges with his distrust of abstraction—whether religious, sexual, or patriotic—that he renders trivial the power of the situation he has created. The reader need not fathom the relationship between games and the development of religions from the bottomless past to admit that games and rites have precise similarities: a regularized pattern of behavior, an actual or psychological withdrawal from the everyday world of time and space, a temporary release from anxiety, an emphasis upon communal activity. Though in our society the one partakes of the serious situations of life and the other, of the profane, in each, man is "carried outside himself and diverted from his ordinary occupation and preoccupation."

The image of the game dominates beginning, middle, and end, the most minor as well as the most potentially moving moments of the narrative. The novel's opening underscores Santiago's multiple influence upon the boy, his guidance in the intricacies both of the sometime sport by which the old man earns his bread and of the foreign amusement called "the baseball." When no danger threatens within the action, a gentle humor emanates from his ability to pontificate upon "the baseball," to recall the magical presence in Cuba of its greatest "heroes," to derive satisfaction from the rumor that the father of "the great DiMaggio was a fisherman." And the boy's admiration for Santiago's uniqueness within his natural vocation and for Durocher and Mike Gonzalez as managers of the sport tend to fuse and confuse a way of life with a mode of entertainment. Whereas "faith" is necessary for catching fish, especially when one is supposed to be "unlucky," "faith" is also a concomitant to the skill of the Yankees; one must have faith in their ability to win and *they will win*. To remember the ancient tie in archaic religions between games of chance and divination is to understand this old man's prelogical desire that his disciple "buy a terminal of the lottery with an eighty-five." The day that he goes to pursue his "big fish" is his eighty-fifth without luck. He at once assigns a predictive value to the lottery and makes the game a symbolic reflection of his own human situation. The excruciating simplicity that functions to lessen his success as a consciousness through which we experience the events of the narrative is, paradoxically, made credible by his childlike concern for "the great DiMaggio," by his exaggerated respect for "gambling," by his mystical belief in luck. If Manolin, who has gone to a "lucky" boat, were his son, he would "gamble," take the boy out on the eighty-fifth day with a confidence equal to that with which he places money upon the number of a lottery.

Once the life-and-death struggle between man and fish begins, once the old man becomes obsessed by the intimacy between himself, who was "born to be a fisherman," and the victim, then the story demands some recognition of the mystery involved in each human destiny. But Hemingway's nagging suspicions about RELIGION seduce him into a constant apology that takes the form of overt statement or metaphorical reduction. First, the old man must insist that he is "not religious"; he must manifest this fact by saying his prayers "mechanically" or "automatically"; he must, in effect, justify his lapse into belief. For his author forgets that he is not Jake Barnes, he does not have to rationalize from a sophisticated perspective of the world his apparently illogical combination of Christian prayer and pagan participation in rites of the kill. And having dramatized a genuinely religious man—albeit a devotee of a primitive religion—Hemingway's initial instinct to connect church and society, the religious and the social, within the boat is sound. But his emphatically male bias makes the purposive mingling of game and rite ridiculous; not only has the game he chooses no suggestion of cult participation or identification (as the bullfight has in *The Sun Also Rises*) but also the reader finds it impossible to spiritualize the too-human celebrities that he has read about in sports pages and gossip columns. Human interdependence is reduced to a diversion. Perhaps it is artistically valid that the old man, who earlier was the prophet of "the baseball," should lament on his second day tied to the dying fish because he does "not know the result of the *juegos.* . . ." That he values his endurance, however, because it makes him "worthy of the great DiMaggio who does all things perfectly even with the pain of the bone spur in his heel," that he dilutes life and death—even that of fighting cocks—to such thinness, indicates that Hemingway has failed to gage the possibility of the comparison. Masculine admiration substitutes for aesthetic judgment. When the sharks come, Santiago's brooding upon the death of the marlin seems perverse. "But I must think . . . because it is all I have left. That and baseball." Given the quality of his previous thought, such a juxtaposition is gratuitous. When "sin" becomes the concept to occupy his thoughts, he rejects it because "there are people who are paid to do it . . . [He was] born to be a fisherman as the fish was born to be a fish. San Pedro was a fisherman as was the father of the great DiMaggio." Santiago knows that a man who was "born to be a fisherman" is not adept in meditating upon sin, but Hemingway cannot resist the temptation to "yoke by violence together" the persons of Saint Peter and the "father of the great DiMaggio." The reader senses that the apotheosis of the fisherman is not far distant. The image calculated to turn the elderly protagonist into a Christfigure does come, but the author intrudes awkwardly into the text probably to soften the patent attempt at manipulating our responses. "'*Ay*,' he said aloud. There is no translation for this word and perhaps it is just a noise such as a man might make, involuntarily, feeling the nail go through his hands and into the wood." The disturbing violation of tone stems both from the unnecessary allusion to a sympathetic culture hero and from the movement from Santiago's consciousness to Hemingway's. The consequent sentimentalization of the old man is harder to accept than his fabulous endurance. Again, the Christ-image ludicrously jars our awareness, primarily because the old fisherman has already canonized the great DiMaggio. Nor does his insistence that he thinks about baseball in order to take his mind off his suffering reconcile us to the banal range of his perceptions. The context in which rites and rules function together to characterize the ordered world of Spain and to serve as a contrast to the disorder of the Jake Barnes circle does not exist here. Since the old man is very much in harmony with his physical environment, his religious world view is debased to the level of the game that, unfortunately, is only a game.

Avoiding the temptation to dramatize the hunt from the too simple eyes of Sam Fathers, whose knowledge, like Santiago's, is limited to his intuitions, William Faulkner chooses as the center of narrative consciousness the boy Ike. Even as a ten-year-old child he is acutely aware of historical and social phenomena. The hunting of bear is no longer required for the subsistence of any group. Though it has become a sport, the reader is never allowed to forget its religious implications. Described as a "yearly pageant-rite of the old bear's furious immortality," it has no part of the routine of our time-space world; clocks and compasses are useless in the "great gloom of ancient woods." Instead, the game is set against the bigger life of Nature; it occurs at the "year's death." Moreover, Faulkner makes a subtle distinction among his characters; there are those for whom sharing in the hunt no longer confers any spiritual value and those for whom the ritual anticipates some personal crisis. The swampers, the townsmen in new clothes who gather to watch the kill do not count at all; they are mere spectators of the "yearly rendezvous." Ike's belief in its unique mystery invests the very drinking of liquor with a meaning relevant to this "ancient and immitigable contest according to ancient and immitigable rules":

> There was always a bottle present, so that it would seem to him
> that those fine fierce instants of heart and brain and courage and

wiliness and speed were concentrated and distilled into that brown liquor which not women, not boys and children, but only hunters drank, drinking it moderately, humbly even, not with the pagan's base and baseless hope of acquiring thereby the virtues of cunning and strength and speed but in salute to them. Thus it seemed to him on this December morning not only natural but actually fitting that this should have begun with whiskey.

The use of phrases like "it would seem to him" indicates that it is Ike's eye that suffuses the event with solemnity. "To him, they were going not to hunt bear and deer but to keep yearly rendezvous with the bear which they did not even intend to kill." Given these assumptions, how he and Sam Fathers act out the various stages of initiation becomes one subject of the first three parts of the narrative. He must discover that this world in which all the ancient rules and balances of hunter and hunted had been abrogated provides him with the possibility of coming to terms symbolically or really with his personal and historical past. Sam's marking him with the blood of his first buck is one link in the long chain of rites that will ultimately connect him to the past of Nature and divorce him from that of Western history.

The other Southerners, who regard the hunt as an exercise of skill and sportsmanship rather than an acting out of mythical events, possess inferior knowledge for interpreting facts. Rules not rites dominate their world. When Major de Spain learns about the separation of the frantic mare from her colt, he immediately assumes that Old Ben has broken "the rules." The body of the colt causes the proven hunters to continue to deceive themselves, but the boy does not realize until much later why Sam understands and they do not. "Afterward the boy realized that they also should have known then what killed the colt as well as Sam Fathers did. But that was neither the first nor the last time he had seen men rationalize from and even act upon their misconceptions." Finally, Cass and Major de Spain misjudge the role that Sam's willed death plays in the rite. In a harmonious cosmos where "the distance between man and mythical being, which was at best slight, disappears altogether in the moment of ritual," Boon's killing Old Ben during the "yearly pageant-rite" is the symbolic killing of Sam. Whether Boon does in fictional actuality kill Sam, as Cass believes and as Faulkner later stated, is ultimately irrelevant for the wilderness world. That Cass insists upon knowing, even while he claims that he would have done the same had Sam requested it, is his carrying into the woods, into the space of identification and participation, the ethical standards of a society that emphasizes a "responsible" self. He cannot accept Sam's death as the boy does, as the logical consequence of ritual action, but rather regards it as a crime against a social structure that mediates between orthodox Christianity and some divinely sanctioned moral order presumed to be objective.

Until he is sixteen, then, the boy immerses his Christian self in ritual action. Twice a year for two-week periods he moves from the daily routine of his culture, from a society whose religious values are expressed in worldly institutions, from a belief in a transcendent deity and in individual salvation by grace and in man's corrupted nature, into the timeless woods. And he goes influenced by his own class's idea of the hunt as a game. Faulkner, however, insists again and again upon the boy's unlearned response, his anticipation that has nothing to do with either godlike foreknowledge or Calvinist predestination (though Part IV may make the critic think so) or with the rules of the game. His intuition is similar to what W. E. H. Stanner has called The Dreaming: the tendency among primitive religious men to prefigure in "a time out of time" extraordinary creatures, both human and animal, who "have capacities beyond those of ordinary men as well as being the progenitors and creators of many particular things in the world." So Old Ben is perceived imaginatively long before his physical presence is seen.

> It ran in his knowledge before he ever saw it. It loomed and towered in his dreams before he ever saw the unaxed woods where it left its crooked print, shaggy, tremendous, red-eyed, not malevolent but just big. . . .

> It seemed to him that he could see them, the two of them, shadowy in the limbo from which time emerged and became time: the old bear absolved of mortality and himself who shared a little of it.

Like the no-time of "The Dreaming," the mental experience explains what happens in the real fictional world; Old Ben, as mythical ancestor, and his final destruction by puny men have already happened before they are acted out in ritual.

Ultimately what his heritage denotes as a game becomes for him a way of being; momentary ritual transforms life. Nor is it mere chance that the last hunt must be extended beyond the usual temporal limits of two weeks. Such an extension symbolically marks the encroachment of ritual time (or "everywhen") into Christian historical time. Again, the moment of Old Ben's death—the destruction of the incorruptible by corruptible man—and the discovery of his grandfather's immorality occur approximately at the same time in our calendar-world: he is sixteen. His society's participation in the deaths of his spiritual father, Sam Fathers, and of the totem animal, who is his ancestor, is but another manifestation of original sin, like slavery and incest. When at twenty-one he relinquishes his land, he not only repudiates his culture's depravity; he emotionally substitutes one religion for another. He denies the religion of sin and individual salvation through grace because of the very corruption that it posits and assumes, too late in the movement of history, one that promises unity among all natural things.

To insist that Ike and Santiago are like Christ or Adam before the Fall, to insist upon their innocence, is to falsify the facts of the novels: neither is finally innocent. Both undergo ritual acts that separate them from their routine experience, that provide them with the special knowledge to cope with their situation. Santiago's ritual allows him to assent to his suffering, as he does to the marlin's, to anticipate with resignation the transformation from life to death; Ike's participation in what may seem like a game but which is really a ritual reenactment results in knowledge that causes him to reject the self that is based on a belief in man's flawed nature, in order to identify himself completely with those who are incorruptible because they do not accept a Christian ontology. Faulkner's impulse to make Ike a carpenter, like Christ, is fortunately, not pursued. At no other point is Ike equated with Christ. Neither do Santiago and Ike reveal essentially American material. Each's story manifests, not Western, but primitive religious action and structure. The animal that each faces is local, but what is indigenous is imbedded in a motif that appears in most oral traditions unencumbered by European sophistication.

SHELDON NORMAN GREBSTEIN

Hemingway's Craft in The Old Man and the Sea

The Old Man and the Sea, published in 1952, was the last major work of fiction by Hemingway to appear in his lifetime. Although several years of creative effort remained to him before his death in 1961, the writing of those years is not likely to either enhance or materially alter his reputation—at least in the opinions of Carlos Baker and Philip Young, who have examined the writer's unpublished papers. If this is indeed the case, *The Old Man and the Sea* will probably solidify its position as the final boundary of Hemingway's career, just as *In Our Time* marks its beginning. The judgment of the Nobel Committee, which singled out *The Old Man and the Sea* for special praise in its award of the 1954 Literature prize to Hemingway, has proved to be unusually percipient.

Nor have the critics neglected the work. Soon after its publication it became the subject for serious and generally sympathetic commentary, continuing to this moment. Some have hailed *The Old Man and the Sea* as Hemingway's affirmation and reconciliation of man and nature; others have interpreted it as Hemingway's reiteration of man's tragic or ironic defeat by insuperable forces. The story's allegorical dimensions have also been examined, especially its use of Christian symbolism and the parallels between Santiago's ordeal and Christ's, or that of a mythic quest hero. An early and persistent reading holds that the novella poses a parable of Hemingway's own

From *The Fifties: Fiction, Poetry, Drama.* © 1970 by Warren French.

literary fate, with himself as the gallant fisherman and his career as the splendid marlin devoured by bloodthirsty shark-critics. In sum, *The Old Man and the Sea* would not seem to be a neglected work.

Nevertheless, while the story's themes, characters, and dominant symbols have been carefully examined, as in the recent study by Bickford Sylvester which also reviews the various critical interpretations, many of the work's vital elements of structure and some of its most effective techniques remain unnoticed. This despite the common agreement that Hemingway's narrative art has never been better than in *The Old Man and the Sea*. I am convinced that much of the hostility to Hemingway, seemingly more virulent and frequent with each passing year, and the oft-heard and influential view of him as a minor writer of narrow range and scanty achievement, derive from too much emphasis on his ideas, his world view, the "meaning" of his work. However important the Hemingway "Code" and the Hemingway "Hero" have been to our literary imagination, we are a little tired of hearing about them. Literature will owe more to his technique than to his vision of life; after him the writing of prose narrative was not the same. It is the craft, then, of *The Old Man and the Sea* that this essay proposes to treat.

One of the characteristic effects of Hemingway's good work is that of wholeness, completeness, symmetry. What has usually been attributed to the Hemingway Code, the sense of rigid control over painful or turbulent feelings, is as much an attribute of form—of a violent pattern of action contained within a strong but unobtrusive structure. This structure must never be ignored in the reading of a Hemingway narrative, yet, surprisingly, one finds relatively little attention to it.

First, the essential design of *The Old Man and the Sea* can be compared to that of the drama, for the narrative moves through three distinct phases of action which are symmetrically proportioned in relation both to one another and to the whole. In the first part, or act, Hemingway establishes the old man's relationship with the boy, Santiago's uniqueness and potentiality for tragic stature, the ethical values to be tested, and the voyage out to sea. This part occupies almost exactly one-fourth of the entire work. The second section, act two in the drama, is introduced by Santiago's twice-repeated "yes" and begins at the moment when the great marlin takes the fisherman's bait. It proceeds to describe the harrowing combat between man and fish, and concludes with Santiago's killing of the marlin. This section is virtually twice the length of the opening phase and occupies the middle half of the work. The concluding section, the dénouement, completes the symmetry for it is the same length as part one. It narrates the voyage back, the destruction of the marlin by sharks, and the old man's reconciliation with the boy. Thus the story comes full circle. This sequence of action, then, in its proportional arrangement, comprises the work's basic architecture. However, this is hardly its only structural principle. The large frame is reinforced by other, more intricate designs.

Among the essential symbolic patterns which support the structure of *The Old Man and the Sea*, as of other Hemingway narratives, is the movement from inside to outside, or, conversely, from outside to inside. This movement sometimes applies literally as the progression from in-doors to out-of-doors (or the reverse), from nature to dwelling or dwelling to nature, as in "Indian Camp," "Three-Day Blow," "An Alpine Idyll," and many others. In some instances the pattern has only two phases, in others three, with the action returning to the place or sphere of origin. The inside-outside pattern has many ramifications, of course, which break through the literal naming and which inherently convey deep emotional associations and values: in here—out there, home—abroad, familiar—strange, tame—wild, predictable—unpredictable, and so on.

Furthermore, the values which gather around each of these polarities are themselves ironically ambivalent, alternately desirable or repugnant, good or evil. For example, in "Indian Camp" the out-of-doors—especially the lake which Nick Adams crosses to and from the Indian settlement—represents the seeming peace, serenity, and infinity of untrammeled nature, which the naive boy contrasts with the dark hut where a woman has screamed in the agony of childbirth and a man has cut his throat. The symbolic possibilities of the contrast are manifold: Eden before and after the Fall, marriage and single life. Yet the placid lake which assures Nick of his immortality is but a mirror of his innocence. It may be immortal; he, of flesh, is not.

In *The Old Man and the Sea* the same pattern applies but in a slightly different form. Here the movement is from shore to sea to shore, and we have at once a credible imitation of life (is this not the way of fishermen?) and the archetypal associations which sea and shore inspire. Carlos Baker has rightly insisted that the simultaneous creation of a vivid surface reality and strong symbolic undercurrents is fundamental to Hemingway's method and among his greatest achievements. This is in part what Hemingway meant when he spoke of the "iceberg principle," a famous but not wholly understood phrase.

But these associations, as I have noted, are more complex than they may seem at first. Irony and symbolism, E. M. Halliday reminds us, are often inseparable in Hemingway. Shore means home, safety, comradeship; it is the locale for the story's portrayal of the love between Santiago and Manolin. It represents peace, rest, even perhaps an ultimate destiny, in two senses: first in the untranslatable but portentous image of lions playing on African beaches, second in the possibility that (as Bickford Sylvester argues) Santiago returns to die. The shores's negative or hostile function is emphasized when we recall that here Santiago lives in total poverty and is mocked by other fishermen, and that here, at the end, obtuse tourists mistake the marlin's skeleton for a shark's—the very monster which destroyed it. If the shore is thus the affirmative symbol of the closest human relationship Santiago has ever known, it also represents corrupt and confused standards of judgment.

Just as Hemingway establishes paradoxical values for the land, he bestows even more ironically ambiguous meanings upon the sea. As the vast arena for Santiago's struggle with the great marlin, it is that sphere in which man becomes most intensely alive, most severely tested, most heroic. The sea is beneficent, the source of peace and nourishment, and of inexpressible grandeur. But it is a trap, too, the element populated by deceptively beautiful yet poisonous creatures such as the Portuguese Man-of-War, and by the vicious sharks. The sea succors and exalts man even as it overwhelms and ruins him. This is what Santiago means when he says repeatedly in the book's concluding section that he has gone out "too far." The sea becomes, finally, the objective correlative for the abstractions we name Nature, Fate.

Thus the work's narrative pattern and frame, the land-sea-land movement, embodies also the polarities of its meanings: the known against the unknown, the human against the infinite. Furthermore, Hemingway strengthens the principal narrative pattern by interweaving two other sub-patterns, which serve to reduplicate the three-part structure: together-alone-together, darkness-light-darkness.

In the together-alone-together design the narrative opens with its depiction of Santiago's intimate comradeship with the boy, takes him out to sea alone, then closes with the renewed and intensified love of the boy, who resolves henceforth to defy his natural father and always accompany his spiritual father. Whatever one's interpretation of the significance of Santiago's solitary trial against marlin and shark, affirmative, negative, or ironic, the final phase of this design seems to allow little ambiguity; from his aloneness on the sea Santiago is restored to human love on shore. We surmise, too, that other fishermen will no longer mock him for his bad luck. The secular prayer the old man utters recurrently during his exhausting contest, "I wish I had the boy," is fulfilled at the story's end. He will have the boy for as long as he lives, and the boy—as he did at the beginning—is keeping him alive, with food, admiration, and hope. Structure becomes parable; our children extend us.

The second related pattern, darkness-light-darkness, is clear enough in its literal or realistic appearance but contains subtle implications. That is, as fishermen do, Santiago sets out before dawn, captures his fish in daylight (though not of the same day), and returns to port at night. Because the quest itself begins and ends in darkness, the response elicited would seem to be tragic, with darkness functioning first as foreshadowing and then confirmation of failure, loss, defeat, or, at the extreme, the fisherman's death. In darkness also the sharks complete their savage work, as we associate darkness with bestiality and sin. Yet here is the paradox. That the marlin is first hooked and then killed in daylight, that the first shark attacks when the sun is still high, as in daylight Santiago begins to question the ethics of his actions, all suggest that slaughter and moral awareness occur simultaneously and that both are forms of illumination. Indeed, Santiago's reflections upon the joy, the pride, and the evil of killing, ideas stated in full consciousness (in broad daylight, as it were) rehearse a life-long preoccupation of Hemingway's and perhaps his most profound and disturbing literary idea. The killing of the fish, another of Hemingway's deaths in the afternoon, and the old man's thoughts about it remind us of Hemingway's overt statement of that idea in the opening pages of the earlier book: that for him the most intense, the truest art, occurs in the presence and with the inspiration of violent death.

The narrative and symbolic pattern of light-darkness can be studied in further detail, for it serves in the story both as simple external frame and as internal imagery. As frame, the story begins and ends in daylight, from the late afternoon of the eighty-fourth day Santiago has gone unlucky to the afternoon three days later, when the tourists comment ignorantly while Santiago sleeps exhausted. More important, Hemingway uses a recurrent imagery of light and darkness. The sun on the sea hurts Santiago's eyes but it also warms him and helps unclench his crippled left hand. He dreams of white and gold beaches where the lions play. He is fed by white turtle eggs and gold and silver-sided fish. The moon and stars are his friends, and he associates the great fish with the celestial bodies. He knows he cannot be lost at sea because he will be guided by the glow of lights from shore—related, too, to the land-sea symbolism. But silver is also the color of extinction, as the marlin changes from its regal and vibrant blue-purple of life to the pale hue of death: "the color of the silver backing of a mirror." The sea, in contrast, is always and only dark. In fact, the word assumes almost the significance of leitmotif. I count "dark" (or darkness) used thirty times in the story, usually in connection with sea or water, yet never obtrusively. It works as a subtle form of incremental repetition, underscoring the sea's inscrutability, its archetypal mystery, for example in Santiago's thought: "The dark water of the true gulf is the greatest healer that there is."

We must consider, finally, the techniques by which Hemingway portrays his hero, and here again there appears a kind of ambivalence. That is, Hemingway commends Santiago to our affection and admiration; at the same time, he carefully foreshadows the story's tragic or ironic outcome and demonstrates the protagonist's frailties as a man. Hemingway's method is dual: first, he establishes the old man's attributes through a series of contrasts and associations which convey both strength and weakness, innocence and guilt; second, the writer makes his hero intimately familiar to us by his skillful use of a particular narrative perspective.

It was noted earlier in this essay that one of the important functions of the story's opening section is to elevate the fisherman to heroic stature. The most obvious means is direct statement, and three such assertions occur in the work's early pages. Hemingway tells us that Santiago's eyes remain "cheerful and undefeated;" the hero says of himself, "I am a strange old man;" the boy utters the highest tribute: "There are many good fishermen and some great ones. But there is only you." These statements convince us, despite their honorific content, because they are balanced against Santiago's age, scarred hands, tattered shirt, and simple humility of speech. Even more persuasive and revealing, however, are the characteristics suggested by the difference or contrast between the old man (and his relationship with the boy) and other men.

Santiago is unlucky; others, such as the boy's present master, are lucky. The boy's father "hasn't much faith;" the boy and the old man do. The boy's present master has poor vision, does not allow the boy to help him carry the boat's equipment, and fishes close to shore. The old man has keen eyes, welcomes the boy's help, and goes far out. Other men speak of the sea as neutral or enemy; Santiago feels the same kinship with it one has with a woman. The old man drinks shark liver oil for its healthful properties; other men hate it. The old man talks to himself for company; others have radios. Santiago fishes correctly and precisely; other men tend their lines carelessly. He thus becomes a kind of natural aristocrat of fishing, as his idol DiMaggio is a true prince of baseball. Even the old man's white lies to the boy contribute to his nobility, for he wishes no pity or charity; and the very poverty of his shack enhances the nobility of his character and the magnificence of his dreams.

Yet it must be shown that Santiago is a flawed mortal, one of the race of Cain, born to kill his brothers and to suffer. Hemingway reminds us of the hero's human imperfection by emphasizing the theme of treachery, betrayal, deception, from the start. It begins innocently enough with the old man's mention of his "tricks" as a compensation for his waning physical strength. Although this means simply his craft, his skill and intelligence as a fisherman and man's principal claim to superiority over other animals, the word itself has a sinister and negative connotation which Hemingway deliberately plays against its surface sense. The same word is repeated a few pages later, and here Hemingway establishes as the corollary for man's tricks the cruelty and unpredictability of the sea, nature, and the unknown agency ("they") which makes some creatures "too delicately" for survival. From this point on in the story recurrent emphasis is given to deception, betrayal, and treachery, especially man's treachery. It was "treachery" to pursue the great marlin in the deep water beyond the usual range of fishermen, as it is "unjust" to kill him. Santiago's left hand behaves traitorously throughout much of the combat with the fish. Though men hunt fish for food, Santiago concludes that they are unworthy of their prey. And once the old man has conquered the fish, the mode of conquest becomes a cause for shame. "I am only better than him through trickery and he meant me no harm," Santiago thinks as he begins the voyage home with his dead fish-brother. The connection between trick and treachery, between intelligence and sin, is now unmistakable.

In consequence, the return to shore can be compared to Santiago's penance for his crime, though full expiation is not possible because the fish is dead. The sharks, evil in themselves, assume the ironic function of moral agents: they inflict the necessary punishment. Their appearance comes sufficiently as a surprise to intensify the story's action, yet it has been foreshadowed. Subconsciously we have been waiting for them. In the novella's opening pages sharks are associated with vile smells; they are mentioned again, twice, on the voyage out, and once more after Santiago has hooked the marlin. Both their participation in the action and their moral function are specifically given when, late in the second day of the combat, Santiago says, "If sharks come, God pity him and me." And, finally, their appearance produces in him the same response as one suffering the tortures of crucifixion: in answer to the boy's question at the story's close, "How much did you suffer?" Santiago answers, "Plenty."

At last, regardless of profound symbolism and fascinating ambiguities, we must *know* the old man; we must share in his experience. The chief method by which Hemingway joins us to him—even more, by which we enter into him—is the masterly use of that narrative mode called "selective omniscience." In this mode, properly employed, the artist retains the objectivity and freedom of the omniscient, third-person, outside narrator, but takes advantage of the immediate and intimate responses—the "I am there" sense—of the first-person, inside narrator. The writer achieves this through careful selectivity and consistent focus upon one (or a few) of his characters, subtly integrating his voice and vision with theirs. Although Hemingway did not invent this mode, he refined it early in his career and used it with peculiar skill. Furthermore, he is able to avoid detection in his shifts from third-person to first-person narration, or, to say it another way, avoid discordance in his various narrative voices, by using essentially the same linguistic structures, the same level of language and diction, that his characters would naturally employ. Interior monologue thus becomes almost indistinguishable from outside narration. It is a technique that Scott Fitzgerald, for all his superb talent, never wholly mastered. Although a complete study of Hemingway's use of this technique would require more space than available here, a brief explanation is essential.

With a single exception (when we dip quickly into the mind of the boy), the third-person mode is scrupulously maintained during the book's first twenty pages which treat events on shore. We know the *contents* of Santiago's thoughts by Hemingway's statement of them but we do not share in them directly. However, once Santiago is alone and rows out to sea we enter into his mind with increasing frequency, sometimes moving from outside to inside with the traditional Hemingway cues, "he thought," "he said," sometimes gliding over directly from third person to first person. In other words, we get to know Santiago better when we have him alone. The initial instance of Santiago's voiced thought is indicated by quotation marks; after that the author uses no typographical markers except for what is actually spoken aloud. Thus to the reader third-person and first-person narration seem visually the same, as they do aurally. Likewise, the seams of the narrative, the transitions in voice, are kept from intruding upon the reader's attention. For example, here is a typical passage:

> The fish moved steadily and they travelled slowly on the calm water. The other baits were still in the water but there was nothing to be done.
>
> "I wish I had the boy," the old man said aloud. "I'm being towed by a fish and I'm the towing bitt. I could make the line fast. But then he could break it. I must hold him all I can and give him line when he must have it. Thank God he is travelling and not going down."
>
> What I will do if he decides to go down, I don't know. What I'll do if he sounds and dies I don't know. But I'll do something. There are plenty of things I can do.
>
> He held the line against his back and watched it slant in the water and the skiff moving steadily to the northwest.
>
> This will kill him, the old man thought. He can't do this forever. But four hours later the fish was still swimming steadily out to sea, towing the skiff, and the old man was still braced solidly with the line across his back.

Surely the passage appears simple enough and wholly characteristic of Hemingway, yet this seemingly transparent and artless prose employs, in sequence, four distinct narrative modes. It begins with third-person narration, but with the writer occupying the same point in time, space, and outlook as his character. It then shifts to direct utterance, set off by conventional punctuation and introduced by a conventional phrase. Next, however, there is a passage of interior monologue without any cues, followed immediately by another brief passage of outside narrative, followed in turn by a passage which integrates cued interior monologue and third-person narration.

Even in this kind of purely rational analysis of narrative technique, which allows nothing for the momentum of previous action, for the reader's already initiated identification with the protagonist, or for the rhythms of the language (note the repetitions in the passage, and the use of parallelism and balance in the sentence constructions), Hemingway's craft impresses us as remarkably *right*, totally congruent to its subject. It has been said before but it cannot be said too often: no one has written better about such things than Hemingway.

What is true of *The Old Man and the Sea* is true at large. Who does not know Hemingway's writing? Yet who can profess to understand exactly how it is made, or unriddle the secrets of its special magic? We want to know more, for at its best, as in *The Old Man and the Sea*, it partakes of the miracle of enduring art: that it can never be exhausted by critic or reader, but that it renews itself and its audience perpetually.

LINDA W. WAGNER

The Poem of Santiago and Manolin

I sometimes think my style is suggestive rather than direct. The reader
must often use his imagination or lose the most subtle part of my thought.
—Ernest Hemingway, "A Man's Credo"

Some recent criticism of Hemingway's work indicates that readers might
now—ten years after his death—be more open to his posthumously
published comment. Hemingway as *suggestive*, as poet of the American novel,
is a new portrait for many readers. Yet if we can let ourselves see him as the
craftsman he was, teeth cut on Pound's Imagist-Vorticist energies and Ford's
Impressionist anxieties in the *Transatlantic Review* office, then perhaps we can
more accurately read his writing. In the same way that paraphrasing poems
is dangerous, since no one-to-one equivalent exists for the compression
inherent in a poem, so a simple distillation of Hemingway's writing is often
misleading.

I do not intend in this essay to trace the relationships between the
Imagist and Vorticist poets and Hemingway. We know that the younger
writer first wrote poems, and then moved cautiously to the stories and
prose vignettes that comprised *In Our Time*. By his own account, when
Hemingway began *The Sun Also Rises*, he was "still having a difficult time

From *Ernest Hemingway: Six Decades of Criticism*. © 1987 by Linda W. Wagner.

writing a paragraph"—precisely because he was, from the beginning, so terrifically conscious of "getting the words right." And although his first novel was a masterpiece, as were *A Farewell to Arms* and *For Whom the Bell Tolls*, Hemingway could never rest on laurels. Yet, after *The Old Man and the Sea*, he tended to be more at peace; in fact he wrote in August of 1952 about the Santiago story, "It's as though I had gotten finally what I had been working for all my life." The focus in this essay, then, is on Hemingway's last great satisfaction, the lyric novel that may be his greatest because in it all segments of the book—structure, imagery, word choice, characters, plot—create a single organic whole. Hemingway began as a poet and so he ended—and, well aware of Dylan Thomas' remark that the greatest poems have in them both love and death, he captured in *The Old Man and the Sea* several great loves, and a truly noble death.

T. S. Eliot may have been thinking of Hemingway's writing as well as Djuna Barnes's when he commented in his introduction to *Nightwood*, "it is so good a novel that only sensibilities trained on poetry can wholly appreciate it. A prose that is altogether alive demands something of the reader that the ordinary novel-reader is not prepared to give." With Hemingway's fiction (as with the Imagist poems that preceded it by a decade) each word counts. Years before he created the iceberg theory, he operated under its premises but with perhaps even more attention to making each word do several things. In this, Hemingway's admiration for Joyce and Pound was no doubt of greater influence than his shorter-lived friendship with Gertrude Stein.

In considering each word's significance, the writer was also constrained to create an active, moving focus. Literature could never exist as a static picture. Verbs were prized; adjectives made useful. The Imagists had initially made these suggestions and Pound's work with Chinese ideograms intensified their interest. For Hemingway, the principle of active writing operated at a double level in *The Old Man and the Sea*. There are many verbs and surprisingly few adjectives, considering that much of the novel is description. And, in a broader sense, Santiago's struggle is always a dynamic one. There is movement, verve—even when only the stars are moving. The book's original title (*The Sea in Being*) suggested this dynamism, reflecting the source of Hemingway's later pride as he commented that "the emotion was made with the action." Had Santiago not cared so much, he would not have gone out so far; had he not revered the fish, he would have cut the line and come home; had he not come to love it, he would not have struggled so valiantly to save little more than its carcass. Just as every word in the book is there for a purpose, so is Santiago's every act. His dialogue with his left hand is a vivid reminder of the importance of each gesture, each movement.

By focusing on the immediate action, Hemingway follows Imagist doctrine and also avoids the sentiment inherent in his choice of hero. Santiago is pure pathos—alone except for an unrelated boy, poor, comfortless, unlucky, and old; yet because Hemingway presents him as proud and courageous, aligned with the arch young lions, that is the way we see him. (As Pound commented, the poet can at least partially control his readers' reactions, as the journalist cannot.)

Perhaps this is one of the most difficult of the Imagist tenets to employ, the fact that the author controls without interfering. He presents, he renders the story; but his control is limited to the selection of details. Pound had discussed (in a 1914 essay on Joyce) the dangers of both realism and impressionism:

> There is a very clear demarcation between unnecessary detail and irrelevant detail. An impressionist friend of mine talks to me a good deal about "preparing effects," and on that score he justifies much unnecessary detail, which is not "irrelevant," but which ends by being wearisome. . . .
>
> [Joyce] excels most of the impressionist writers because of his more rigorous selection, because of his exclusion of all unnecessary detail.

Pound's summary tone suggests that anyone can tell when detail is irrelevant, but only the master craftsman—here, Joyce; later, Hemingway—knows the line between necessary (and superfluous) detail. It becomes a matter of both quantity and kind.

Hemingway's choice of the singular noun *shirt* in his brief opening description of Santiago is one such essential detail:

> Once there had been a tinted photograph of his wife on the wall but he had taken it down because it made him too lonely to see it and it was on the shelf in the corner under his clean shirt.

The reader is led quickly through the impressions—a photo, and colored at that, must have been a great tribute to his love; then Hemingway recreates his sadness, in removing the photo; then he reinforces Santiago's poverty: *the* shelf may well have been the only shelf, just as the single shirt was his only change. In one sentence Hemingway has conveyed both Santiago's passion and his poverty.

The same care with detail is even more evident once Santiago is in action, fishing. Many of Hemingway's paragraphs follow the pattern of (1) large narrative statement, then (2) accumulation of reinforcing details, and finally (3) the summary statement that gives the otherwise objective paragraph its determination. When Santiago baits his hooks, Hemingway leaves no question that the old man is expert.

> (1) Before it was really light he had his baits out and was drifting with the current. (2) One bait was down forty fathoms. The second was at seventy-five and the third and fourth were down in the blue water at one hundred and one hundred and twenty-five fathoms. Each bait hung head-down with the shank of the hook inside the bait fish, tied and sewed solid and all the projecting part of the hook, the curve and the point, was covered with fresh sardines. Each sardine was hooked through both eyes so that they made a half-garland on the projecting steel. (3) There was no part of the hook that a great fish could feel which was not sweet smelling and good tasting.

The final tone, established through the adjectives "sweet smelling and good tasting," comes as no surprise to the reader, even though he has been reading about baits, because earlier in the description, Hemingway had used the words *solid, fresh*, and particularly *half-garland*. The reader is thus viewing the entire process as Santiago would—the fish are beautifully fresh, the act of fishing is a ritual.

Working in a nearly poetic condensation, Hemingway turns frequently to figures of speech—often patterned in a series—as a way of giving extra meaning to his seemingly simple descriptions. Our initial picture of Santiago depends largely on this use of connected images. We first see his patched sail, looking when furled "like the flag of permanent defeat." Then Hemingway gives us Santiago's scars, "as old as erosions in a fishless desert." *Defeated, fishless*—the images are rapidly taking us one direction until the author moves, quickly, to Santiago's eyes: "Everything about him was old except his eyes and they were the same color as the sea and were cheerful and undefeated." The identification with the sea, coupled with the direct contradiction of "undefeated," establishes the tone Hemingway wants. But we also have the facts—and it is not because of the existing facts that Santiago is whole, but rather because of his spirit.

Operating throughout the writing in *The Old Man and the Sea* is a kind of rhythmic identity, evident in this excerpt, which William Gass has recently described in his discussion of Gertrude Stein:

> Her success in uniting thought and feeling in the meaning and

movement of speech showed that rhythm is half of prose, and gave
it the power of poetry without the indecency of imitation. . . .
Sometimes she brings prose by its own good methods to the
condition of the lyric.

As his experiments with language in his earlier novels had shown,
Hemingway was also concerned with this rhythmic identity as an integral
part of the whole effect. The rhythm of *The Sun Also Rises* is laconic, abrupt;
of *For Whom the Bell Tolls*, moderately smooth, with much longer sentences.
Hemingway's attempts to use the Spanish language, and the more personal
pronoun forms, were ways of attaining the flavor—at least partially a
rhythmic concern—of the Spanish people (the duration of the word *thee* is
longer than *you* no matter how slowly the latter is said). Even Richard
Cantwell's crudities help create the disjointed, even staccato measures of
Across the River. But nowhere does Hemingway match so well the language
of his persona with the narrative voice of the novel. Santiago's tranquillity
sets the pace for *The Old Man and the Sea*, in keeping with his slow, chary, and
deceptively uncomplicated speech.

The passage describing Santiago's baits also illustrates the somewhat
idiosyncratic use Hemingway makes here of the compound structure,
particularly the connective *and*. In its simplest position, the *and* coupling
suggests that there is no judgmental relationship between the clauses
connected: "He was an old man who fished alone in a skiff in the Gulf
Stream and he had gone eighty-four days now without taking a fish." It is
not *because* he fishes alone that Santiago has caught nothing. The simple
statement of apparent fact does what it purports to do, puts down the facts,
with no causation or blame.

Hemingway achieves the same kind of objective tone when he uses
the structure in more emotional situations, "The old man had taught the
boy to fish and the boy loved him." Perhaps Manolin did love Santiago
partly because of his having taught him, but rather than oversimplify the
relationship, Hemingway again uses the simple coupling which leaves more
to the reader's own insight. The structure—for all its apparent simplicity—
is thus suggestive.

At times several of these compound sentences must work together as
a unit to help reinforce the impression the reader will probably draw from
the first sentence. In his description of Manolin and Santiago stopping for
a beer, Hemingway sketches the milieu of the fishing village in two such
connected sentences:

They sat on the Terrace and many of the fishermen made fun of

the old man and he was not angry. Others, of the older fishermen, looked at him and were sad.

That Santiago was not angry is a bit ambivalent—is he beaten or indifferent,
or has he "the peace that passeth understanding," the wider tolerance? The
follow-up sentence shows that the latter interpretation is the one
Hemingway intends to reinforce.

It is one matter to look at single words and sentences and nod sagely,
thinking, "Yes, that's Hemingway's 'one clear sentence,' and there is the 'no
ornament except good ornament'"; it is more impressive to see all these
single elements joined into a longer passage which works, and conveys
surprising richness. The page of dialogue between Santiago and Manolin
essentially presents their past relationship, their present love for each
other—and the effect that love has on Santiago—all amid more common-
place detail about the village and the fishing process.

> "How old was I when you first took me in a boat?"
>
> "Five and you nearly were killed when I brought the fish in too
> green and he nearly tore the boat to pieces. Can you remember?"
>
> "I can remember the tail slapping and banging and the thwart
> breaking and the noise of the clubbing. I can remember you
> throwing me into the bow where the wet coiled lines were and
> feeling the whole boat shiver and the noise of you clubbing him
> like chopping a tree down and the sweet blood smell all over
> me."
>
> "Can you really remember that or did I just tell it to you?"
>
> "I remember everything from when we first went together."
>
> The old man looked at him with his sun-burned, confident
> loving eyes.
>
> "If you were my boy I'd take you out and gamble," he said,
> "But you are your father's and your mother's and you are in a
> lucky boat."
>
> "May I get the sardines? I know where I can get four baits
> too."
>
> "I have mine left from today. I put them in salt in the box."
>
> "Let me get four fresh ones."
>
> "One," the old man said. His hope and his confidence had
> never gone. But now they were freshening as when the breeze
> rises.

In Manolin's comparatively long memory of the fish, Hemingway writes his usual active prose, relying on the many -*ing* words, but he more importantly resolves the boy's memories happily. Even though Santiago is "clubbing" the fish, his action seems as natural to the boy as "chopping a tree down," and the heavy blood smell he recalls as "sweet." That a five-year-old child had such a reaction to what must have been a gory and frightening scene shows clearly the trust he had in Santiago. Hemingway gives us further proof of the old man as trust-inspiring in his description of his "sun-burned, confident loving eyes," and then goes on to show in turn the power of Manolin's love on him, with the closing image. By placing the descriptions of Santiago throughout the section, Hemingway keeps the old man before us, even when Manolin carries most of the dialogue. And by establishing tone through nature images, he reinforces the impression of Santiago as sea-like, old, strange, proud, and unbeaten.

The relationship between Manolin and Santiago is poignantly done, particularly when one considers that the boy appears in only one-fifth of the novel—in the first eighteen pages and the last six. The structure of the book is thus like that of *The Sun Also Rises*, with Jake and Brett together in Parts I and III, as are Manolin and Santiago. Yet when Santiago is alone, he thinks often of the boy, and his thoughts of him become a kind of refrain.

It begins, "I wish I had the boy," and then modulates into "If the boy were here"; finally reaching its climax in a threefold repetition, as the coils of line tear Santiago's hands,

If the boy was here he would wet the coils of line, he thought.
If the boy were here. If the boy were here.

Santiago has no time to pray, he tells God in his humorous attempt to bargain, but his thoughts of Manolin come at points of crisis and—structurally—seem to substitute for the prayers another man might be saying. That this effect is intentional—Manolin as Santiago's only hope, only love—is restated later when Santiago justifies killing the marlin.

Besides, he thought, everything kills everything else in some way. Fishing kills me exactly as it keeps me alive. The boy keeps me alive, he thought. I must not deceive myself too much.

Using structure as well as immediate presentation, Hemingway drew this all-encompassing love relationship, perhaps the most convincing of those in any of his novels. When Manolin says, "I remember everything from when we first went together," we accept his exaggeration, as Santiago does, as evidence of his selfless love for the old man. His willingness to bargain, to beg, to steal for food and supplies for him—and to go against his parents' wishes—is further evidence of that generous relationship. With Hemingway's definition of love as generous giving, the similarities between Manolin's devotion to Santiago and Maria's to Jordan and, to an even greater degree, Renata's to Cantwell, are evident. Sex aside, much of each of these relationships exists in the near-reverence of youth for the enduring wisdom of age. In *Across the River*, Renata wants to learn from Cantwell; true, she thinks his talking about war will in some way exorcise his bitterness, but her thirst for information must have some basis in interest as well. The closest parallel to the love between Manolin and Santiago, of course, is that between Jake and Brett. Also sexless, that love was proven chiefly in Jake's desire to give whatever he could toward Brett's happiness—and only because society finds bullfighters more objectionable than cups of coffee did Hemingway's first novel fail to have its appropriate effect.

Manolin wants everything good for Santiago; there is no jealousy between competing fishing boats here. He is confident in his position with the old man; there is no timidity or artifice. One of the best evidences of the latter is the fantasy Santiago and the boy create about the yellow rice and fish. Only very confident lovers joke (as Santiago does with God). Such scenes create the aura of tranquillity, of surety, that this novel maintains throughout. Like Shakespeare in *The Tempest*, Hemingway has realized the value of humor in the midst of the life-and-death struggle that the book really is, and he uses it well: the old man's thoughts about Joe DiMaggio's bone spur, and his childlike wondering about it, occur at some of the highest peaks of action. And the comic dialogue between Santiago and Manolin about fear is a skillful touch of the raspberries to any former Hemingway reader. To come from Robert Jordan's near-obsession with fear, fear as an index of manliness, to Santiago's mocking comments on the baseball teams is progression indeed:

> "The Yankees cannot lose."
> "But I fear the Indians of Cleveland."
> "Have faith in the Yankees my son. Think of the great DiMaggio."
> "I fear both the Tigers of Detroit and the Indians of Cleveland."
> "Be careful or you will fear even the Reds of Cincinnati and the White Sox of Chicago."

Santiago—and Manolin in his tutelage—seems to be almost beyond man's usual concerns with mortality—hence, his "strangeness" and perhaps his complete resolution (Cantwell's ability to spit might be an intermediate stage in this progression). Yet Hemingway includes enough detail to show that Santiago is a realist, not a romantic; he knows he will have to use "tricks" on the fish because his strength is not what it was when he was young. And he accepts his fate realistically, too, knowing that he "went out too far." The fish—though an impossibility—was not impossible to catch; it was only bringing it back such a long distance, unscathed, that was impossible.

Admittedly, Santiago shares many traits with the best of Hemingway's heroes, Jake Barnes and Robert Jordan. He does not admit to a limited set of hopes for man; there are no impossibilities. The central image occurs near the center of the story when Santiago, bemused at the size of the marlin, considers man's "luck":

"I have never seen or heard of such a fish. But I must kill him. I am glad we do not have to try to kill the stars."

Imagine if each day a man must try to kill the moon, he thought. The moon runs away. But imagine if a man each day should have to try to kill the sun? We were born lucky, he thought.

This is the same kind of reversal in our normal perception of events that Hemingway emphasizes as Santiago sits cramped all night in the cold boat, "The sack cushioned the line and he had found a way of leaning forward against the bow so that he was almost comfortable. The position actually was only somewhat less intolerable; but he thought of it as almost comfortable."

Calling it optimism is too pale. Santiago's outlook is stoicism at its best, somehow infused with a living, growing hope. And the presentation of it is amazingly effective, partly because of the author's shifting point of view.

Trying to categorize Santiago's philosophy makes one eager for generalities, and we tend to summarize all the Hemingway heroes, noticing how few suicides there are in any of the fiction, although nearly every character at some moment has a right at least to contemplate the act. One of the difficulties with identifying with Jake Barnes was our sparse knowledge about his real feelings, the restrictions of using first-person point of view with a laconic and rather toughsounding narrator. By the time of *The Old Man and the Sea*, Hemingway had learned not only to move easily between first person and omniscient (and here to include dialogue for more necessary insights); he had also learned to give the reader didactic help at crucial moments. Rather than have us believe what Santiago says—that the pain is nearly comfortable—Hemingway tells us how it really was. And rather than have us slide over the moon-sun passage, he adds a summary image a few pages earlier, so that Santiago's position is crystallized in our minds. It is all hopeless.

> The old man had seen many great fish. He had seen many that weighed more than a thousand pounds and he had caught two of that size in his life, but never alone. Now alone, and out of sight of land, he was fast to the biggest fish that he had ever seen and bigger than he had ever heard of, and his left hand was still as tight as the gripped claws of an eagle.

Soon after this, we have one of the few flashbacks in the book, as Santiago thinks of his Indian wrestling with the strongest man on the docks. They had gone one night and one day, and, for no rational reason, Santiago had won. So Hemingway tells us, in effect, that spirit can go a long way. It cannot, however, overcome everything.

Santiago is never broken, but then Hemingway has also told us that "man is not made for defeat. . . . A man can be destroyed but not defeated." What is new in this novel is the explicit injunction to think. Contrary to the earlier admonitions of Barnes, Henry, Morgan, Jordan, Thomas Hudson, and Cantwell that they not think—because, we suppose, Hamlet-like, they would be too fearful to act—Santiago in all his wisdom admits, "But I must think. . . . Because it is all I have left." Then he improvises the weapons he has lost, and later repeats, "Think of what you can do with what there is." In this synthesis of thought and action, Santiago works just as Jordan surely has, to the best of his ability, using what he has but never mourning, as Cohn might have, for what he did not have and could not hope to obtain. Hemingway's theme has changed little throughout his writing, but his method of expressing that theme has been modified toward greater directness and greater emphasis on the final effect. The latter part of *The Old Man and the Sea* is the most didactic of any of Hemingway's writing.

The "Cuba" and "Sea" sections of the posthumously published *Islands in the Stream* run a close second, however, and in the Thomas Hudson story is found the same emphasis on endurance. By depriving Hudson of his three sons, two at the close of the "Bimini" section and the third during the "Cuba," Hemingway has set up a different kind of endurance test, a torture of the heart rather than the body. Hudson, describing life as a series of tests, thinks to himself that all will be well "if we can get by this one and the next one and the next one." As he summarizes his own position, "Get it straight. Your boy you lose. Love you lose. Honor has been gone for a long time. Duty you do." Again Hemingway gives us a man who has known love—like Santiago—but is now bereft of it all. (The first part of *Islands* works largely to establish how great his devotion to his sons is and how lost he is in their absence.) Unwieldy as some parts of the novel are, and unfinished, the book is still a moving study of man's bereavement. Just as Santiago loses parts of the fish to the sharks, so Hudson loses parts of his own life until finally, as his behavior in the "chase" section suggests, that life means little. His actions show that all he has left is duty. (Once injured, in another reasonless aberration of fate, Hudson does think of his painting—"life is a cheap thing beside a man's work"—but it seems to be a definite afterthought.)

The transfer of emotion from this mass of writing, loosely connected as the "sea novel," to *The Old Man and the Sea* is evident. Whereas Hudson is concerned with his love for his sons and his first wife, Santiago has Manolin. The somewhat inarticulate conversations between Hudson and his boys seem stilted (one exception is young Tom's reminiscence of his early days in Paris) compared with the direct expressions of Manolin and Santiago. But then these characters are simpler, and their laconic language is borne out by substantiating actions. In *Islands*, so many people are involved that giving any one of them sufficient emphasis is difficult. The situation may have been closer to the author's own, but it was much harder to achieve artistically than the single man-single boy of *The Old Man and the Sea*. Only once in *Islands* does Hemingway achieve a similar concentration, when David tries to land the fish. There also the action is meaningful: it is focused on only several characters (with Hudson's position as separate, yet horribly involved, clearly drawn), and the scene moves quickly. Like Santiago's feeling for the marlin, David's reaction to his fish is compelling—his injured hands and feet, his feeling of union with the fish, his reticence, and his love for it. The boy's experience is, however, finally less effective than Santiago's because of the constant interruptions from the other six people on the boat and also because Hemingway uses third person point of view to convey the boy's reactions.

In *Islands*, too, the fishing experience is primarily an initiation process giving us greater insight into Hudson's fears for his sons—fears that the novel shows, perhaps too quickly, were well founded. The scene ends when the fish breaks away. In *The Old Man and the Sea*, by extending the story much further, by taking us past the excitement of the catch, the fight, and the possession, Hemingway emphasizes what a man can endure (just as in *Islands*, the successive two parts of the novel do this for Hudson). By shifting emphasis from catching the fish to staying with it, Hemingway changes the nature of the story. In the course of *The Old Man and the Sea*, he shows repeatedly Santiago's doing what he as man "had to do," and much more, until he finally waits, unarmed, for the last sharks, wondering "what can a man do against them in the dark without a weapon?"

It has been called existential, the fact that Hemingway gives his hero this dilemma, and makes him face it. But how similar the whole situation is to that of the scene in Faulkner's *The Unvanquished* when Bayard Sartoris asks, "How can you fight in the mountains, Father?" and the answer comes, "You can't. You just have to." *The Old Man and the Sea* is the novel Faulkner admired. For it is the first one Hemingway had written in thirty years in which the hero stood it all. And lived.

The catharsis here, in this spent resolution of Santiago's struggle, must remind any reader of the effects of Greek tragedy. The classic intensity of focus is evident in the limitation to three characters, the nearly single setting (village, ocean, village), the three-day time span (unified by the single action), and the resolution of that single action. So tightly unified is the story, in fact, that some of the telescoping of time is so heightened that it creates irony. As Santiago pulls on the line, for example, Hemingway writes,

> This will kill him, the old man thought. He can't do this forever. But four hours later the fish was still swimming steadily out to sea.

The juxtaposition of time information with Santiago's incorrect "knowledge" does more than convey fact; it also foreshadows the falsity of many of Santiago's expectations. And we are reminded again of the Hemingway thesis: even the greatest of men can seldom be in complete control of all circumstances.

Structurally, too, Hemingway emphasizes this axiom. It takes Santiago ninety-four pages to get the fish and only eighteen to lose it to the various sharks. The concentration, even in terms of space and detail, falls on Santiago's purely voluntary exposure to danger. For the first time in twenty years, the hero of a Hemingway novel was not chafing under "orders." (As Hudson said, in the passages written immediately after *The Old Man and the Sea*, "There are worse places to be than on your own.") Santiago could not complain about the higher powers—except the highest fates of all, those that willed him toward his destiny. Like Jake Barnes, Santiago's duty is only to himself and his ideals; similarly, only those who know him well, who understand him, can judge him. Therefore, Hemingway concludes the novel by letting Manolin give his reaction to Santiago's experience, fittingly, in actions as well as in words: crying, warming and rewarming Santiago's coffee, and keeping guard as the old man sleeps. Here love is a secure and confident relationship.

The actual ending of *The Old Man and the Sea* works perfectly to complement the rest of the book. It is no deliberate Christian ploy to have Santiago carry the mast up the hill (on page 26 he carried it down), and then lie face down on his bed (this is the falling action of an exhausted man, not a person going to bed). For those who read these last ten pages as evidence of Hemingway's Christ symbolism, one must suggest that Santiago's not saying the promised prayers provides an antidote to that interpretation. Instead, we must view the last few passages as (1) summation of the theme that runs, obviously and yet skillfully, throughout the book—man's incredible ability to survive, and more, to dare; to make it, whole in spirit and body; (2) a return to the enduring love that Manolin gave and Santiago lived for; (3) a necessary ending to the apparent "plot"—Santiago alive, his reputation vindicated, and the marlin skeleton disposed of; and (4) one of the most masterful of Hemingway's exercises in juxtaposition.

Once Santiago is asleep, focus shifts again to Manolin whose tears of joy and sorrow, occurring three distinct times, are the best single testimony to Santiago's courage. Then the last few pages of the novel shift setting kaleidoscopically: Manolin watching Santiago, going for coffee, talking with the crowd gathered near the skeleton, talking with Santiago, and then again returning to the village. As the boy hurries back and forth, we sense the reactions of the entire village and even of the outsiders—those uninitiated observers who usually appear in a Hemingway novel, but often to the detriment of any total effect. Here, however, after the laconic dialogue of Manolin and Santiago, with even his evident suffering described only as "Plenty," the ending image of the tourists' ignorance has a triple-edged effect. The evidence of Santiago's greatest catch is now garbage and, as such, has no meaning for any but the initiated. Even when the waiter tries to explain what has happened ("Tiburon." "Eshark"), the tourists hear him incorrectly. In the vapid "I didn't know sharks had such handsome, beautifully formed tails," Hemingway has caught the tone of facile indifference he despised. Yet in this novel—rather than belabor the ignorance, or admonish, or let Manolin comment—he instead moves quickly back to the sleeping Santiago, strangely at peace with his pain, the pain which signifies life, dreaming once again of the lions, as Manolin stands watch. We are given Santiago's peace in the envelope of Manolin's concern.

The relationship between Santiago and the marlin has been made much of, and rightly so, for the sense of wonder, the immensity, the brotherhood is beautifully conveyed. But, as the structure and imagery of *The Old Man and the Sea* prove, it is the love between imperfect human beings that lies at the core of Santiago's experience. It is that love that redeems Santiago; and it is that love to which he returns.

G.R. WILSON JR.

Incarnation and Redemption in
The Old Man and the Sea

That the heroic fisherman of Hemingway's *The Old Man and the Sea* carries a heavy burden of Christ symbolism has been widely recognized, but critics have disagreed markedly about the extent to which this identification functions in the novella and about how this symbolism is finally to be interpreted. In addition to the well annotated references to the crucifixion itself and to the other events of Passion Week, the author has, however, provided some helpful clues quite early in the book—clues that previous commentators seem to have overlooked and that may contribute to some clarification of this critical problem.

As the novella opens, we are told that Santiago "had gone eighty-four days now without taking a fish," and, in the second sentence, we learn that during "the first forty days a boy had been with him." If we add to this eighty-four day period the three days covered by the book's action, we get a total of eighty-seven days. Shortly thereafter, the boy recalls, "'But remember how you went eighty-seven days without fish and then we caught big ones every day for three weeks.'" In this way, Hemingway establishes two separate time spans of eighty-seven days that are important in the old man's life. The "forty days" and the three days covered by the novella's action are clear references to the Fasting in the Wilderness (and thus to Lent) and to Christ's Passion, respectively, and have been so noted by nearly every critic

From *Studies in Short Fiction* 14:4 (Fall 1977): 369–73. © 1977 by Newberry College.

to address himself to this aspect of the work, but, since this author's choice of details is rarely capricious, one wonders immediately about the possible significance of the two eighty-seven-day spans.

If one pursues the hint of the reference to forty days and looks carefully at the Christian liturgical calendar, it appears that Hemingway may have had something quite definite in mind when he selected this number. Two particular periods in the church year suggest the figure. The first is the entire Christmas Cycle from the first day of Advent, 27 November, to the last day on which Septuagesima Sunday can fall, 22 February; the second is from Ash Wednesday to Ascension Thursday, a period that constitutes all but the last ten days of the Easter Cycle from Lent through Paschaltide. While these correspondences may, of course, be merely coincidental, it seems unlikely; we know that Hemingway was familiar with the liturgical calendar, and the basic fact that he chose to make such heavy use of Christian symbolism in *The Old Man and the Sea* argues against coincidence. At any rate, the implications of these correspondences might well be worth exploring.

The first of these two time spans in the old man's life, the eighty-seven days followed by the three fruitful weeks, suggests the liturgical Mystery of the Incarnation. During this period, in terms of Christian myth, the liturgy commemorates Christ's assumption of his earthly life and the establishment of his claim as the Son of God. Similarly, it is during this time span in Hemingway's parable that Santiago establishes his claim to heroic stature in the eyes of the boy Manolo and becomes, in fact, the hero incarnate. We can see, for example, in the dialogue concerning doubt and faith that immediately follows the mention of this time span the existence of a master-disciple relationship between the old man and the boy, as Carlos Baker, among others, has pointed out. In citing specifically three weeks during which the old man and the boy "caught big ones every day," Hemingway may well be alluding to the three years of Christ's public ministry during which he was both a fisher of men himself and an instructor to his disciples in how to be fishers of men, a role paralleled by Santiago in his instruction of Manolo. Furthermore, the way in which Christ established his divinity among the faithful was by performing miracles, and, similarly, Manolo's faith in Santiago seems clearly to be founded on the apparent miracle of three weeks' bounty after the long barren period. A later reference, also tied to a discussion of faith that immediately precedes it, identifies this eighty-seven-day span as a "great record" in the eyes of the boy, just as Christ's life on earth, as attested in the Gospels, constitutes a great record in a different sense of the word. And when, to the boy's comment, the old man responds, "'It could not happen twice,'" he underlines the unique nature of his incarnation as hero. Finally, the importance of all this is to be found in the theological concept that only through the Incarnation of Christ, through his assumption of human form, can his eventual sacrifice have redemptive value for mankind; were he only divine, the Passion could have no human meaning because it would involve no sacrifice. Similarly, Hemingway seems clearly to be establishing Santiago's "great record," which concluded with three triumphal weeks' bounty, to render more meaningful the second eighty-seven-day span, which is to end with three days of agony and apparent defeat.

If the first time span suggests the Mystery of the Incarnation, then the second span, that including the eighty-four days that the old fisherman has gone without taking a fish plus the three days described in the novella, would seem correspondingly to suggest the Mystery of the Redemption. The many symbolic details linking Santiago (and the marlin, for that matter) with Christ and the crucifixion have, of course, already been noted by various critics and need not be rehearsed here. It is important, however, to recognize that the focus of this second span is limited; as indicated above, we are here concerned with that period of the liturgical calendar beginning on Ash Wednesday and ending on Ascension Thursday. This period includes the mortification and death of Christ, the instruction of the disciples in the meaning of Christ's sacrifice by his repeated appearances during the forty days following Easter, and two of the three mysteries that are subsumed in the Paschaltide Season—the Resurrection and the final Ascension into Heaven; it does not include the third mystery, that of the Descent of the Holy Ghost, which is not celebrated until Pentecost, ten days later.

If we look at *The Old Man and the Sea* with this in mind, it may clarify several matters. First, the old man, like Christ, achieves a triumph in apparent defeat. While Christ's triumph is over physical death, Santiago triumphs over the *dentuso* and the *galanos* which, though they destroy the great marlin, cannot diminish the heroism that has led to the union of man and nature climaxing the battle between fisherman and fish. In addition, Santiago is able, again like Christ, to return to his disciple with the evidence of the hero-deed that he has accomplished. This is necessary in order to make clear the significance of that deed for all men, a significance that is, of course, expressed in the novella's theme of tragic affirmation: "'But man is not made for defeat. . . . A man can be destroyed but not defeated.'" The redemption that Santiago brings back to the world is to be found in a recognition of the deep resources of human strength made possible when man is properly attuned to his world, a strength that the old fisherman has painfully and heroically exemplified. And, although this message is not yet widely comprehended, (as underscored by the tourists at book's end) just as Christ's message was not grasped outside the faithful few, the disciple perceives completely the significance of the old man's final adventure. That it is, in fact, his final adventure, that Santiago is about to die when we last see him, although disputed by some critics, seems supported by the fact that this second eighty-seven-day period ends on Ascension Day, for, just as the Ascension is the crowning event of Christ's earthly ministry, so Santiago's sojourn in the world must be concluded once he has imparted his message of redemption. Finally, the omission of the celebration of Pentecost suggests that the redemption postulated by Hemingway in his parable is an entirely human one requiring no infusion of a mysterious outside force to be operative. That is to say that the period here paralleled is one that focuses only on the incarnate member of the Trinity, and, correspondingly, the suggestion seems to be that the hero is important because he displays the grandeur of which man is capable without the help of any external or mystical power, save that embodied in his comprehension of the union with nature that he has achieved.

Finally, it might be helpful to remember that Christ is one avatar of the figure whom Joseph Campbell calls "the hero with a thousand faces," and Santiago, obviously, can also take his place in that particular pantheon. A comparison of the events of *The Old Man and the Sea* with Campbell's summary of the pattern of his so-called monomyth reveals a close correspondence. The hero sets out with the aid of a helper (Manolo), crosses the threshold of adventure, ("'I went out too far,'" says Santiago) and meets a trial that can take many forms including the brother-battle, dragon-battle, crucifixion, and a night-sea journey, all of which can be seen as applying in some way to the old fisherman. The adventure culminates again in several possible ways, one of which is a sacred marriage, closely analogous to the union established between man and marlin at the conclusion of Santiago's epic battle ("'I have killed this fish that is my brother,'" he says). The hero must endure tests (the sharks) before his return to the world to which he brings some sort of boon, in Santiago's case the knowledge that man, who can be destroyed, cannot be defeated.

The liturgical gloss of incarnation and redemption outlined above is important because it strongly underlines this mythic dimension of *The Old Man and the Sea*—the dimension in which the book's power resides. Contrary to those critics who would minimize this work, the Christian symbolism is not simply a pat overlay attempting to give weight to an otherwise mundane story, but rather it constitutes the basic technique by which Hemingway presents his view of man as a coherent and intrinsically important part of the cosmos in which he must find value. This vision of man goes far beyond that revealed in Hemingway's earlier work.

In place of the code hero, who accepted a nihilistic universe more or less passively and whose only effort was to try to come to terms with that dark vista through some personal accommodation, we have here the hero incarnate, who achieves meaning, not only personally but universally, by a full commitment to his world and through an intimate relationship with that world's creatures. Only because of this unity with nature can Santiago exercise, indeed expend, his strength and endurance as a man to achieve his final symbolic but meaningful triumph in the face of literal disaster, a triumph that carries a redemptive message for all who share the human condition. In the effective artistic communication of that redemptive message lies the brilliant achievement of *The Old Man and the Sea*.

JAMES H. JUSTUS

The Later Fiction: Hemingway and the
Aesthetics of Failure

M an as victim in a world at war is, arguably, the fundamental twentieth-century vision, and its most compelling spokesman is Hemingway. If he was not the first American writer to appreciate this permanent condition—it is already a settled conviction in Dreiser, Crane, and London at the turn of the century—he was the first to articulate it without the pretension of intellectual theorizing, instinctively aware even in the early 1920s that to fit the disturbing truth into a framework of theoretical structures was itself a kind of softening of the truth. And despite the perceptible shift in emphasis from the buttoned-up stoicism of Jake Barnes and Frederic Henry to the acknowledged need for communal co-operation in Harry Morgan and Robert Jordan, the original insights and the usable metaphors remained the same in the work of the 1930s and after: in a life of warfare, man suffers.

Indeed, nothing in the later work can support the contention occasionally voiced that Hemingway's 'growth' can be traced in his sequence of protagonists, that there is a steady ennobling process, from the nihilistic entrapment of man to his victory through tragic transcendence. For all the bathos of one and the noble self-sacrifice of the other, Harry Morgan and Robert Jordan are linked with the earlier protagonists in trying to fight through delusion and personal inadequacies to some clear picture of the reality of inevitable loss. And lest we accept too readily the notion of a

From *Ernest Hemingway: New Critical Essays*. © 1983 by Vision Press Ltd.

mellow Hemingway in *The Old Man and the Sea*, the rhythms of mythic parallels, the quasi-biblical diction, and the stark Homeric courage of its protagonist cannot disguise the central fact of the fable: the grand victory is brief. Santiago *loses* the great fish, and for all the skeletal proof of his catch, he is still an old man with only residual skills, a failure who must retreat to dreams of youth and vigour. What we learn from Hemingway in the 1920s is what we learn from Hemingway throughout his career: the fact of failure is the one clear-eyed and undeviating purchase on reality in the midst of falsifying stratagems, poses, masks, and those defensive bursts of justification that weave together author and authored, life and art. Man is doomed to failure; he must run a race whose outcome is already known; 'they' who finally 'get you' are often not indifferent but apparently malevolent; man must live with violence and pain in a sustained anguish that comes from a realization of his only temporary survival; fear is a constant, and while courage is possible, heroism is not. There is not a single Hemingway protagonist who is not wounded, sometimes physically so, always psychically. Because loss is their permanent condition, these protagonists are prey to nostalgia and fantasy and reconstituted versions of the self, dodges and substitutionary acts that somehow function as temporary comfort and assurance.

A catalogue of Hemingway's characters from Nick Adams to Thomas Hudson, as well as the narrative situations that document their difficult adjustment to lives that are only minimally self-directed, shows a remarkably consistent record of human failure. In addition to a physical disability that he knows is permanent, Jake Barnes betrays his own best instincts and violates his own carefully devised code of personal conduct. Nick Adams never quite recovers from the traumas of childhood violence, the suicide of his father, and his own wounding in Italy. The rain that symbolizes the death of his lover and child is also Frederic Henry's own symbolic future of unrecoverable loss. Harry Morgan is one of the spiritual and economic Have-Nots whose general failure is merely ratified by his formal death in a hail of bullets. And if Robert Jordan is, according to Philip Young, the first of Hemingway's protagonists to conquer his 'incapacitating nightmares', we should not forget the end of his story; our final glimpse of him, a peripheral figure in the failed struggle for Spanish freedom, is of supine man whose final act is gestural rather than definitive. What he loses are his love, his cause, and his life. While much of Colonel Cantwell's last phase is marked by revaluation, reminiscence, and rewriting of the record to strengthen his place in it, the picture is one of sad depletion and the often quirky energy of the dying. The heart of Santiago's spiritual victory would seem to be sheer endurance of the fact of failure. And the evidence of the short fiction is similar. The protagonists in the most memorable stories—'The Snows of Kilimanjaro,' 'The Killers',

'The Short Happy Life of Francis Macomber', 'The Undefeated', 'The Gambler, the Nun, and the Radio'—are caught in a context in which they or a third party engage in a recital of their failures or where victory is brief.

Given such a grimly consistent vision, we may well ask what *are* the possible counters to it? The work of the late Hemingway, like the early, reveals *no* satisfactory alternatives to the vision of failure—indeed, now that we have available the biography of, letters from, and assorted memoirs about this intensely autobiographical writer, we might well suspect even darker hues in that vision in the later fiction. That this is not the case is the triumph of Hemingway the artist over Hemingway the man. In both *The Old Man and the Sea* and *A Moveable Feast*, the writer who always complained of the difficulty of writing invented and managed to maintain the pace of certain rhetorical rhythms which in the first instance dignify and elevate the fable of failure and in the second disarm the reader's instinctive distaste for what the author reveals of his own selfishness, competitiveness, and mean-spiritedness. Style, that is, becomes one strategy of countering content.

In a sense, *The Old Man and the Sea* is now a lesser achievement than it was once thought to be because of the transparency of the device. The choice of a simple old fisherman who is down on his luck but who still proudly exercises his long-used skills is an explicit dalliance with sentimentality, a situation containing a ready-made, built-in poignancy not unlike that found in the pages of *The Reader's Digest* or *Guideposts*: in short, the inspirational value—the human spirit triumphing over adversity—is inherent in the very subject itself. What remained for Hemingway was the manner of telling, a style simultaneously detailed and generalized, calling upon his own specific familiarity with Gulf Stream fishing and a heightened form of the kind of translated English he had brilliantly but sporadically used (mostly for comic effects) as early as *The Sun Also Rises*. It is no wonder that *The Old Man and the Sea* was praised extravagantly when it appeared in 1952, and that the best critics correctly perceived that the victory was one of style. That, of course, had been the single greatest achievement of the early Hemingway, too—the forging of an uncluttered style that became the most influential of the twentieth century. Now, in the Santiago story, the stripped-down diction, the simple syntax, the repetitions, and the use of the conjunctions for rhythmical purposes had been redirected away from the blunt, tough-guy mannerisms into something akin to the scriptural.

But anterior to a famous literary style that gives a patina of success to the sequential fables of failure is an equally famous personal style that provides the illusion of success within a vision in which failure is a given. The story of Hemingway's art is the spectacle of failure both personal and existential. The story of Hemingway's career as man and artist is the search for techniques to neutralize if not overcome failure. No protagonist wins, since none can win, but the famous dichotomy between the Hemingway hero and the Hemingway code hero, the imaginative splitting apart of The Way It Is and The Way It Should Be, is one obvious means for handling the fact of failure. Figures such as Manuel Garcia, Ole Andreson, Rinaldi, Santiago, Pedro Romero—and the Ernest Hemingway of the public press—are flesh-and-blood exempla who show how, in the face of certain defeat, man's only nobility consists in personal conduct, an integrity that allows him to face his defeat with dignity.

This personal style in its largest sense is anterior and analogous to the crafted precision of Hemingway's literary style. In this respect the competing values of style and vision become an important source of the undeniable vitality that even readers not notably sympathetic to Hemingway admit they find in the best of his work. What we often note in the Hemingway hero is a dramatized instance of that tension between style and vision, a structuring of human responses into aesthetic patterns that constitute creative counters to the gloomy fact of failure. His projected but never completed Book of the Sea is neither the best nor the worst of Hemingway's work, but even in its post-humous, edited state it reveals considerable interplay between vision and craft; and as 'late Hemingway' it may illustrate some final creative state-ment in that interplay which from the beginning characterizes its author's approach to his art—and to his life.

One measure of the decline in Hemingway's creative energy for the last fifteen years of his life is the gap between the works he ambitiously planned and worked on and those he actually completed. In Carlos Baker's descrip-tion of the unfinished novel Hemingway called *The Garden of Eden* (some of it cannibalized for *Across the River and Into the Trees*) we find that to the usual difficulty of composition was added the apparent loss of authorial judgement generally. Personal engagement with his subject in *The Dangerous Summer* was no guarantee against slack, self-indulgent writing, embarrassingly evident even in the heavily edited excerpts that *Life* (but not Charles Scribner) saw fit to publish. Embedded in the 'Cuba' segment of *Islands in the Stream* is what may well be the author's own self-mocking gloss on his failure to make anything of another large project. In his preparations for his day off in Havana, after a lengthy time at sea, a fretful Thomas Hudson asks himself: 'What the hell is wrong with you? Plenty is wrong with me, he thought. Plenty. The land of plenty. The sea of plenty. The air of plenty.' For several years Hemingway planned a grand trilogy of novels with the vague rubric of "Land, Sea, and Air'. Within that plan, the Book of the Sea itself consisted of four independent novels, three of them devoted to Thomas Hudson and a briefer fourth to Santiago. From the testimony of friends and the evidence in the *Selected Letters*, the only piece of writing from the last period that came without agony was *The Old Man and the Sea*, for which Hemingway interrupted the writing of 'Bimini' and 'Cuba'; after completing the Santiago story, intended from the start as a coda for Hudson, he returned to the final sea-chase segment, now titled 'At Sea', which he wrote in the spring of 1951. After editing and cutting by Mary Hemingway and Charles Scribner, Jr., the three Hudson parts of the Book of the Sea were published in 1970 as a single novel, *Islands in the Stream*.

Although the narrative discontinuity between *The Old Man and the Sea* and *Islands in the Stream* is clear, more significant is their thematic and psychological continuity. If, following the author, we consider the two novels as a single work issuing from a common period of composition (irregularly from 1946 to May 1951), and if we remember that Hemingway interrupted his Book of the Sea to write *Across the River and Into the Trees* (1948), what we most dramatically see is the functional interrelation of the author's life and art. That intimate connection is of course the hallmark of Hemingway throughout his career, evident to everybody during his lifetime despite the author's own annoyed disclaimers. But this cluster of work is different. These titles are an old man's books. Though Hemingway was only 47 when he began this work, as the biography sadly documents, he was already a prematurely ageing man. One sign in the fiction is the prominence of nostalgia, the recurrence of dreams, the bouts of reassessments, and the impulse to reshape old mistakes into more acceptable forms. All three heroes are manifestations of a battered lifetime of constant threats, tests, and disappointments, and a few victories that are memorially rehearsed to help shore up defences against a larger defeat to come. Explicitly, Cantwell and Hudson have perceptibly moved beyond the expectations of youth and the accommodations of maturity, from the nagging moral question of how shall a man live? to the starker one of how shall a man die? If Santiago, a simpler man, is not given to such lofty meditations, it is only because his creator is still being faithful to a realist's creed of credible characterization; the fable itself and the modest self-assessments of the old man are implicit articulations of the same thing.

Given the circumstances of Hemingway's creative life during the composition of his Book of the Sea, the wonder is that it possesses what vitality and coherence it does. No other of his works is more consciously *composed* than *The Old Man and the Sea*, the coda segment. It is not merely that, to follow Gertrude Stein's famous observation on Hemingway's early writing, it smells of the museum. In this case, the classical and biblical analogues of epic endurance are retold with austerity and restraint. While its control, its willed perfection, its rigorous excision of anything left to chance are its obvious strengths, they also make *The Old Man and the Sea* finally less interesting than the other parts of the sea story that became *Islands in the Stream*. Unlike the taut structure and the calculations of style in the Santiago story, with its air of a rhetorical exercise, the Thomas Hudson story is *under-written*: the shapely but flexible patterns of its structure can still surprise, and the more varied, less processed style accommodates a wider range of human complexity.

Two similar episodes—Santiago's successful struggle with the marlin and David Hudson's unsuccessful struggle with a broadbill—suggest the general differences in the two works. Even though the David episode is the dramatic centre in 'Bimini', it is preceded and followed by other incidents, other characters, other anxieties. Its pacing and its placement meet our conventional expectations of the novel form; that is, it has context. In *The Old Man and the Sea* the landing of the marlin is also central, the first necessary stage in a continuous drama, but it is its own context. While the sense of place is firm, the action seems to occur in some realm of storybook time. Partly because of its rigorous adherence to the old unities, Santiago's drama is fablistic, not novelistic. What passes for its narrative extension is really symbolic, mythic, even allegorical, a characteristic that explains why ordinary copy-editors at *Life*, where it was first published, were instantly able to see something more in this work than a simple, primitive story exquisitely told. Its 'upper' level of meaning is as insistent as its 'lower' level of story. Unlike *The Old Man and the Sea*, *Islands in the Stream* is complex in its narrative situations, its characterizations, and its sense of a society in a specific moment in time as well as a sense of place. As many readers have shown, *Islands in the Stream* is also shot through with hints of a larger symbolic significance, but they are merely intimations and they remain firmly subordinated to narrative.

Despite its considerable editing—the first by Hemingway himself—*Islands in the Stream* retains enough narrative patterning to make it struc-turally and thematically coherent. Each of the three-part narrative has its own architecture, and each is designed to display different facets in the drama of human decline. Each book is dominated by the fact of death as Thomas Hudson, without fully understanding his sons, wives, and lovers, undergoes the searing experience of deprivation of those he loves, until, at the end, he himself lies dying. One critic has perceptively commented on Hemingway's technique of representing literally Hudson's progressive narrowing of his life in 'At Sea', in which 'at last in a channel along the Cuban coast, where the mangrove presses close on either hand, he finds his death'. 'Bimini' economically supplies all that we need to know—and the most we will ever know—of the circumstances behind this twentieth-century 'grief-hoarder'. Its narrative rhythm is established by alternating segments of repose and action. The obscure tensions, both cultural and personal, that culminate in the ugly fight on the Queen's Birthday; David's narrow escape from a shark; and David's heroic bout with his fish: these three dramatized episodes reveal the protagonist as spectator. With a stability all too precarious, Hudson is unable to affect events; his is a recuperative sensibility whose major threat is the eruption of the very emotions that make men human: rage, love, remorse. In between these scenes of action are moments of repose, carried mostly by beautifully rendered conversations in which Hudson meditates on his vulnerability and stands exposed to a fate he cannot change.

'Cuba' is an extended segment of repose whose only action—patrol duty—is background. It consists of talk—conversation, story-telling, reminiscence—and functions as the first available, and finally inadequate, counter to suffering. The other available counter is the commitment to duty, the action of 'At Sea', although Hemingway implies that in the overall scheme there is finally little relationship between the purgative and what is being purged. Indeed, the swiftly paced action of the sea-chase in part three, like the sustained talk in the repose of part two, is merely substitutionary. While both telling and acting have their own integrity, they are modes that ultimately make no difference. Grief, loss, suffering are existential, and they are paramount in the emotional structure of the novel. When Hudson and his first wife are reunited in 'Cuba', the happiness is momentary, doomed already by their individual personalities and by the fact of their son's death; being suddenly summoned for sea duty is almost irrelevant in an uneasy relationship that is already spoiled. 'Get it straight', Hudson tells himself. 'Your boy you lose. Love you lose. Honor has been gone for a long time. Duty you do'. Patrolling the Gulf Stream looking for Nazis is, potentially at least, an action in the service of a higher cause, the stuff of conventional World War II films, but *duty* here is grimly personal. He does not have to like chasing Nazis, Hudson reminds himself; he merely has to do it well. The emotional state of the protagonist is the consistent focus throughout the novel, and depletion is its most telling note. Texturally, the novel is studded with the diction of defeat: *unhappiness, suffering, loss, sorrows and cries, grief, hopelessness, blankness, wickedness.*

This study of failure is pervaded by a mood of imminent social and cultural collapse, an aura of dread that provides a context for, even as it condenses into, the personal collapse of Thomas Hudson. 'Bimini' opens on the Queen's Birthday, an anachronistic event whose honouring by irrelevant celebrants is noisy, vulgar, and violent; with a sick gusto Mr. Bobby collaborates with Hudson in projecting the painter's masterpiece, 'The End of the World', a Caribbean version of Hieronymus Bosch that will of course never be painted; the wealthy tourists from the yachts are 'trash', but even Hudson's friends are 'a pretty seedy lot', not bad but 'worthless'. Roger Davis, the closest of these friends, is another of Hemingway's walking wounded, a burnt-out case when we last see him looking, with neither enthusiasm nor hope, for a new start in the west. The atmosphere of dread takes on a metaphysical cast whenever Davis and Hudson, brothers in pain, are by themselves. Davis suffers from guilt arising from the failure of responsibility (in the death of his younger brother and with a succession of women) and the prostituting of his talents, but he tends to transfer such personal problems into the public realm. After his fight with an obnoxious tourist, Davis admits his regret in succumbing to violence:

> 'There's a lot of wickeds at large. Really bads. And hitting them is no solution. I think that's one reason why they provoke you. . . . You know evil is a hell of a thing, Tommy. And it's smart as a pig. You know they had something in the old days about good and evil.'
>
> 'Plenty of people wouldn't classify you as a straight good', Thomas Hudson told him.
>
> 'No. Nor do I claim to be. Nor even good nor anywhere near good. I wish I were though. Being against evil doesn't make you good.'

They both agree that the wealthy tourist was an 'awful type', and as a final comment, Davis observes:

> He couldn't have been any worse than the last one on the coast. The trouble is, Tommy, there are so many of them. They have them in all countries and they are getting bigger all the time. Times aren't good, Tommy.

The evils are real, of course. They include natural disasters, such as waterspouts and hurricanes, sharks, and Nazis as well as spoiled vacationers and corrupt Hollywood tycoons; but, more importantly, they include personal demons, the dark nightmares of nearly all the adult characters in *Islands in the Stream*. Davis recognizes the principle: 'I was against it and then I was evil myself. I could feel it coming in just like a tide'. Hudson is not only not exempt; he is Hemingway's prime example of the fragile remnant, a human being victimized as much by his own inner deficiencies as by any of those assorted external evils. Roger Davis is a reminder of his own darker self, a figure sapped of self-confidence and self-control and occasional hostage to self-pity. But there is another side to this relationship. Davis has squandered his talent and has made himself vulnerable by loving others. The poignancy here is that even in his ruin he may be superior to Hudson. It is not surprising that a tactful Hudson hesitates to preach too readily or too directly to his friend; Davis's squandered talent may be greater than Hudson's husbanded one.

Throughout 'Bimini', the only section in which Hudson's profession is treated, Hemingway establishes the grounds by which we can be assured that Hudson is trying to be a good artist in a bad time. The assurances are not convincing. Despite his protagonist's early friendship with fellow artists in Paris—Picasso, Braque, Miro, Pascin—the author gives no real evidence that Hudson is anything better than a passably decent artist, commercially successful enough to maintain an agent but imaginatively deficient. His most admired painting, hanging behind the local bar, is of three water-spouts and three men in a dinghy; his most heartfelt painting, generated by his son's struggle with a broadbill, tries to capture transient reality in a moment of actual loss; and Mr. Bobby, though his aesthetic judgement may be suspect, gives what is clearly intended to be an unsentimental summary of Hudson's *oeuvre*:

> People paying money for pictures of Uncle Edward. Pictures of Negroes in the water. Negroes on land. Negroes in boats. Turtle boats. Sponge boats. Squalls making up. Waterspouts. Schooners that got wrecked. Schooners building. Everything they could see free. They really buy them?

The professional perfunctoriness of island genre painting is only a part of Hudson's general personal failure. The summary is additionally resonant, coming as it does after Mr. Bobby's exasperated wondering aloud why Hudson and his friends 'stay around this island'. The painter's precise calibration of his island life can also be seen as a tucked-tail retreat, rehabilitation, or escape.

If Roger Davis's other problem is loving too freely, Hudson's is his emotional penuriousness. To love is to make the self vulnerable. That sad truth of human relationships explains both Davis and Hudson: if the first is ravaged by too much giving of the self, the second is desiccated from giving too little. Like the 'carapace of work' he has devised to protect himself, Hudson's stoic imperturbability protects him against further emotional lacerations. While Roger displays all the scars of psychic hurt, Hudson carefully, formally, maintains the disjunction between his equally serious psychic hurts and the external self he shows to the world. We never see or hear him without the full 'Thomas Hudson', an attribution that formalizes the emotional distance between reader and protagonist. He once observes an officer from the Headquarters code room in Havana: 'He looked healthy and his unhappiness did not show'. This is the same sort of desperate adjustment that Hudson himself makes, and one that dates not from the time he is massively visited by the disasters of fate—the loss of his two younger sons at the end of 'Bimini' and that of his oldest son in 'Cuba'—but from our initial glimpse of him.

Like many other Hemingway protagonists, Hudson lives a life of psychic recuperation, remembering fitfully his past disappointments and failures in the midst of the necessary compromises of the present. 'You have to make it inside of yourself wherever you are', he reminds himself, and to Davis, who expresses a need to get away, he says: '"Geography isn't any cure for what's the matter with you"'. But making it inside, laudably realistic as it is, requires even for Thomas Hudson an almost systematic manipulation of the outside. His chief failure is his first marriage, the breakup of which he mentally returns to again and again. Although we are told that he 'had long ago ceased to worry' about it, having 'exorcised guilt with work insofar as he could', his 'work', though he takes it seriously, is always regarded as an activity just slightly better than therapy:

> He had been able to *replace* almost everything except the children with *work* and the *steady normal working* life he had built on the island. He *believed* he had made something there that would last and that would *hold* him. Now when he was lonesome for Paris he would *remember* Paris *instead of* going there. He did the same thing with all of Europe and much of Asia and of Africa. (italics mine)

What is striking about both syntax and diction in this passage, a piece of authorial exposition internalized by the protagonist himself, is its provisional character, Hudson's own awareness that he must rely on surrogates, not to regain anything but simply to keep from losing everything. The make-do stability only barely disguises desperation, and the desperation is disguised not at all by the explicit patterns, order, and rhythm that Hudson arbitrarily imposes on himself. From larger concerns—such as alternating segments of work and reward in a discernible predictability—to smaller ones—such as the little ritual he makes of burning driftwood in his fireplace—Hudson devises and cherishes willed activities 'that would hold him'.

For many of the residents Bimini is a boring stasis; for Hudson the island, a refraction rather than a true reflection of the actual world, is simultaneously an eden, a purgatory, and a refuge. '"It's a good place for a guy like you that's got some sort of inner resources"', says an admiring friend, but Hudson's cool surface is hardly an accurate indicator of either the depth or variety of those inner resources. His characteristic position at the Floridita is itself the language of wary defensiveness: 'He took his seat on a tall bar stool at the extreme left of the bar. His back was against the wall toward the street and his left was covered by the wall behind the bar'. His heavy dependence upon alcohol and seconal and his insomnia suggest a fragile psychological balance that is threatened as much as it is strengthened by the emotional adjustments he must make for his sons' visit. Although his proprietary airs and patrician condescension instantly establish Hudson as a valued Bimini resident, not a transient, his own internal musings reveal a more ambiguous status. He is still a foreigner living alone, a spiritual alien adjusting as well as he can to the condition of human separation. Every detail of his biography is a reinforcement of his spiritual rootlessness: he is thrice divorced, the father of three sons by two wives, the owner of three houses but no home—the solid, prominent Bimini house that has withstood three hurricanes, a Finca in Cuba, a ranch in Idaho—and a boat with a flying bridge that ranges all over the Gulf Stream, first for fish, finally for German submarines.

Hemingway's extraordinary attention to sensuous details in *Islands in the Stream* functionally underscores his protagonist's need, since they are often his points of stability in a wavering world. The preparation, colour, taste, feel, and smell of his drinks—the Tom Collinses, the frozen daiquiris, the Gordon's gin with lime juice, coconut water, and bitters—are precisely, lingeringly itemized. The description of Honest Lil's complexion—'She had a skin that was as smooth as olive-coloured ivory . . . with a slightly smoky roselike cast . . . [like] well-seasoned *mahagua* lumber when it is freshly cut, then simply sanded smooth and waxed lightly'—comes naturally from a consciousness that has long contemplated the object. The discipline of description, always a hallmark virtue in Hemingway, here is exquisitely fitted to the protagonist, who not only has, literally, a painter's eye but who must also cultivate it compulsively for his own emotional good, for by this practice an indifferent and disparate nature can be spatially disposed, 'a lot of the wickeds at large' can be blocked out or compositionally transformed, and his own griefs and guilts can be exorcised.

"'I've learned how to live by myself pretty well and I work hard"', Hudson tells a friend, and his hard work is not limited to his painting; he works hard to keep a general routine; to drink, fish, and party in planned segments, and to disallow, if he can, any untoward occasions which would drain his emotional resources. Even little pleasures are planned: Hudson puts away the Mainland newspaper 'to save it for breakfast'. The high point of his summer at Bimini is his sons' visit, but it is potentially the most draining.

Knowing the customary disorderliness of youth allows him to prepare for a
house disrupted by scattered clothing and fishing gear:

> When a man lives in a house by himself he gets very precise
> habits and they get to be a pleasure. But it felt good to have some
> of them broken up. He knew he would have his habits again long
> after he would no longer have the boys.

But the inevitable results of his sons' high energy and spontaneity and
their relational chemistry among themselves and others cannot of course be
fully planned. Before the boys leave David narrowly escapes an attack by a
hammerhead shark and undergoes a gruelling day trying to land a swordfish;
and the emotional toll is greater for the damaged father than for the resilient
son. By himself Hudson is unable to fill the customary parental role, which
functionally is shared by not only Roger Davis, a kind of shadow version of
Hudson and David's tutor in the fighting chair, but also Eddy, the alcoholic
cook who kills the attacking shark when Hudson's aim proves faulty. What
Hudson *can* do is to paint two pictures of David's fish that got away. This
after-the-event tribute is anticipated during the action, when Hudson maintains his distance on the bridge, seeing David's ordeal from a 'foreshortened'
perspective, and when, finally, after he descends to the 'same level as the
action', his observation of his son's 'bloody hands and lacquered-looking
oozing feet' is more painterly than fatherly. Hemingway clearly intends the
lack of discipline in Davis and Eddy to be more blatant versions of the
disabling flaws that the protagonist only by great dint of effort has managed
to control.

The cost is high. A life of enforced habits, of measured pleasures, is also
a life of emotional barrenness, as we see in Hudson's adjustment to the loss
of his sons. No amount of self-discipline can fully prepare him for being
hostage to fate, but it is the only kind of behaviour he knows. Despite having
little 'interest in the game', he tells Eddy: "'We'll play it out the way we can'".
Aboard the *Île de France* the grief is blunted by drinking, reading, and exer-
cising until he is tired enough to sleep. He also learns that *The New Yorker* is
a magazine 'you can read on the fourth day after something happens'.

In both 'Cuba' and 'At Sea' the self-discipline is that of a zombie.
Whatever bouts of pleasure were possible in 'Bimini' are nowhere in
evidence in the second and third segments, but what is even more
pronounced is the grim game itself. And although Hudson and his crew play
the game reasonably well in their search for the Nazis, they make tactical
mistakes that put the chasers at the mercy of the chased, and they impulsively
kill rather than take prisoner a German sailor, an act that in Hudson's mind

renders all their efforts useless. From small details to the larger structure, most of what Hudson undertakes as action is substitutionary. He carries his .357 Magnum between his legs: '"How long have you been my girl?" he said to his pistol'. And he uses it to blast a land crab on the beach who, like him, was doing nothing more than 'practicing . . . his trade'. 'There is no way for you to get what you need and you will never have what you want again', Hudson tells himself. 'But there are various palliative measures you should take'. These measures are talking to and sleeping with his favourite cat; long, ritualized drinking sessions at the Floridita; curiously detached sexual acts; and doing his 'duty'—service for the Navy. With his sons he can play the game of rummy for the shocked delectation of the tourists at Mr. Bobby's; without them at the Floridita he plays a cheerless game of the dignified rummy telling 'happy' stories to Honest Lil. To Hudson's credit nowhere does he engage in that most stereotyped palliative—talking out his grief. He tells Honest Lil: '"Telling never did me any good. Telling is worse for me than not telling"'. Rather his stories—fanciful concoctions—are aesthetic displacements; when he is forced into conversation about direct matters that hurt, the information is as sparse, oblique, and clipped as the speech rhythms. One of Hemingway's devices for showing the desperate nature of these palliatives is the frequency of flashbacks. In 'Bimini', when he has the quiet joy of his sons' companionship, the memories of Paris are collaborative—young Tom remembers, too—but after their deaths Hudson's memories return more compulsively to the past—to happier days at the Finca and the exploits of his cats, to other love affairs, to earlier days in North Africa, the Middle East, and Europe. Despite the 'carapace of work' and doing his duty 'well', Hudson's is characteristically memorial living.

The Book of the Sea is of course about the author just as the most generative energy in all the previous books, fiction and non-fiction alike, had been autobiographical. Hemingway's dismay in 1952 that his simple story of Santiago was immediately read as parable and allegory of the author grown old, harassed by enemies but still equipped with the finest skills of his contemporaries, was understandably half-hearted and ambiguous. The Old Man and the Sea accurately, sensitively, depicts the psychological status of its author, whose view of human possibilities and whose devices for countering that gloomy assessment had not been changed by Depression America, Fascist Spain, or an entire World War. The logic behind the aesthetic of contest (big-game hunting, deep-sea fishing, bull-fighting) is precisely the fact that the chaos of living—with violence at its centre—can be mitigated only through human efforts to give it shape and purpose, that is, arbitrarily, by the imposition and acceptance of rules, procedures, and conventions in which the playing of the game itself is its own significance. If there is any 'victory' in Santiago's story, it comes because the old fisherman plays out his given game with whatever determination and energy are left. The 'victory' in the Thomas Hudson story is even grimmer, and its poignancy lies in the very closeness of protagonist and author.

Gregory Hemingway and James McLendon have shown the extent to which the novelist made use of his Caribbean experiences in the 1930s. Following his usual penchant for the techniques of the *roman à clef*, the method in *Islands in the Stream* is even more transparently autobiographical than it is in earlier work, most notably in his frank use of his wives and their sons, but also including the friends, bores, and islanders, even Honest Lil, the long-suffering whore who likes to hear happy stories, and the author's favourite cat that gets the honour of keeping his original name, Boise. Even the episode of the pig that commits suicide by swimming out to sea is based on an incident during 1943 when Gregory and Patrick stayed on Cayo Confites while their father took the armed *Pilar* on sub-scouting expeditions. Commenting on the fact that the episode of David and the shark attack in *Islands in the Stream* stemmed from an incident involving himself, the younger son (rather than Patrick, the middle), Gregory Hemingway adds: 'Papa almost always changed the situation a little and usually improved on it slightly but mainly he used material that had actually happened.'

We are now able to see the autobiographical basis of Hemingway's art with greater clarity than we were thirty years ago, but, more importantly, we are also able to see the logic behind that fact. With more intensity than most writers Hemingway wanted no biography written, no letters collected. He wanted only his published works to be read and admired. In retrospect this may have been an aesthetic instinct as well as personal choice. A biography must have struck him as redundant: he was all there, in better versions usually, in the works themselves. What is bothersome in the later fiction is the apparent loss of authorial judgement generally, such as the garrulous posturing of Hudson in 'Cuba'. But it is a weakness that appears as early as *Green Hills of Africa*, in which dramatic thrust is calculatedly cast aside in favour of an artificial 'interview' situation featuring a straight man and a Papa who knowingly pronounces his judgements on literature, sports, nature, and the meaning of life. It is a posture that recurs in *Across the River and Into the Trees* and, with minor adjustments, in *A Moveable Feast*; and the pattern establishes the basic autobiographical basis of Hemingway's art, so much so that Papa the Hunter, Colonel Cantwell, and Thomas Hudson are merely variations of a single identity; further, the Hemingway of Paris in the early 1920s is a variation, too. All these characters are projections, idealized figures put to the service of a writer whose primary creative energy was necessarily his own life.

The emotional honesty especially evident in Thomas Hudson as self-portrait may not say as much for Hemingway's conscious judgement as for his psychological agony. But even here, at his most transparent, the matter of real life is usually adjusted into more shapely patterns than real life supplied, and the impulse behind the reshaping was aesthetic more than biographical: the need to show, not the need to conceal. Again, we have Gregory's testimony: 'My father had a tendency to improve on even the best of real stories.' Hemingway's early traumatic experiences, his loves and hates, his wars, his sporting exploits, his sensitivity to place are recounted from *In Our Time* to *Islands in the Stream* in ways that are both autobiographical and aesthetically artifactual. Finally he projected his best version of his own death in *Across the River and Into the Trees*, an event quintessentially Hemingway, since it dramatizes the extent to which man can control, shape, arrange that major moment that, except for suicides, lies beyond human agency.

GERRY BRENNER

A Not-So-Strange Old Man:
The Old Man and the Sea

O f *The Old Man and the Sea* Hemingway said, "I tried to make a real old man, a real boy, a real sea and a real fish and real sharks." Try though he did, no critic commends this novella for its realistic writing, subject, or hero. And understandably so, for especially when the sharks mutilate his gigantic marlin, Santiago's philosophic resignation is not realistic. It is certainly not when set next to the behavior of the anonymous man in the anecdote that grew into the novella: "He was crying in the boat when the fishermen picked him up, half crazy from his loss, and the sharks were still circling the boat."

A symbolic character, Santiago embodies only virtues that ask for moral approval of him as an idealized Papa. He is selfless, thoughtful, courageous, durable, reliable, and, above all else, gentle. Ever thoughtful of his "brother" the marlin, at one point he wishes he "could feed the fish," at another is "sorry for the fish that had nothing to eat," and still later deeply grieves when the first shark mutilates the fish's beautiful body. He shows no anger toward the fishermen who make fun of him. And he respects Manolin's father's decision that the boy fish with someone else after forty fishless days with Santiago. Even his dreams are innocuous, filled with mating porpoises and frolicsome, not fierce, lions. He is violent only when killing the attacking sharks. But such actions, in defense of his "brother,"

From *Concealments in Hemingway's Works.* © 1983 by the Ohio State University Press.

sanctify hostility. Finally, Manolin's adoration shows the absence of any punitiveness in Santiago's role as his substitute father.

To do other than approve and admire the old man would be unseemly, if not blasphemous. Yet Hemingway is excessively protective of his "saint," does everything artistically possible to immunize the "strange old man" against adverse criticism. Even Santiago's "sin" of "going out too far" we are to hallow for its noble effort and the moral truths the old fisherman learns from it. But I keep hearing Santiago's refrain: "'I wish I had the boy. . . . I wish I had the boy. . . . I wish the boy was here. . . . I wish I had the boy. . . . I wish the boy were here.'" Santiago utters these wishes, of course, because he needs help with the huge marlin. And Hemingway asks us to hear them as prayers. With one ear I do. But with the other I hear their resentment and anger: that the boy, Manolin, is not with him, that Manolin obeyed his parents' orders to fish in another boat, that Manolin has not vowed disciple-ship to Santiago. The malice in Santiago's wishes makes me ask, is he truly a "strange old man," as he calls himself; or is he quite ordinary, as much a hypocrite as the next person, as deficient in self-awareness as the rest of us? And do Santiago's actions, like ours, harbor unconscious wishes that are incongruent with the phosphorescent nimbus that circles, like a halo, his skiff? Can he be read antithetically?

If Santiago loves the marlin as much as he declares, must he kill it? An ordinary fisherman would, of course. But neither hunger, poverty, his iden-tity as fisherman, his reputation of being "salao," nor the marlin's condition requires him to kill it. A truly "strange old man" or even an extraordinary fisherman might have released the marlin once it rolled over on its side next to the skiff, for that would have proved the fisherman's domination of it. Santiago's killing it questions the sincerity of his declared love and his benev-olence. And it shows a sizeable lack of intelligence. Surely a wise, old, expe-rienced fisherman would know that he would have to harpoon the huge marlin, that he would not be able to boat the fish but would have to lash it to the side of his skiff, that, consequently, the blood from the wound would quickly lure hungry sharks, and that he would have to fight them off or let them feed.

Must Santiago return with the mutilated carcass? If he genuinely loves the marlin, he should be loath to let it suffer the ignominy of becoming either "garbage waiting to go out with the tide" or a spectacle to stupid tourists: "'I didn't know sharks had such handsome, beautifully formed tails.'" Were Santiago really selfless, strange, he would have unleashed the marlin at sea, for a saint has no need to vaunt his achievement before his fellow men. Or does he stand to gain something by bringing home the carcass? Naturally he regains community regard. But he also gains what he has wished for in five of the nineteen wishes that flood the novella—Manolin: "'I told the boy I was a strange old man. . . . Now is when I must prove it.'" Unquestionably the boy can best continue to learn the skills of fishing from Santiago. So Santiago's wish merely extends Manolin's. But two other men have legitimate claim to Manolin—his father and the fisherman he has been fishing with the past forty-odd days. Santiago brings home the mutilated carcass, then, because without proof of his exploit he can not show his superiority to such lesser men. Nor can he wrest Manolin from their parental authority without confronting them. Nor can he compel Manolin's pledge of discipleship: "'We will fish together now for I still have much to learn.'"

I also question why *brother* dominates Santiago's word-hoard. He confers brotherly status on the marlin, on porpoises and flying fishes, even on the stars. His fraternity should also enroll the man-of-war bird, the lions on the beaches of his dreams, the "negro of Cienfuegos," and bone-spurred Joe DiMaggio. Although Manolin is a boy, Santiago treats him as a brother, an equal, and acknowledges their interdependency. In contrast, the other fisherman whom Manolin's parents ordered him to fish with treats him as an "inferior" and "'never wants anyone to carry anything.'" Manolin's concern for Santiago portrays him as a good brother, too: "I must have water here for him, the boy thought, and soap and a good towel. Why am I so thoughtless? I must get him another shirt and a jacket for the winter and some sort of shoes and another blanket." Indeed, despite some local fishermen who laugh at Santiago, brotherhood is the dominant chord of the novella, reiterated in the generosity of Martin, the proprietor of the Terrace, and of Pedrico, who cares for Santiago's skiff after his return. The story's very emphasis upon Santiago's two hands—in contrast to his one-armed predecessor, Harry Morgan—underlines with synecdoche the importance of brotherhood: "There are three things that are brothers," thinks Santiago, "the fish and my two hands." This implies that Santiago's wishes for Manolin to be with him are wishes for a brother, since a *mano*(lin) is literally a little hand, figuratively a small brother.

By taking Santiago at his word, we should see brotherhood in its ideal form, agape, and should realize that the archetype that Hemingway assigns him is brother's keeper. Santiago's attitude toward Manolin, the marlin, and *la mar* vouches for his wish to be brother's keeper to virtually all creation.

An antithetical reading of Santiago's fraternal ethic finds it self-serving. It grants Santiago and any who embrace that brotherly ideal a measure of irresponsibility not available to people who must fulfill the role of parent, spouse, or child. Quite simply, a brother's responsibilities have only the force

of religious commandment; psychologically self-imposed, they are not oblig-
atory. A brother can honor fraternal responsibilities and bask, modestly or
immodestly, in the self-satisfaction of his supererogation. Or a brother can
ignore those responsibilities without feeling guilty. But children and spouses
lay legitimate claims and responsibilities at parents' and mates' feet; and guilt
pursues them, frequently whether they honor or dishonor those claims. Children feel guilt too. They are plagued by the compulsion to measure up to
parental values and by the virtual impossibility of doing so—because of the
contradictions in those values, of the tortuous ways of their own experiences,
and of the rebelliousness of their own impulses.

These considerations explain why Santiago is a widower, has begotten
no children, and in neither dream, memory, nor statement traces his lineage
to father or mother. The absence of parents, wife, and children eliminates
filial, conjugal, or parental obligations. That absence also frees Santiago from
compulsory duties to his fellow man. And that absence tells me that self-
serving ingredients foul the air of his apparent altruism and show that he is
"one of us," someone who wants to be thought better of than he deserves. He
is our ordinary, not our strange, brother, even though we indulge ourselves
in Hemingway's fantasy of Santiago's nobleness.

Far below the conscious surface of the novella, like the marlin beneath
Santiago's skiff, are other proofs of an antithetical reading of Santiago as not
so strange, as a man with normal, sublimated, aggressive, and erotic drives.
For example, Santiago acts out, and so shares, parricidal wishes. Notwith-
standing his age or his scars, "as old as erosions in a fishless desert," Santiago
is an interesting version of the parricidal son. By defeating at arm wrestling
"the great negro from Cienfuegos who was the strongest man on the docks"
and whose "shadow was huge," Santiago defines early the parricidal nature
and purpose of his actions. His deep regard for the marlin before and after
he kills him, his lack of aggression toward him, and his failure to show
delight in conquering him, though, all reveal a sympathy and concern
uncommon in the Oedipal clash. But parricide is parricide. Santiago
obliquely admits this when he equates hooking the marlin with "treachery"
and when he recalls the time he bereft a male marlin of his mate by catching
and killing her, calling it "the saddest thing I ever saw." The love and respect
Santiago professes for the marlin, then, are insidious because he disguises
them with piety. Like the pretense of the cast net and the pot of yellow rice
with fish, Santiago's regard for the marlin is also a pretense that conceals
antithetical feelings of filial hostility. Similarly the ordeal, the suffering, and
the wounds he must endure conceal his motives for killing it.

Santiago seems without a motive for killing the marlin, merely trying to survive as a Gulf Stream fisherman. His ordeal and suffering, as the story's chronology of events indicates, are simple results of catching such a large fish. But psychologically the ordeal antedates hooking the marlin, as Santiago's old, "deep-creased scars" indicate. One motive for catching and killing this surrogate father, then, is to avenge the suffering it has previously inflicted upon him. And any prospect of reconciliation with it is nullified by what happens to (what Santiago wishes to happen to?) that once-noble marlin. Repeatedly mutilated, when beached it is a mere skeleton, making highly visible to Santiago's community his literal—and to a psychoanalytic community his symbolic—achievement. And his exaggerated defense of the marlin's carcass, just one of many instances of reaction formation, makes evident his guilt and the wish underlying that guilt. The sham of Santiago's brotherliness, then, is again confirmed when he kills the marlin. That act shows that his exaggerated fraternal feelings screen an unconscious fratricidal wish. And since such a wish displaces more primary father-son hostilities, it partly represents parricide. Moreover, by slaying the gigantic marlin Santiago figuratively executes the fathers who have demanded Manolin's obedience and who have impugned his own abilities. Another version of Saint George's dragon, Jack and the Beanstalk's giant, or Tom Thumb's ogre, Santiago's marlin shows once again that whether heroically defeated, fiercely slaughtered, gruesomely butchered, or piously slain, a dead father is a dead father.

One thing that dignifies Hemingway's novella is its refusal to celebrate the victory with a happy ending. And one thing that secures its identity as adult literature is that parricide is not its only wish. Because Santiago performs his deed in full view of the third person expected in all Oedipal triangles—in this case *la mar*—an erotic fantasy accompanies its aggressive one. In its simplest, if perhaps crudest, form, the erotic wish is for an epic sexual orgy. Whereas the giant marlin is the father in the parricidal fantasy, in an incestuous one it is the phallus. Once hooked, the huge marlin's sustained underwater voyage disguises an episode of gigantic penetration in those warm currents of *la mar* "which is what people call her in Spanish when they love her. Sometimes those who love her say bad things of her but they are always said as though she were a woman. . . . The old man always thought of her as feminine and as something that gave or withheld great favours, and if she did wild or wicked things it was because she could not help them." In the parricidal fantasy Santiago's esteem for the marlin is reaction formation that conceals hostility. In the erotic fantasy it is self-admiration: "Never have I seen a greater, or more beautiful, or a calmer or more noble thing than you, brother," Santiago immodestly admits. Climaxing the erotic fantasy, Santiago drives in the harpoon, "leaned on it and drove it further and then pushed all his weight after it," whereupon the marlin "came alive," "rose high out of the water showing all his great length and width and all his power and his beauty," then "sent spray over the old man and over all of the skiff."

Such gargantuan, libidinous pleasures belong to a god. Half-gods and mortals who seize them must pay, be they Prometheus, Adam, or Santiago. When the son, however disguised, desecrates the "mother" and the taboo forbidding sexual knowledge of her, he sets into motion the inevitable anxiety that accompanies the Oedipal complex: castration. The first to react to the desecration should be the father who, tyrannical and vindictive by nature, can mutilate the son in the name of justice. True to form, the first to hit the marlin is the mako shark, "the biggest *dentuso* that I have ever seen," says Santiago. And it strikes "in the meat just above [i.e., forward of] the tail," the marlin's genital area. Its inward-slanted, eight rows of teeth are "shaped like a man's fingers when they are crisped like claws," Santiago tells, vivifying the mako's castrating instruments in imagery reminiscent of the sharp talons of that eagle that fed, circumspectly, upon Prometheus's liver. As the mako approaches Santiago's now-quiescent marlin, properly lashed in place alongside his skiff, Santiago thinks, "I cannot keep him from hitting *me* but maybe I can get him." I italicize the pronoun because it unequivocally identifies the marlin as a part of Santiago. So does Santiago's subsequent thought that "when the fish had been hit it was as though he himself were hit." Consistent with the castration fantasy are the later attacks by the various *galanos*. If the father is unable or unwilling to avenge fully the sexual outrage, then the brothers assume the task, also punishing under the aegis of justice the brother who has performed the very act they themselves only dreamed of doing.

Whether father or brother figures, the mutilating sharks avenge the wrongs committed in both the parricidal and incestuous fantasies. But the sharks disguise another principal who directs their castrating forays. *La mar*'s agents, they act on her behalf to deny her willing participation in incest. Killing the second *galano*, Santiago tells it, "'slide down a mile deep. Go see your friend, or maybe it's your mother.'" Just as the superego, seeking to preserve the mother's immaculate image, denies the id's hunger for incest with her carnal image, these ambivalent attitudes toward the mother as angel and whore, as gratifying lover and castrating bitch, also show up in the incestuous fantasy. The vision of a three-day orgy with mother is, to the fantasizing unconscious, beatific, especially when it glorifies the huge organ whose strength contributes to such colossal delights. But the reality is brutal. Santiago hopes for a quick conquest: "Eat it so that the point of the hook goes into your heart and kills you, he thought. Come up easy and let me put the harpoon into you." But he gets a grueling ordeal, not a suppliant female but a fierce antagonist. Just as Santiago asks whether he has hooked the marlin or it him, the narrative asks whether Santiago's antagonist is the marlin or a female power that uses the marlin to disguise her sadistic designs; for once coupled, Santiago must submit to her dominance, to his partner's ruthless impulses. In the dark of the first night she makes a lurch "that pulled him down on his face and made a cut below his eye." Her second lurch, cued at the moment he calls her "a friend," nearly pulls him overboard and cuts the flesh of his hand. She enjoys humiliating him by making his hand cramp: "A cramp, he thought of it as a *calambre*, humiliates oneself. . . ." She even delights in trying to nauseate him: with her third lurch and nocturnal leaps "he had been pulled down tight onto the bow and his face was in the cut slice of dolphin and he could not move." Back bent in agony, hands lacerated to mush, body exhausted so that he grows faint and sees "black spots before his eyes," Santiago's orgy is a sadomasochistic nightmare. And his only escape from it and from subsequent sexual torture is self-mutilation. This he inflicts with his harpoon. Wrathful at his act, the *dentuso*'s subsequent mutilation represents the male dread that a women's genital orifice conceals castrating teeth: the vagina dentata. I truly hope that "the old man looked carefully in the glimpse of vision that he had!"

Unlike Santiago, tenaciously holding one taut line, my reading must seem to dart to and fro, like the sucking fish that lash about eel-fashion, around the great fish. One moment I hold onto a father figure, the next to a phallus, then to *la belle dame sans merci*. One moment I see the mako as father and the *galanos* as brothers. And then I see both kinds of sharks as finny versions of the Erinyes, those avenging Furies who sprang into being when as goddesses of guilt, the blood of Ouranos, castrated by his son Kronos, fell upon Gaia-earth. But in fiction and dreams, of course, identities and relationships are neither static nor single. Dynamic and multiple, they not only tolerate but invite interchangeable readings. To do less is to shortchange the complexity of a writer's psyche and creative imagination. Call it condensation, Freud's term for a dream's superimposition of different, even contrary components or ideas onto one composite structure or image. Or call it ambiguity, New Criticism's derivative catchword for a literary work's multiple meanings, a symbol's several referents Either way, the critic's and analyst's task is to see things in both and ways, to find what is latent in what is manifest, to trust the tale and not the teller.

Despite what may seem like psychoanalytic prestidigitation in my reading, then, it follows the Oedipal constellation of parricide, incest, and castration and so is internally consistent. And by arguing repeatedly that

Santiago is not strange, I intend for my antithetical reading to enrich Hemingway's novella, not to impoverish it. After all, Santiago is a richer character for having complex motives, however much his simplicity appeals to us.

My reading does impoverish Hemingway, though, for there is psychological imbalance in *Old Man*. Hemingway reveals it partly by sentimentalizing Santiago. Spurred by his own affiliative wish, Hemingway insists that his old fisherman be acknowledged as strange, be well liked, and be seen as brother to all creation. And contrary to Hemingway's usual technique of letting readers infer their own conclusions on the basis of what he shows or dramatizes, here Hemingway pushes his conclusions by telling, by assertions. He tells us that Santiago has "confident loving eyes" that are "cheerful and undefeated." He tells us that Santiago had "attained humility" even though "he was too simple to wonder when he had" done so. He tells us that Santiago has "strange shoulders," that his cramped "left hand was still as tight as the gripped claws of an eagle," and that he looks "carefully into the glimpse of vision that he had." And he tells us that the novel should tell us something about going "too far out." This lack of subtlety, this excess of statement, unusual in Hemingway, exposes Hemingway's imbalance because it shows him struggling to repress anxieties that conflict with his wishes.

Among the reasons for Hemingway's excess here is a wish to idealize himself. Long accustomed to the role of "Papa"—as all intimates, regardless of age, sex, race, or blood, called him—he seeks through Santiago to portray his best self. And the novella's insistence upon fraternal relationships expresses Hemingway's affiliative wish and his wish to escape the guilts that plague, as I mentioned, fathers, husbands, and sons. Of course, Jake Barnes, Frederic Henry, Harry Morgan, and Robert Jordan are men whose actions are well flanked with fraternal motives. But Santiago is archetype to their prototypes. And since Santiago's fraternal ethic is self-serving, then Hemingway's valuation of it is too. Confident that his creation of Santiago is without irony, I also suspect that Hemingway identifies with Santiago's sense of mission because it lets him again dodge, Christ-fashion, any familial wrongs he is culpable of. I allude to Jesus' response when told that his mother and brothers are waiting to speak with him: "Who is my mother? Who are my brothers? . . . Whoever does the will of my heavenly Father is my brother, my sister, my mother." Surely Hemingway would identify with Santiago, able to justify any conduct by invoking his life's mission, declaring, "Now is the time to think of only one thing. That which I was born for." Santiago's statement may be nobly appropriate to the occasion, but it also insinuates that he—and an author whose primary allegiance is to the Muse— be pardoned for any domestic neglects.

The neglect that ignites Hemingway's anxiety is his neglect of his own three sons. He can be deservedly proud of his resourcefulness and devotion during both Patrick's concussion and recovery in the spring of 1947 and Gregory's emergency appendectomy in June of 1949. But a father is more than handyman in a medical crisis. More typical of Hemingway's relationship to his sons is the Christmas of 1950 at the Finca, just before he began writing *Old Man*: "Patrick was there with his new wife Henny; Gigi appeared with a girl whom Ernest did not like. There was a constant stream of visitors, including Winston Guest, Tom Shevlin, Gary Cooper, and Patricia Neal. . . ." There is nothing unusual about this instance of Hemingway domesticity. Filial visits crowded by notables and intimates was the perennial pattern for the Hemingway sons. And so their relationship with him was seldom more than a holiday one.

Although Hemingway's guilt for neglecting his sons is partly shown in his creation of a man whose excessively fraternal duties excuse his irresponsibilities, it is also shown by his preoccupation in the other two works he composed during the winter and spring months of 1950–51. Like the second and third sections of *Islands in the Stream*, drafted on either side of the novella, *Old Man* is deeply preoccupied with the loss of a son. That preoccupation stems partly from Hemingway's loss of influence over his three sons at precisely the time he was writing these three works. His oldest son, John, was still soldiering, "the only trade he knows." His middle son, Patrick, had just married and was preparing to leave the States for Kenya. His youngest, Gregory, was growing more difficult and rebellious than before. Only he was bold or naive enough to challenge his father's parental and marital behavior. And the death of his mother, Pauline, in October of 1951 gave him the occasion to bear a long grudge against his father's treatment of her—and of himself.

It takes no large leap of imagination to see that Manolin's separation from Santiago after forty fishless days expresses Hemingway's anxiety over his loss of influence on his departing or defecting sons, whatever his neglect of them had been. That anxiety also explains Santiago's perseverance with the marlin and his willingness to go "out too far" for it. Both behaviors are projections of Hemingway's wishes: to compensate for his shortcomings, his "salao" as a father, and to believe that he would go far out to regain his sons or his influence over them. Indeed, as Wylder notes, Santiago's conflict is with Manolin's "parents for control of the life of the boy," partly showing that Santiago's motives are aimed at regaining Manolin's discipleship. Hemingway heightens this parental conflict by having Santiago wrest Manolin from two fathers, his legitimate one and the fisherman he had been "ordered" to fish with.

Finally, because excessive behavior always signals antithetical wishes,

Santiago's excessive benevolence reveals the most repressed wish in *Old Man*, the wish common to all the work of Hemingway's last decade, filicide, the wish to kill or have killed his sons. The marlin is brother, father, and phallus. But it is also son, as the fish and the boy's nearly identical names suggest. Manolin's forced separation from Santiago is mirrored in the marlin's attempted separation from Santiago's skiff, line, hook, and harpoon. The fish, then, is Manolin's virile double, and Santiago's ordeal, killing and returning home with its mutilated carcass, reveals his perseverance in acting out his filicidal wish.

Old though he is, through "trickery," intelligence, and experience Santiago can subjugate any male, regardless of strength or disguise, who challenges his supremacy. And what of a son who entertains thoughts either of freeing himself of his father's influence or of finding a replacement for his father? Since both thoughts are latent in Manolin's departure after forty days of luckless fishing, that son would be well advised, if fiction were prophetic, to recognize the alternatives of acting out such thoughts of defection. He must escape altogether or return, vowing discipleship. Otherwise, he may end up dead, a skeleton "among the empty beer cans," "garbage waiting to go out with the tide." Santiago's act of killing the marlin, then, is ultimately an act of fratricide, parricide, and now, filicide. And Santiago should stand revealed as a not-so-strange old man, one who expresses in sublimated ways those deeply submerged wishes all humans share but suppress.

Perhaps I present the idea of filicide too abruptly and assign to Hemingway an utterly alien wish. But it is felt in his hostility toward his youngest son, the complications and difficulties of whose person were, and continued to be, a problem to Hemingway, according to his wife. And it is invariably present in the makeup of the human psyche. As dramatized in that "most meaningful synthesis of the essential conflicts of the human condition," Sophocles' *Oedipus Rex*, filicide is a central, precipitating factor in the character and destiny of Oedipus and so of all humans. Responding to the dire prophecy that their child would slay his father and commit incest with his mother, Laius and Jocasta pierce their child's feet and order him to be killed or abandoned when only three days old. Oedipus's subsequent parricidal and incestuous acts, then, issue directly from his parents' attempted filicide and his unconscious wish to avenge their wrong to him. The circular blame of this situation acknowledges reciprocal anxieties that all parents and children have of being rejected, harmed, or abandoned. And it follows that every family situation of a father, mother, and child will contain the repressed wishes of filicide, incest, and either matricide or patricide or both. There is nothing intrinsically hideous or abnormal about filicidal wishes in Santiago, Hemingway, or anyone else. They become abnormal only when they are strongly denied or when there is an undue if not compulsive need to express only benevolent wishes, as Santiago's case nearly shows.

Although I emphasize that Hemingway's filicidal wishes are unconsciously aimed at his three sons, they are also self-directed. More precisely, as the works of the fifties will show, Hemingway feels increasingly responsible—and so increasingly guilty—for his father's suicide. Because suicides always act out upon themselves the homicidal feelings they have for others, Dr. Hemingway's suicide expresses a filicidal wish toward his neglectful son. And Hemingway unconsciously owns that his father's wish is just. For as I mentioned in the previous afterword, Hemingway was absent during the ordeals of his father's last years. In one formulation Hemingway's guilt for his absence issues in the fantasy that Santiago-as-father—old, luckless, alone, and struggling against great odds—can overcome vicissitudes, be they of *la mar*, the sea as terrible mother, or of life with Grace Hemingway. In a second formulation Hemingway's guilt for his absence issues in Santiago's indictment of Manolin: "'I missed you.'" A bland indictment? I think not. After all, the tears and grief of Manolin-as-Hemingway already show the mental mutilation caused by his guilt for having been absent during Santiago's ordeal. The old man's words will surely reverberate deeply in Manolin's conscience. And should Santiago die because of his ordeal? The already lachrymose Manolin will flagellate himself for not having vowed discipleship earlier to Santiago. All his life he will feel responsible for Santiago's death and will feel remorse for not having responded to the old man's affiliative needs.

DAVID TIMMS

Contrasts in Form: Hemingway's
The Old Man and the Sea *and Faulkner's 'The Bear'*

It is paradoxical that while most of us feel diffident about formulating definitions of the novel, we are confident about which texts we wish to call 'novels'. No wonder we are reluctant to offer definitions. The novel's bastard nature was acknowledged early: *Joseph Andrews* is famously a 'comic epic poem in prose'. That the novel is 'mimetic' or tends towards the 'referential' would be an area of agreement even for critics of widely divergent aesthetics: Erich Auerbach and Roman Jakobson perhaps. But the very fact that the world comes so insistently into the form makes it more obviously the ground for contesting ideologies. This suggests that it is impossible to make a list of necessary qualities we would all agree on. Even Forster's unfashionably unambitious definition, that the novel is 'any fictitious prose work over 50,000 words,' has been contradicted by Nabokov's *Pale Fire*, which opens with a substantial verse section. But it seems that as readers we find it easy to recognize 'family resemblances' between novels. Texts as different as *Tristan Shandy* and *Middlemarch* are clearly siblings, but *Gulliver's Travels* is equally clearly only a cousin.

But oddly, the opposite seems to apply with regard to the novella. Here, we can find defining characteristics. Length is the most obvious. Mary Doyle Springer in *Forms of the Modern Novella* (1975) refines Forster when she says that the novella is 'a prose fiction of a certain length (usually 15,000

From *The Modern American Novella*. © 1989 by Vision Press Ltd.

to 50,000 words)'. That is fair enough: novellas are that length, otherwise they are short stories or novels. But what about ascribing particular works to the class of novellas? James's 'The Death of the Lion' seems unproblematically a novella, especially since he gives his own *imprimatur* to the description. But 'The Aspern Papers' or 'The Turn of the Screw'? They are both within the word-limit. Conrad provides a more striking instance. I would call *The Nigger of the 'Narcissus'* a novella, but not *Heart of Darkness*.

These examples hint that the difference may be one of value, and indeed that distinction has been offered by plausible voices. F. R. Leavis, for instance, jibbed at the word '*nouvelle*' for Lawrence's *St. Mawr*: 'that description, with its limiting effect, has a marked infelicity. It certainly doesn't suggest the nature or weight of the astonishing work of genius that Lawrence's "dramatic poem" is.' Nabokov is thinking in similar categories when he suggests dismissively that the writer of novellas operates by 'diminishing large things and enlarging small ones'. James on the other hand would not have accepted this conflation of 'novella' and 'novelette'; he referred to the *nouvelle* as a 'blest' form.

Certainly a qualitative distinction will not do to separate *The Old Man and the Sea* and 'The Bear' either from other prose fictions or from each other. In a most useful examination of the history of the term 'novella' Gerald Gillespie includes both works as distinguished modern examples of the form:

> William Faulkner's 'The Bear' is still very close to the 'simple' *novella*, to Hemingway's 'Old Man and The Sea', because it demonstrates through the creature hunted and the participants of the hunt a natural order that becomes visible precisely in the confrontation with the particular symbol.

This seems to me to raise exactly the kind of problem I refer to above. While Gillespie's general comments on the nature of the novella are unobjectionable, this particular ascription of texts seems to me unsatisfactory. I hope an explanation of that unsatisfactoriness might be suggestive not only about the texts themselves, but also about the nature of the novella.

2

It is evident at the outset that *The Old Man and the Sea* and 'The Bear' have similarities beyond their roughly equal length. Gillespie's brief description of the thematic content of the two texts places them both in a tradition of American fictions that begins as early as Cooper's *The Pioneers* (1823) and has been expressed in both 'high' and 'low' culture ever since. Michael Cimino's *The Deer Hunter* (1978) is a recent example. The tradition tells the story of a man's confronting nature and expressing in the confrontation elements of nobility that match what he confronts, and contrast with the society that surrounds him outside the forest or on the shore. It is a theme characteristically American, in more than one sense, as 'The Bear' makes clear:

> There was always a bottle present, so that it would seem to him that those fierce fine instants of heart and brain and courage and wiliness and speed were concentrated and distilled into that brown liquor which not women, not boys and children, but only hunters drank, drinking not of the blood they spilled but some condensation of the wild immortal spirit, drinking it moderately, humbly even, not with the pagan's base and baseless hope of acquiring thereby the virtues of cunning and strength and speed but in salute to them. Thus it seemed to him on this December morning not only natural but actually fitting that this should have begun with whisky.

This view of the hunter is very specific. As the text points out, it is not at all 'pagan', and that is confirmed in anthropological works. According to James W. Fernandez, the 'Fang', a people of western equatorial Africa, use metaphors that make an analogy between men good at hunting and men who are good judges generally. He suggests that this is straightforward common sense and economic hard-headedness: 'Everyone knows the difference between a good and a bad hunter. The evidence comes home in his bag.' But in 'The Bear', though it is a measure of Boon Hogganbeck's inferiority that he is in a position to shoot the bear and misses, it is a measure of Ike McCaslin's superiority and worthiness that he is in a position to shoot the bear and won't. While Santiago in Hemingway's story does kill the fish, he is like McCaslin above the concerns of cash. He does not get it home, and even though the meat would have brought him a great deal of money, his concern that the sharks have 'ruined' the marlin has nothing to do with economics. It is not even that being a 'hunter' carries a mark of social distinction, as it does in Britain. In both texts being a hunter is like being a priest.

If this is a characteristically American view it is also characteristically male. Richard Poirier commends Faulkner's careful balance of negatives in this very passage from 'The Bear' and tries to tell us that 'the description of things being dismissed by the negatives is never foreshortened or contemptuous.'

Could he really make that assertion if he read 'as a woman' the bracketing of
their sex with boys and children? Simone de Beauvoir in *The Second Sex*
(1949) suggests that in a patriarchal culture hunting is the initial source of
male status: superiority 'has been accorded in humanity not to the sex that
brings forth but to that which kills'. Faulkner is not even that positive here:
the real force of the negatives is that 'hunter' equals 'minus female'. His
drink is defined as that which women do *not* drink. The hunters do not use
sheets but sleep under blankets, whose 'rough male kiss' Rupert Brooke
noticed in another context. They have no interest in the virtues of good
cooking, traditionally defined (at least in its domestic context) with women.
Bizarrely, given his appearance, the figure of Boon Hogganbeck underlines
this devaluation: within the symbolism of the text, he is female. The dog
Lion 'don't care about nothing or nobody', but Boon 'knelt beside him,
feeling the bones and muscles, the power. It was as if Lion were a woman—
or perhaps Boon was the woman. That was more like it . . .' We should not
be surprised then to find he does not drink reverentially but immoderately,
and cannot shoot straight. He stresses his alliance with the non-hunters in
the final words of the book: he lays claim to the squirrels ('They're mine')
when 'proven hunters . . . scorned such'.

Though women appear only as concepts in the central experiences of
'The Bear' and *The Old Man and the Sea*, what might be called 'the Female'
is everywhere. Nina Baym identifies a recurrent pattern in 'the' American
tradition:

> . . . the rôle of the beckoning wilderness, the attractive landscape,
> is given a deeply feminine quality. Landscape is deeply imbued
> with female qualities, as society is: but where society is menacing
> and destructive, landscape is compliant and supportive. It has the
> attributes simultaneously of a virginal bride and a non-threat-
> ening mother; its female qualities are articulated with respect to
> a male angle of vision: what can nature do for me, asks the hero,
> what can it give me?

These precise female identifications are not entirely accurate for 'The Bear'
or *The Old Man and the Sea*, but in both cases, landscape is seen as female,
inviting and sexually compliant:

> [Santiago] always thought of the sea as *la mar* which is what
> people call her in Spanish when they love her . . . the old man
> always thought of her as feminine and as something that gave or
> withheld great favours, and if she did wild or wicked things it was

because she could not help them. The moon affects her as it does
a woman, he thought.

For Ike McCaslin, what he experiences in the woods is 'the existence of love
and passion and experience which is his heritage and not yet his patrimony',
and the taste of it is the same as when 'entering by chance the presence of
perhaps even merely the bedroom of a woman who has loved and been loved
by many men'. This world is properly at the disposition of the genuine male
principle. Old Ben is called colloquially 'the head bear . . . the man' by Sam,
his votary, and the maleness of the great swordfish is grossly Freudian. In this
world the 'natural' order of male over female is rigidly maintained: Ben rakes
the shoulder of the bitch who dares to look at him; only a male dog is able to
hold him. The lords of the landscape are distinguished by a superior indifference to the female of their own species: both Ben and the great marlin are
solitary, and their single state is imitated by their accolytes.

Not so in the social world ever closing in on Santiago and McCaslin. It
is the world of commerce and industry, lumber factories, locomotives and
fish-canneries, and its voice is feminine. From his relationship with the bear
and Sam Fathers, Ike learns that he must 'repudiate' the legacy of 'his' land,
because the whole notion of 'ownership' of the land is tainted. But his wife
tempts him with sexual favours to repossess it, and withdraws them when he
refuses. In *The Old Man and the Sea*, too, a woman speaks for society when
she sees the skeleton of the marlin on the beach among the 'empty beer cans
and dead barracudas'. She asks a waiter what it is and the waiter offers
'Tiburon . . . Eshark' in explanation of what happened to the great fish. She
misunderstands, and thinks that she is looking at the skeleton of what the
book has taught us to associate with what is sneaking and evil:

> 'I didn't know sharks had such handsome, beautifully formed
> tails.'
> 'I didn't either,' her male companion said.

For a double reason women cannot be *aficionados*, and besides getting the
facts wrong, the woman here diminishes what the reader is supposed to have
experienced as a struggle of tragic proportions to a question of aesthetics.
She reduces the 'value' of the fish as surely as the sharks did. Both texts
conform to a definition offered by Judith Fetterley: 'To be American is male;
and the quintessential American experience is betrayal by a woman.'

Annette Kolodny has reminded us that a view of the landscape as
female and compliant is anything but 'natural' if you are yourself a woman,
and she has also stressed that the verbal appropriation of the landscape by

men was matched by its physical appropriation, from which women were largely excluded. Given this exclusion, if 'The Bear' yet again excuses Adam and blames 'the woman' for the fall from grace, it must be hypocritical . . . but does it, at least in simple terms?

In *History, Ideology and Myth in American Fiction, 1823–1852* (1984) Richard Clark has suggested that 'the' American tradition shown to be a construct by recent feminist critics might be seen to have a more particular ideological function than simply to affirm patriarchy. He schematizes the form of the characteristic myth retold by texts in this tradition as 'Civilisation threatens Adamic Innocent living in harmony with Edenic Nature.' It cloaks the actuality, which was an attempt to make 'Eden' economically profitable. The myth has a relationship with history rather like the relationship of dream and reality in Freudian theory: it can represent actual situations 'the other way round', with the purpose of providing 'a wish-fulfilling image of man's relationship with nature'.

> Where in historical reality we know that blacks and Indians were exploited and expropriated by the whites, in the mythic representation we are offered the famous couples—Natty and Chingachgook, Ishmael and Queequeg, Huck and Nigger Jim—in which the innocent white man is symbolically allied with his victim in opposition to the advance of white civilisation. Evidently the figure of the white innocent has been produced by condensation and displacement of both material and ideological elements and can be interpreted as acting either as a denial of real conditions . . . or as a recuperation of them.

If this operates for blacks and Indians, it also operates for women in both *The Old Man and the Sea* and 'The Bear', at least in my representation of it so far. But that representation is limited, and this simplified statement of myth does not hold good for Faulkner's story as a whole. 'Civilisation' in the shape of old Carrothers McCaslin predates the Adamic Innocent. Ike McCaslin overtly confronts precisely those historical facts Clark identifies, but while Ike has moral stature at some points of the story, at others he seems ludicrous and his ideals naïf. The woods do indeed have their noble prelapsarian aspect, and Old Ben is an expression of it; but the Garden also already contains the serpent whom Ike calls 'Grandfather' near the end of the work. The complex represented by 'The Bear' will not conform with Clark's scheme, except in a way that is so partial as to raise more questions that it answers. On the other hand, there are no such complications in *The Old Man and the Sea*. It has one digression, in the shape of the episode of Santiago's arm-wrestling with the huge black. This digression however does not obscure the issue but clarifies it, since it functions in a straightforwardly alle-gorical way to the main story.

I suggest that it is on the complications of 'The Bear' and in the anti-thetical singleness and clarity of *The Old Man and the Sea* that the satisfac-toriness or otherwise of the description 'novella' depends. Todorov suggests that 'there is no time, in reading a short work, to forget it is only "literature" and not "life"'; but the novel classically encourages us 'to find Swann's/Way better than our own', as Randall Jarrell put it. Though the two texts are alike as to length, *The Old Man and the Sea* follows the aesthetic principle the novella's brevity hints at, while 'The Bear' does not.

3

Definitions of the novella must take into account its most eloquent modern apologist, Henry James, and the suggestions about the form in his prefaces offer what he himself would probably have called a *point d'appui*. In connection with 'The Death of the Lion' he recalls the relief with which he greeted his editor's advice that he need not confine himself to the 'six to eight thousand words' usual in periodical publication:

> Among forms, moreover, we had had, on the dimensional ground—for length and breadth—our ideal, the beautiful and blest *nouvelle*; the generous, the enlightened hour for which appeared thus at last to shine. . . . For myself I delighted in the shapely *nouvelle*—as, for that matter, I had from time to time here and there been almost encouraged to show.

I should like to concentrate on the two features James picks out: length and shapeliness.

Many critics, following Lukacs, have suggested that the novel uniquely gives the sense of lives shaped not simply by events but by the passage of time itself. This is not to say that all novels do, of course, but those which do not seem conspicuous in not doing so. In an essay on this topic Eleanor Hutchens notes that such novels 'make up the body of the anti-novelistic novel.' That is not to say that the events in novellas do not sometimes take place over long periods of time: 'The Beast in the Jungle' is a case in point. But novellas differ from novels in that they do not give a sense of the expe-rience of the passing of time. They will pick out only significant moments. In the novel, it is the very inclusion of events of lesser significance, of periods of time with no highlights, that gives the sense of time passing. The line of least resistance for the novella is to do as Hemingway's does, and confine action to a short period, in the case of *The Old Man and the Sea* some three days and nights. 'The Bear' is quite different in this respect. At different points of the narrative Ike appears as a small boy and as an old man, 'uncle to half a country and father to none'. Look for instance at this comment on his gun:

> He had his own gun now, a new breech-loader, a Christmas gift; he would own and shoot it through two new pairs of barrels and one new stock, until all that remained of the original gun was the silver-inlaid trigger-guard with his and McCaslin's engraved names and the date in 1878.

The focus is on Ike's central experience with the bear, but passages like this encourage us to do what Eleanor Hutchens notes of reading novels, even those with central figures like Clarissa Dalloway or Leopold Bloom: we put one event always in the context of another, reconstruct a whole life in the experience of reading.

Analogous to the inclusion of 'inessential' events in plots of novels is the inclusion of 'superfluous' details in describing settings. Such details function by virtue of their very irrelevance; as Barthes notes, it reminds us of the contingency of life and therefore testifies to the 'reality' of the world the novel represents. On this point 'The Bear' and *The Old Man and the Sea* diverge once more. Events in 'The Bear' take place in many locations besides the woods, and of all of them we are given some physical sense. Of course the whole situation of Santiago—he is far out at sea and is materially impoverished anyway—is one that admits of little in the way of physical description, but then that is my point: the novella is well-adapted to such narrow settings.

The same is true of character, partly in simple quantitative terms: the novella finds it hard to accommodate a large cast. *The Old Man and the Sea* abides by the suggestions of the form in having only two major parts (the fish and the man), one supporting actor (Manolin), and a few bit-parts. 'The Bear' on the other hand has not only two star rôles (Ike and McCaslin) but two large animal parts as well, and one for a good supporting small dog. There are a number of important 'character' parts (Boon, Sam Fathers, Major de Spain, Ash, the educated black), an opportunity to introduce a starlet, and a large cast of extras. There is a difference qualitatively, too, for the form surely does not encourage psychological complexity. Where an individual's psychology is the subject (as in 'The Beast in the Jungle' once more) the tendency is to treat a single issue. *The Old Man and the Sea* obeys this principle and is not 'psychological', the emphasis being on what the old man does, rather than on what he thinks: on the moral status rather than the springs of his actions. A great deal of 'The Bear' is given over to Ike's motives, and attention is paid to the way in which a whole range of events shape his psyche. Perhaps I should say 'happenings', for Ike is a very passive hero, especially in contrast with Santiago. 'The Beast in the Jungle' comes once more to mind; Ike is more like one of James's heroes than one of Hemingway's.

The Old Man and the Sea deals with a single theme: the possibility of creating significance through dignity and courage in a natural and social world devoid of inherent meanings. The marlin's world is full of sharks; the old man's world is full of people like Manolin's parents who put cash reward above loyalty, or the woman tourist who cannot tell an ignoble fish from a noble one. Gerald Gillespie traces the lineage of the novella from the Latin *exemplum*, and notes the contribution of the Italian *novellino*, the little anecdote that has a moral. Erich Auerbach, too, notes that the *novellino* has the form of an *exemplum*, and comments that the style is 'flatly paratactic . . . with the events strung together as though on a thread, without palpable breadth and without an atmosphere for the characters to breathe in'. The dismissive tone apart, this seems to me an adequate description of *The Old Man and the Sea* in terms of style, plot and setting. But it is surely appropriate to present such a theme in paratactic language and by means of a paratactic plot: this is a world without a teleology or even an eschatology, where the only inherent organizing principle or end product is blank sequence. The only way to make such a world meaningful is to force life and death into a context of your own manufacture where they are not arbitrary; for Santiago the assumed moral imperatives of a ritual contest between his own cunning and experience and the fish's strength. In a well-known letter to H. G. Wells, James expressed something similar: 'it is art that *makes* life . . . makes importance.' But as Walter Benjamin stresses, in the 'story' (and he explicitly includes the novella in this category), '*one* hero, *one* odyssey, *one* battle', and in *The Old Man and the Sea* this singleness is evident in language and narrative style.

Once more 'The Bear' is quite different. It includes a variation on Hemingway's single theme, but Faulkner has ancilliary themes that have a more or less independent existence. The race issue, for instance, branches in several different directions. It is not simply another instance of the damage wreaked by the original sin of presuming to own land and buy and sell it. 'The Bear' deals with the issue of the exploitation of female slaves, and the right to inheritance of the black descendants of slave-owners. It deals with the usefulness or otherwise of 'educating' blacks without giving them proper means of subsistence. It deals with the distinctive qualities of blacks as a racial group, and refers to the different stresses of having black and Indian, or white and Indian ancestry.

If the style of *The Old Man and the Sea* is consonant with its single theme, that of 'The Bear' is appropriate for its complex and multiple ones:

> And He probably knew it was vain but He had created them, and He knew them capable of all things because He had shaped them out of the Primal Absolute which contained all and had watched them since in their individual exaltation and baseness and they themselves not knowing why nor how nor even when: until at last He saw that they were all Grandfather all of them and that even from them the elected and chosen the best the very best He could expect (not hope mind: not hope) would be Bucks and Buddies and not even enough of them.

The language here is hypotactic and grammatically embedded. Ike's wish to find exactly the right word, which goes to the extent of referring to the near relatives that will not do ('not hope mind: not hope'), paradoxically makes the semantics more obscure. The whole, content and style, encourages the reader to see Ike McCaslin's life and problems as complex and confusing—and indeed it is one of Ike's failings that he does not recognize this himself, believing that the simple act of renouncing his land will restore the Garden to order.

This complexity is enormously increased by the fact that 'The Bear' does not maintain a single angle of vision or attitude towards its themes and characters, as *The Old Man and the Sea* does. The attitude the latter wishes to encourage in its reader is like Manolin's at the end: a sort of sad, admiring resignation. It is made bitter-sweet by the introduction of the woman tourist, a member of a crass out-group that serves to define the membership of the sensitive in-group: Santiago, Manolin, narrator and reader. Once more 'The Bear' is very different. While Santiago is not a conventional hero he is consistently heroic and is never presented in a light that will show him as either mean or laughable. He belongs in a tradition of 'naturally noble' American fictional heroes that goes back at least to Natty Bumppo. But Ike McCaslin's naïvety is often laughable, and he does not even have the digni- fied simplicity of a Huck Finn, say. This is clear from his cousin's antiphonal responses when Ike catalogues black virtues:

> 'They are better than we are, stronger than we are. . . . Their vices are aped from white men. . . .'
> 'All right. Go on: promiscuity. Violence. Instability and lack of control. Inability to distinguish between mine and thine—' and he

'How distinguish, when for two hundred years mine did not even exist for them?' and McCaslin

'All right. Go on. And their virtues—' and he

'Yes. Their own. Endurance—' and McCaslin

'So have mules:' and he

'—and pity and tolerance and forebearance and fidelity and love of children—' and McCaslin

'So have dogs.'

Ike's tone here is too righteous and too humble for us to be convinced that the text is wholly behind him; McCaslin as the voice of the common man is too tart and too humorous for the reader simply to dismiss him as a self-interested cynic.

The grandness of Ike's renunciation has a comic and even farcical corrective in the story of Uncle Hubert's bequest. Ike's indigent uncle had nobly promised to leave his nephew a silver cup full of gold coins, which he ceremoniously sealed in a burlap package before the whole family. Over the years, Ike had noticed unaccounted-for changes in the shape of the package, and in its sound when rattled. He discovers the reason for the alterations only when the burlap is unsealed on his twenty-first birthday. Uncle Hubert had 'borrowed' the gold coins one by one, and replaced them with I.O.U.s. Finally he had exchanged the precious cup for a tin coffee-pot. Romance has turned to broad humour, but humour itself turns to irony when Ike pragmatically finds the coffee-pot useful: the silver cup would have been merely ornamental. Something similar happens on a more local level when McCaslin asks Ike why he did not shoot the bear when he had the chance. It is a serious topic, and Ike replies seriously by quoting Keats's 'Ode on a Grecian Urn', implying something like 'Heard melodies are sweet, but those unheard/Are sweeter.' But can this reference remain serious in the context of Uncle Hubert's silver cup, or when we remember that Keats's poem is partly about a man not catching a young woman, when Ike is obsessed with his Grandfather's catching them too often?

Robert Scholes's contribution to a most useful collection of essays, *Towards a Poetics of Fiction* (1977), proposes a diagram that classifies fictions by genre. He gives us a diagram based on an inverted triangle.

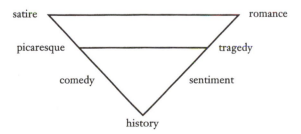

Any fiction can be placed relative to others somewhere in the triangle. Fictions that represent life as it actually is are 'histories', and others vary according to whether they tend to represent life as being better than it is (romance) or worse than it is (satire). Traditional 'novels' are all placed within the bottom two-thirds of the diagram, below a line drawn between picaresque and tragedy. They are mixtures: indeed the fact that they are mixtures is constitutive of their being novels. Where would *The Old Man and the Sea* and 'The Bear' fit? In different places, I suggest. I would place *The Old Man and the Sea* above the picaresque-tragedy line, near tragedy rather than romance. The position of 'The Bear' is more problematic, but certainly it would be below the line, not above. It is drawn down towards 'history' by its complex plot and characterization and its multiple themes, and by its seeing them in both comic and tragic lights: by its seeing life mimetically, 'as it is', in fact.

Novellas as a class would not simply occupy a zone within the area taken up by novels as a whole in Scholes's triangle. Many of the most characteristic would fall outside that area, whether they tend towards satire on the one hand, or towards romance on the other. Another and more famous geometric metaphor for fiction is the circle from James's preface to *Roderick Hudson*:

> Really, universally, relations stop nowhere, and the exquisite problem of the artist is eternally but to draw, by a geometry of his own, the circle within which they shall happily *appear* to do so.

While James's formulation is a just one, it must also be said that the firmer the circle is drawn, the less will be the sense of the multifariousness of life; the more heterogeneous the world included, the less clear will the outline of the circle be, if the shape is maintained at all. The novella is surely a form that stresses the circle, both by the obvious measure of length, and by the less obvious measure of 'shapeliness'. To that extent it gives less of the sense of heterogeneousness that is characteristic of the novel form. I hesitate to offer a reductive definition, but what seems to be the case is that the novella is a form that operates within a narrower technical and thematic range, and that this influences its generic possibilities. Brevity encourages this limitation of techniques, themes and generic possibilities rather than enforces it; but it is precisely when a fiction of novella length adopts heterogeneous technical, thematic and genre features that we become unhappy with the description 'novella'. By this measure, *The Old Man and the Sea* is a model novella, and while I have had no intention of trusting the teller rather than the tale, I am glad not to have to go against Faulkner himself, who had the sub-title of *Go Down, Moses and Other Stories* removed from its second printing.

BICKFORD SYLVESTER

The Cuban Context of The Old Man and the Sea

In preparing a line-by-line, word-by-word scholarly commentary on *The Old Man and the Sea*, I discovered many aspects of the narrative thus far overlooked. One pattern of neglected detail refers to workaday practicalities peculiar to the locale, and very often to local customs and habits of mind— to a general Cuban cultural consciousness. Here, as in many of his other works, Hemingway unobtrusively relies on such detail to account for his characters' motivation and to reveal what is actually being referred to in much of the dialogue. In other words, he requires his readers around the world to notice the specific cultural context of his narrative and to familiarize themselves with that context in order to follow what is literally happening in the plot.

This is an approach we accept as a matter of course in reading the works of other modernists—Joyce, Pound, or Eliot, for example. Yet it is a challenge posed so subtly by Hemingway's method that it has eluded us from the very beginning, in "Out of Season" (composed April 1923), his first narrative written in the style that was to make him famous. As I have pointed out, readers can understand that troublesome story only by learning something about the attitudes of provincial Italian villagers living on the Austrian border after World War I. And our failure to recognize Hemingway's challenge to "think in the head" of his various other foreign characters has

From *The Cambridge Companion to Hemingway*. © 1996 by Cambridge University Press.

accounted for many a canonized misreading or marginal understanding of his works. We have tended to forget that Hemingway is at bottom a travel writer, performing the traditional novelist's function of helping us measure ourselves by and against precisely described exotics.

Accordingly, readers have largely overlooked their need to seek a Cuban explanation whenever details puzzle them—or *should* puzzle them—in *The Old Man and the Sea*. In fact, the novel requires non-Cuban readers to do considerable homework if they are to register not only many literal details of the plot, but many layers of meaning-through-indirection. I will discuss several illuminating examples of narrative details that appear extraneous, implausible, or erroneous, tempting us to dismiss them as incidental or to assume some loose symbolic significance. We will find, on the contrary, very literal, specific topical references, references we are invited to supplement by knowledge or research beyond the text. And in undertaking these assignments we will discover in each case information not only solving a puzzle, but exposing an unsuspected dimension of the narrative as a whole. Our findings throughout will suggest, I believe, the value of screening each narrative detail in Hemingway initially for its literal, topical implications before leaping to conclusions as to its symbolic import. Indeed, we will find that concrete, local applicability determines which of the potential literary, religious, mythic, or archetypal allusions potentially plausible in a given instance may in fact be central, and which secondary, peripheral, or irrelevant.

Near the beginning of *The Old Man and the Sea*, Manolin tells Santiago about the bad eyesight of the new fisherman the boy's father has apprenticed him to—a man who never went turtle spearing in the brilliant sunlight, the occupation that most commonly "kills the eyes" of local fishermen. "But," Manolin says to Santiago, who is much older than this new employer, "you went turtle-ing for years . . . and your eyes are still good." Santiago then makes the oft-quoted, obviously laden remark: "I am a strange old man"; and when the boy asks, "But are you strong enough now for the truly big fish?" Santiago replies, "I think so. And there are many tricks."

We have thought here of the tricks of the trade that the old fisherman will soon use to compensate for his waning physical strength in his struggle against the marlin, tricks that years of experience have taught him: the products of disciplined attention to a craft that for him is also a passion. We have known, too, that in Hemingway the word "strange" almost always refers to something defying conventional understanding, a mystery of nature. The word consistently refers as well to those rare people and creatures who understand the "strange" (i.e., paradoxical) logic that Hemingway most admires: the dedication to timeless principles of behavior at the expense of all concern for material success or survival. We know that Santiago is about to demonstrate this "strange" vision—this "trick," or psychological device for survival—during his ordeal with the great fish; and we assume we have grasped all the implications of his remark that he is a "strange" old man.

But when the boy asks him if he is strong enough for a big fish, Santiago's mind is still partly on how he had managed to preserve his eyesight during his years of turtle-ing. And he has a particular trick in mind, known to very few readers. In the most common method of turtle-ing in the Caribbean, the hunter drifts in a small boat, peering beneath the surface for turtles to harpoon; as a result, the damaging tropical sunlight reflected by the water shines constantly into his eyes. Yet English ships exploring the Caribbean in the seventeenth and eighteenth centuries often employed native Indians who avoided this hazard. These natives used remoras (sucker-fish) to locate turtles. The remora is a parasite, which attaches itself to a larger creature like a shark or turtle and eats the scraps drifting back when its host feeds. The native hunter simply captured a remora and put it in the water with a fishing line tied around its tail. When the fish attached its suction-cup dorsal fin to a passing turtle, the hunter could feel the extra pull on his line and had only to follow the line to the remora, quickly spear and boat the turtle, detach the hungry remora, and put it back in the water to find another host. The hunter never needed to scan the water for his prey. Apparently, Santiago's use of this technique accounts for his continuing good vision, in spite of his years spearing turtles. In this case, then, Santiago's appearance as "strange"—a natural rarity—really is a deception, the result of an insider's device, or trick, although later in the narrative, during his ordeal, he will use such triumphs of expertise over physical limitation to supplement his truly extraordinary, or "strange," emotional resources.

Only Cuban readers, of course, and only some of them, are likely to know at first reading about that remora on a leash. Yet the rest of us have been invited to find out exactly how turtle hunting in Cuba hurts the eyes (and in the process discover the traditional method for avoiding that damage). For readers can reasonably be expected to wonder how the "real old man" Hemingway later called this character can still have good eyesight (not symbolic, but physical eyesight) into his seventies, if long engaged in an occupation that "kills the eyes." Readers cannot reasonably be expected to make the automatic, initial assumptions that Ernest Hemingway—of all writers—is taking poetic license. But of course that is what we have silently inferred, as we conveniently glossed over this incident, together with so many others like it in Hemingway's texts. And this oversight matters, because it has allowed us to form a false impression of Santiago. Santiago is truly "strange," truly inspiring, not because he is physically a freak of nature, or because he is emotionally "a saint rather than a man," as Norman Mailer insouciantly presumed. Santiago is strange because he is in every material sense "the real old man" Hemingway later called him. He is real like us, yet he behaves and thinks—with remarkable regularity—as we are able to behave and think only in our very best moments. And that is exalting to us, *because* he is human; he is possible. A man his age who puts himself through the physical and emotional ordeal we see this old man endure will in reality be likely to break "something in his chest" and be dying—as Santiago is, the text subtly specifies. And such a man, being human, will also experience despair when his resolution occasionlly falters, as Santiago's does back on shore, until at the end Manolin/Parçifal revives the old Fisher King's "strange" disregard for material failure.

Allusions like the one to the remora trick are early indications of Santiago's human fallibility, put there to guide us away from seeing him as an icon rather than the convincing, imitable exemplar that he is. And that is an important function of his other endearing fallibilities. But these are traits readers can recognize only by minutely examining every apparently unaccountable detail of Santiago's portrayal, especially in the opening exchanges with Manolin, and by consulting reference books or other sources when still in doubt. Like Hemingway's travel narratives generally, *The Old Man and the Sea* is directed at readers who have either been to its locale, will ask someone who is from there, or will go to the history and geography books about that place and its people—readers who will do research, as we now know Hemingway did himself.

Another case in point is an indirect revelation of actual historical events that we must know about if we are to appreciate fully the symbolic parallels between Santiago and Joe DiMaggio, and the role of the champion in nature and society that these important parallels help define. The information is conveyed indirectly during the early dialogues between Santiago and Manolin, when they discuss an American League pennant race between DiMaggio's team, the New York Yankees, and the Detroit Tigers. This contest is taking place as they speak, in September of a year some scholars have assumed is based on a composite of DiMaggio's 1949 and 1950 seasons and is therefore a fictionalized representation of early fall in that time period. But C. Harold Hurley has recently discovered that the narrative specifies not only the year 1950, but the exact dates in September as well. And Hurley has discovered this narrative revelation by research into the topical, rather than the symbolic significance of the dialogue's details. His attention to such details as references to the numbers 84 and 85 has at last deciphered the specific relevance of this portion of the narrative.

We have wondered why the narrative presents eighty-four as the particular number of days Santiago has gone without a fish, so that the voyage he is about to undertake is his eighty-fifth attempt. And we have wondered why his always-extraordinary confidence seems to be so especially buoyed by this number that he wants to play an eighty-five in the lottery. There has been wide speculation as to possible numerological implications, archetypal and/or Christian, and other symbolic or biographical explanations for Hemingway's choice.

But these numbers have a much more literal and topical frame of reference. They refer to the pennant race the two discuss both before and after Manolin interrupts their conversation to go for bait and food for Santiago. And it will be instructive, for all of us who study his narratives, to observe Hemingway's oblique disclosure of the connection. We are to notice that before Manolin leaves, Santiago's confidence in DiMaggio's leadership and a Yankees pennant victory is stated as an assertion of faith. But when Manolin returns, Santiago tells him: "In the American League it is the Yankees *as I said*" (emphasis added), a reference (obvious, once we notice it) to some new, firm information confirming his earlier faith. Yet all Santiago has done while Manolin has been away is sleep and read "yesterday's" newspaper. ("You study it [the baseball news] and tell me when I come back," Manolin had told him.) We are prompted, therefore, to sift through international press coverage of the Yankees in September of the two years shortly before the novel's composition (1951), and in doing so we find Santiago's good news. His newspaper is that of Monday, September 11, 1950, reporting on the Yankees' game the day before that, Sunday, September 10. On that Sunday, Joe DiMaggio, after a long period of indifferent performance at bat, hit three home runs (a record in Washington's Griffith Stadium), leading the Yankees' to their *eighty-fourth* win of the season. And although the Yankees' eighty-fourth victory coincides numerically with his own eighty-fourth fallow day, Santiago is encouraged by this numerical concordance. For he knows that the Yankees' eighty-fourth win brought them within half a game of tying with powerful Detroit Tigers in the very tight pennant race that year. Further, this tells him as a Yankees follower that the Yankees then had to win only one game of a doubleheader with the mediocre Washington Senators, scheduled for the next day, Monday the 11th, to secure a tie with the idle Tigers. and because DiMaggio's return to form put the Yankees in a position to pull even with their eighty-fifth win, Santiago has renewed confidence in the potential for success of his next voyage, which happens to be his eighty-fifth. For he is preoccupied with permutations of numbers and statistics, not only like baseball enthusiasts everywhere, but as a Cuban characteristically habituated to the lottery. And readers familiarizing themselves with the characteristic mentalities of baseball devotees and gamblers (both intimately known to Hemingway) will know that Santiago's manipulation of numbers here is typical and predictable.

Yet the numerical concordances are ancillary to a more objectively verifiable "tip of the iceberg" identifying DiMaggio's performance in Washington as the single event that confirms Santiago's faith in both DiMaggio and himself. Before we explore in detail Santiago's reaction to this game, then, we should observe how the event is obliquely specified by references to two other Yankee games on days immediately following. When Manolin returns from the Terrace with food for supper, he tells Santiago that the Yankees "lost today." We remember that "today" (present time at the beginning of the novel) is two days later than the event reported in "yesterday's paper." And readers realizing an invitation to read more baseball reports will find that the Yankees did lose a game on Tuesday, September 12, 1950. Next, readers enterprising enough to search for baseball references throughout the balance of the text will notice that during his "second day" at sea Santiago thinks about a Yankees/Tigers game being played at that moment. That is two days after the loss Manolin reported, and four days after the event so inspiring to Santiago. And a Yankees/Tigers game did take place on Thursday, September 14, 1950, four days after DiMaggio's Sunday game. Everything squares. Conclusively, yet entirely by indirection, the narrative places itself in historical time. Almost by "calculus" and certainly by "three-cushion shots" (as Hemingway variously described his method of disclosure), DiMaggio's Sunday game is confirmed as the event Santiago has read of in his "yesterday's paper."

To consider further the event Santiago "happily" cites to confirm his faith that "the Yankees cannot lose," DiMaggio's Sunday game was spectacular: a single event suitably matching in magnitude Santiago's outsize accomplishment, soon to follow. DiMaggio's stadium-record three home runs all traveled over four hundred feet in the spacious park; and they were, as well, part of a statistically "perfect" game (four at-bats, four hits, four runs, and four runs-batted-in). "The great DiMaggio was himself again," indeed. And in the week starting with this game, the Yankees did win their eighty-fifth victory in the doubleheader Monday, as Santiago expected—and their eighty-sixth as well, with DiMaggio contributing three of the eleven runs his team scored in those two games. DiMaggio went on, for the week as a whole, to hit six home runs in eight games, with a batting average of .467. In that single week, out of thirty at-bats he had fourteen hits, scored fourteen runs, and batted in thirteen runs: Statistically, one player accounted for twenty-seven runs, nearly half of his team's total output of fifty-eight. This was an extraordinary feat, particularly for an "old man" in baseball terms at that time (at thirty-five DiMaggio was one of the older players in the league),

hampered by multiple injuries, and with sportswriters calling for his retire-
ment as they had before his comeback in 1949.

But what matters most for the novel is that when DiMaggio came alive
his personal contributions led his team to win six of its eight games that week,
and emerge in first place a half-game ahead of the Tigers, prepared to grind its
way to an eventual pennant. Not until the end of the novel, when Santiago
wakes up Saturday morning after his own extraordinary performance and reads
"the newspapers of the [days] that [he] was gone" (September 13–15), will he
himself learn more details of his aging fellow champion's resurgence at bat, a
sustained performance matching his own at sea. But during this dialogue on
Tuesday, the day before he sets out on his eighty-fifth attempt to catch a fish,
Santiago has particular reasons for being personally reassured by his knowledge
that "the great DiMaggio" has returned to form, and done so despite a fallow
period associated with a number almost matching that of his current, eighty-
four fishless days. For Santiago has earlier gone eighty-*seven* days without a fish.
And if Santiago's power (his "luck") has earlier returned after eighty-seven days,
it will certainly survive the present hiatus of eighty-four. That DiMaggio has
made dramatic comebacks before (in 1949 especially), and has now followed
with another even more dramatic, is doubly reassuring. To Santiago,
DiMaggio's becoming "himself *again*" (emphasis added) includes the meaning
"*once* again." It means that in champions (like DiMaggio and "*El Campeón*"
Santiago) the mastery that makes them them*selves* will survive the onslaughts of
time, not once but repeatedly—until at last that special quality brings them
"alive" even "with their death in [them]" (as it does the marlin, the Mako shark,
and Santiago himself at the narrative's end). And for this fundamental reason,
the new resurgence by DiMaggio gives Santiago confidence in his next day at
sea, or in an inevitable day of success soon after that—even without the numerical concordances he conceives.

All these specific topical considerations explain why it "means nothing"
that the Yankees have lost a game on the day he speaks. What matters is that a
champion's ability to perform, once operative, is not affected (as another, merely
talented performer's might be) by a lapse of confidence over one day's reverses
(or eighty-seven such reverses), any more than over the realities of physical
decline. For at bottom "what makes the difference" in a champion (and sustains
those on his "team") is an ability, recognized by Colonel Cantwell in *Across the
River and into the Trees*, to make "every day a new and fine illusion"—despite the
disillusionment of many a yesterday. And Santiago himself demonstrates this
capacity as he speaks of faith, numbers, consonances, and luck—all of which has
sounded to hasty readers like superstitious self-deception on his part and may
appear to others as fond condescension on Hemingway's part.

On the contrary, the numerical consonances with DiMaggio's record make up one of several "informed" illusions or ritualized fictions Santiago relies upon, not because he believes in the literal context of the fictions, but because he does believe in a cause that requires him to act without hope of material success. And because he is both proud and humble enough to believe that human beings cannot act without hope of material reward, he finds ways of behaving *as if* he will succeed where he most knows he cannot. Despite his accurately portrayed Cuban fascination with numbers and chance, there is no evidence that Santiago believes, literally, in the cosmic significance of such easily (and obviously) manipulated "sings" as numerological consonances. But there is ample evidence that he does believe in a vital connection among the species, depending on the fully extended behavior of rare individual members—creatures oriented to total commitment, without concern for practical success or personal survival. That is the principle of action Santiago exemplifies as he kills the first shark to attack his fish, hitting it "with *all* his strength . . . *without hope but with resolution*" (emphasis added)—performing *as if* he could, by totally committing his resources, keep all the other sharks now coming from destroying his fish, yet fully aware that he cannot. That informed, sophisticated pretense is a "trick" far more rare and difficult than using the remora; it is a trick of the heart and mind, the "strange" way of seeing that Hemingway respected above all other human accomplishments. It is the hard-won, complex vision required of the thinking "champions" in nature's scheme: the human beings in all walks of life who are able to go "far out beyond all people." Maintaining their efforts by every means necessary against their near-debilitating knowledge of the material cost, they inspire and sustain the human race at their personal expense.

As DiMaggio's team "cannot lose" in its struggle, then, neither will Santiago's team. Santiago's eighty-fifth day at sea, ending *his* slump with *his* record result, will in reality gain something precious, if not a materially tangible trophy, for the team he champions—the human species. For we will find that in his struggle with the great marlin Santiago reaffirms once again, as he has so often before, humanity's necessary connection with nature's order. In portraying the roles of Santiago and DiMaggio in the survival of their groups, therefore, Hemingway stresses in both cases the reliance of the many upon the one. This is a theme not only reinforcing the novel's occasional comparison of Santiago to Christ, but commenting on the relation of all human champions to society.

In addition to the roles of the two champions, there is a larger similarity between the Yankees' overall struggle against the resolute Tigers team of 1950 and the old man's entire struggle against the great marlin and the sharks. It is a similarity making the "September stretch" (the closing weeks) of that year's pennant race a particularly apt demonstration of this novel's most central theme: that in the order of nature intensity equals vitality. The champions of each species featured in the novel act according to a natural principle of perpetual tension, thereby maintaining for the others in their species an attunement with nature. The taut fishing line, kept for two complete rounds of the sun stretched just beneath its breaking point, is an objective correlative of that principle, which is being enacted by the man and marlin at opposite ends of that line. And the contest between the evenly matched Yankees and Tigers of 1950 exemplified that principle. During the week timed with the novel's action the Yankees did not surge ahead with DiMaggio's resurgence, to end the tension and anxiety they had experienced all along. Throughout the week of Santiago's ordeal and well into the next week, the lead edged back and forth repeatedly by grudging half-game increments, the two teams locked in a sustained balance of forces like that of Santiago's twenty-four-hour "hand-game" with the "great negro from Cienfuegos." This arm-wrestling scene from dawn to dawn is the novel's second objective correlative of natural order. It demonstrates as well the human community's vicarious participation in that order, as these two regional champions of two villages enact nature's principle of vital tension before their enthralled spectators in the tavern at Casablanca. Hemingway could hardly have synchronized his narrative with a sustained event in contemporary baseball more felicitously objectifying this principle and the intermediary role of human championship. For in this novel, as in the world's stadiums and arenas, it is not the material quarry but the intensity of the quest that is of ultimate value to the many of us who only watch and wait.

Final evidence of the need to read the baseball allusions more carefully is our neglect of a broad and ironic cultural implication. For Cubans like Manolin and Santiago, baseball is perhaps as central to the consciousness—actually mythic—as it is for Americans in the cornfields of Iowa. It is typically Cuban for Santiago's imagination to embody its special vision of championship not only in lions from his Spanish memories of African voyages, but in a baseball player from the American *Gran Ligas*. When Santiago senses that Manolin is tired of listening to an old man's memories, he says "Go and play baseball," acknowledging the national pastime. But although the American "big show" is a dream of glory for young Cubans like Manolin and his friends, it is essentially an inaccessible dream. Santiago mentions two successful players in the majors, Mike Gonzales and the dazzlingly talented Adolpho Luque, both of whom he, with justification, considers the greatest managers in baseball. Yet they manage in the Cuban winter leagues because, as Barbour and Sattelmeyer observe, "an unwritten law" prevented them from managing in the majors. That this is the point of

Hemingway's reference to these two players becomes even clearer when we discover that the unwritten law was racial, barring Cubans whether of mixed race or not, that Gonzales and Luque were accepted because both, apparently, looked white, and that only two other Cubans—Rafael Almeida and Armando Marsans, also "light-skinned"—ever played in the majors until well after the novel was composed in 1951. There is a cultural commentary, then, as well as archetypal symbolism and artistic symmetry conveyed when Santiago, humbly yet proudly aware of his natural aristocracy, takes DiMaggio's resurgence as a personal omen. For although a young man as talented as today's Hispanic superstars may be playing among Manolin's friends in Cojimar, it is to a fisherman's son from San Francisco that Santiago must look for *El Campeón* of baseball.

Predictably, Spanish and Cuban historical and cultural contexts also interact in this novel, more pervasively; and these further demonstrate the primary role of topicality in specifying relevant symbolism. There is, for example, a profound thematic pattern that we have yet to glory in, because it can only be recognized by readers willing to become familiar either with Spanish history from a Cuban perspective, or Cuban history from a Spanish perspective. Much of the novel is directly or indirectly associated with the Virgin of Cobre. Near Cobre, a small town in southeastern Cuba, is the sanctuary of Our Lady of Charity, a small statue of the Virgin Mary. An image of the Virgin hangs on Santiago's wall, as it does in most Cuban houses; the text implies that his wife may, like many other Cubans, have made a pilgrimage to the shrine and brought back this picture. In 1916, Pope Benedict XV declared the Virgin the principal patroness of Cuba. She is, then, a figure associated with Cuba's national identity. Now according to legend, this statue of the Virgin Mary was floating on a wooden board off the coast of eastern Cuba in 1628, when it was found by two Indians and a Creole in a rowboat. And it is an ancient Spanish legend that the body of Saint James (Santiago) also appeared floating on the sea, in its case already inside a boat, and was found off the coast of Spain, near Compostela, where it was said to have come from the Holy Land, even though the boat had no rudder or sail. Thus the legend of the patroness of Cuba parallels, in the Spanish New World, the far older legend of Santiago in old Spain. And Hemingway has again found in history, this time cultural history, a parallel entirely relevant to his plot. For the New World legend of a mysterious boon, or blessing, discovered at sea, by humble Cubans in a rowboat, looks back to the seaborne gift of Saint James' remains off the coast of Spain, and looks forward to the modern Santiago's discovery—while at sea in a rowboat that loses its tiller—of a "great strangeness," or mystery, at the moment of the marlin's death.

Moreover, the relic, or boon from the sea reposited at Santiago del

Prado, Cuba, at the shrine of the Virgin is regarded as a spiritual endowment to the Cuban people, as the seaborne relics at Santiago de Compostela are regarded as a spiritual gift to Spain. And Santiago, the modern fisherman, brings ashore the skeletal relics of *his* "strange" encounter, skeletal remains that spritually enrich those among the people of modern Cuba who are still capable of appreciating his values and accomplishment. As we will later consider in some detail, Santiago lives in a divided community, a village turning from the craft passion of the old Cuba to a ew materialism. But those supporting national pride and old values are sustained by Santiago's circular sea journey in his wooden boat. Their traditional values will last now, in their hearts, until their next champion, Manolin, reenacts the age-old fertility rite, risking everything to maintain the vital contact between the human community and the mysteries of nature—the contact that preserves the community's sense of wonder, despite the encroaching materialism.

The historical quests contribute, as well, to another formal nicety of the work—a pattern of circles or cycles in the structure of the narrative as a whole. There are the cyclical sea journeys of Santiago's youth, from his native Canary Island to the African beaches, where he experienced an epiphany—a mystical sense of identification with young lions, nature's champions—that recurs in his consciousness throughout the narrative. Later there are the circular sea journey and epiphany of Santiago's old age, now as a Cuban. The repetition brackets his life, making it a circle, and at the same time envelops and makes the plot, about a circular voyage and life, become itself a circle. All of these cycles and circles are there for the reader to associate with the annual, cyclical pilgrimages of the Spanish and the Cuban people—to and from the shrine of Santiago in Spain, to and from the shrine of the Virgin of Cobre in Cuba.

Such historical and cultural parallels as these, together with the Consciousness of North America represented by the baseball allusions, make *The Old Man and the Sea* a Cuban book, then, in far more than setting. In particular, the Spanish-Cuban concordances unify the novel by celebrating those native and European ethnic forces unifying Cuban culture: ethnic bonds that for centuries held together the Hispano-Caribbean tradition disintegrating in modern Cuba. I have no doubt that Hemingway had these cultural parallels (and more) in mind when he donated his Nobel prize medal to the sanctuary of *La Virgen de la Caridad del Cobre*, a Cuban national symbol. It was a medal awarded largely because of this novel. And Hemingway called his offering "a tribute of love to the people of Cuba"—as is Santiago's sacrifice within Hemingway's novel, as is, of course, the book itself. Thus Hemingway's gift of his medal is a crowning artistic touch, a final reticulation, outside his text, of that integration of fiction and history that *is* his text.

We turn now to the most arresting narrative fact disclosed through topical details beyond common knowledge. The novel requires readers (even Cuban readers) to do considerable homework if they are to register the surprising narrative fact that "the boy" Manolin is actually a young man of twenty-two, rather than a child somewhere between twelve and fourteen, as we have supposed. His age is unmistakably, if obliquely, specified by Manolin himself when he compares his family life to that of the American baseball player Dick Sisler. "The great Sisler's father was never poor," he says. "And he, the father, was playing in the Big Leagues when he was my age." When *who* was Manolin's age, Dick Sisler or his hall-of-fame father, George? The answer is that it is the father who was Manolin's age, just as our English, word order-oriented ears prompt us to choose, as we respond to the noun nearest the pronoun. Yet Hurley, the only other commentator to do the research this line requires, has assumed it must be the son, *Dick* Sisler, who was Manolin's age when his father was playing professionally. For the great George Sisler was twenty-two when he began his professional career, and retired when his son Dick was ten. Thus, as Hurley correctly deduces, Manolin must be either at least twenty-two or no more than ten, depending upon how we parse Hemingway's sentence. And because like most of us Hurley cannot immediately think of Manolin as considerably *older* than has been assumed, he understandably asserts that the young fisherman must be ten, somewhat younger than has been assumed.

However, it we continue our investigation even further, alerted by certain apparent implausibilities, we discover that it is a physical impossibility for Manolin to be only ten years old. At the same time, we find that the clues formerly leading readers to think of Manolin as a child are—in the context of the boy's native culture—entirely consistent with young manhood. And finally, we realize that as we think of Manolin as a young adult, other details of the narrative fall into place to form an unsuspected level of socioeconomic comment in the novel.

To take the physical evidence first, surely very few adult readers of either sex can imagine themselves carrying from Santiago's boat to his shack a box the size of a large garbage can, filled with coiled fishing line weighing probably over 150 pounds and at the very least 100 pounds. Yet readers careful enough to work out the weight and size of Santiago's lines are required to think of a boy twelve to fourteen doing just that—while somehow managing to juggle the old man's gaff and harpoon. Accordingly, when such readers *also* become aware that they must choose between ten and twenty-two for Manolin's age, their decision is foregone.

Of course, only readers familiar with the local equipment described can be expected to approximate these formidable dimensions immediately. But the rest of us really should become suspicious enough at some point to check on the extent of the boy's burden, even without having researched the historical evidence restricting his age. For the narrative's description of the line's thickness, composition, and enormous length is so meticulous that it eventually calls attention to itself, tempting us to compile the various specifications challengingly scattered throughout the text. Also, specifications for the lines' total length are given in two sets of figures to mark their importance, as is the evidence of the baseball dates. And when we compile them, we find that the old man carries in his boat 660 fathoms of line. That is just short of 4,000 feet (three-quarters of a mile or thirteen football fields end-to-end) of "coiled, hard-braided brown" line, or "cord" "as thick around as a big pencil" (to all of my consultants a description exactly fitting lines five-sixteenths of an inch in diameter). Called "Catalan *cordel*" in the text, this Spanish line of the period was made of natural, rather than synthetic fiber. For general readers its composition is carefully, if indirectly designated as such: After fishing, the old man takes "the heavy lines home as the dew was bad for them," because natural fibers rot, while synthetics do not. And readers consulting specialists will find that natural-fiber line is heavier than modern synthetics, even synthetics with sufficient specific gravity to sink in salt water, as Santiago's lines do. Specifically, *cordel* was made of a bast fiber, a material still used, although rarely, to make fully comparable lines in the United States. We can therefore learn tht 660 fathoms of any such line—braided and five-sixteenths of an inch in diameter—weighs one-hundred-and-sixty pounds after a portion has been in the water. As the text stresses, these are "heavy lines." And the bulk I mentioned is verified by commercial fishermen who daily use hand-coiled line of this length and diameter.

Philip Young, who did compute the lines' length, suspected out of general common sense that a "young boy" could not carry three-quarters of a mile of heavy line—"unless, as we are not told, the lad was actually a giant." What we are told, or course, is that the lad was actually a powerful young man of twenty-two. And had that disclosure registered on Young, he would not have had to conclude, as he did, that Hemingway must simply have been fudging probability.

Yet to my knowledge only Young, after all, has responded to the careful description of Santiago's lines, worked out their length, and been given sufficient pause at least to comment, however precipitously, on the ostensible implausibility. And the reason, I suspect, is that all of us have been distracted from conceiving of Manolin as full-grown, principally because his subservience to his father's demand that he leave Santiago for another fisherman is convincingly childlike to us, and because the references to him as "the boy" become almost a repetend.

Manolin's unquestioning subservience strikes us differently, however, when considered in the light of Cuban custom, especially at that time. In 1970, Lowry Nelson's socioeconomics study, *Rural Cuba*, described a family patriarchy still modeled on that of feudal Spain and strict to a degree that would not occur to American or European readers. Authority was slowly shifting, in some respects, from the family to the individual and the community. But a son's life, regardless of his age, remained dictated by his father until he married and actually set up housekeeping under a separate roof. This subservience was so complete, for example, that a single man did not, in his father's presence, practice the male ritual of smoking.

And during the period described in the novel there was in Cuba an abundance of such chronologically adult, yet patriarchally controlled men. According to UN demographic statistics, in 1953 (only three years later than the novel's action) 88.1 percent of Cuban males between the ages of fifteen and twenty-four were unmarried, and presumably remained dominated by their fathers. Thus in 1950, Manolin's resigned comment about his father, "I am only a boy and I must obey him," and Santiago's agreement that this is "quite normal" both faithfully represent the Cuban attitude toward a vast majority of young men. As for the term "boy," an illuminating indication of what the word means to Manolin himself is a reminiscence by Marcos Puig the Younger, chief among the young Cubans Hemingway had in mind while portraying Manolin. One day, in 1932, Hemingway had come upon Puig and his father (whom Hemingway named as a model for Santiago) as they were bringing a large marlin alongside their small skiff. And when interviewed later about this encounter with Hemingway, Puig remarked: "I was still a young boy then." He was in fact at least twenty-two. Thus Hemingway's first impression was not of a child, but of a young man exactly the earliest credible age for Manolin of the two possibilities absolutely established by the Sisler allusion. And Puig's reference to himself as "a young boy," despite his chronological age, says much about the attitudes of the fishing villages Hemingway was drawing upon in this novel. I am indebted to Allen Josephs for pointing out, moreover, that another acknowledged local model for Manolin—Manolito, a friend of Hemingway's son Gregory and presumably Gregory's age—was twenty-two when the novel appeared. Santiago, of course, refers to himself as "a boy" when he was a seaman "before the mast" at Manolin's age, hardly plausible for a ten-year-old, we note, but just right for a young man of twenty-two. And this is not surprising, when we remember perhaps the most important point of all: that in Latin America the Spanish word *muchacho*, one of the words for "boy" used in Spanish translations of the novel, applies to young males up to their early twenties, as does—in Spain—the word *chico*, also used in translations of the work.

But even apart from these primary cultural reasons for the appellation in this novel, it is characteristic of Hemingway to use "boy" in its international colloquial sense when referring to young adults in many of his works. In Hemingway's canon generally, in fact, "the boy" refers frequently to a male undergoing the very last stage of initiation into the complexities of adulthood. And that, finally, is at once the social and the mythic significance of Manolin's physical and mental maturity in *The Old Man and the Sea*.

At the social level, Manolin's devotion to Santiago, and his parents' demand that he be apprenticed to a more consistently productive fisherman, reflect a major division in the local economic community. It is a conflict between progress and tradition, between craft passion and exploitation—in short, between the old Cuba and a new Cuba that Hemingway saw emerging in the 1940s. Manolin's father has opted for progress. The fisherman he chooses for his son is a middle-aged man, but his minimally competent, cautious methods yield a steady profit. Thus he is associated with the "younger fishermen" who are motivated only by the money they have been making by supplying shark livers for the booming "cod liver oil" industry in the United States in the 1930s and 1940s. These mechanized fishermen represent the decline of the old Cuban fishing culture and the beginning of an exploitative fishery. Actually, in their use of buoys and floats, they are the precursors of the disastrous "long-line" fishery that spread across the Atlantic immediately after this novel was published, and which threatens, some claim, to render all billfish extinct in all oceans by the year 2000. That is the dire prediction recently urged upon suppliers of fuel for these ships by a forthcoming documentary funded by the American Billfish Foundation. The warning demonstrates Hemingway's prescience in sensing the severe consequences of the practice he singled out for attack.

It is this far-reaching struggle between old and new, between true vocation and market-mindedness, that Manolin's adult status functions most importantly to reveal in the novel. Manolin has obviously been a satisfying character when "read" as an endearingly precocious child, attuned to Santiago's values by innate endowment alone. But when we respond to all of the evidence in the narrative, we recognize a realistically portrayed young acolyte, consciously struggling to maintain an adult compromise between his inborn idealism and a cultural paternalism he accepts (as a man) and yet (as a man) resents. With this in mind we can appreciate what Manolin really means when he says of his father's and his employer's attitudes toward him: "It is as though I were inferior." We have assumed that this is simply a child's chafing at being treated condescendingly. But we make sense of more of the novel when we realize that Manolin's father and employer dismiss his opinions because they think he is a misguided young idealist, foolishly drawn to an impractical, outdated way of life. We have a Cuban version of the American or European Babbitt, convinced that his son has foolishly fallen among priests or artists. And it is for this specific, topical reason that Manolin's father has forced him to work for a man "almost blind," metaphysically as well as physically, by Manolin's and Santiago's vocational standards.

Those standards are high, indeed, because for Santiago and Manolin craft passion reflects a sense of participation in natural order, a participation portrayed in both mythical and religious terms in the novel. The practical men against the idealists become the materialists against the mystics. The myth of the Fisher King is dominant in the novel. And as a young adult, Manolin fits into his role in that myth much more effectively than we have been able to recognize, hampered as we have been by our image of him as a child. For only an adult can be a fully credible Parçifal-figure to Santiago's Fisher King/grail keeper: a pure and potent young knight whose belief rejuvenates the aged master's failing resolution toward the end. Specialists tracing that pattern elsewhere in Hemingway's canon will find that the rejuvenating tyro is always a young adult.

In this novel social interaction shades into myth, then, and thence into religion (and vice versa). Manolin is only one of a circle of young men in the community who are devoted to sustaining Santiago, the pure craftsman, scorned though he may be by the dominant new materialists. The names of this cadre of what might be called political supporters in the community's *ethical* conflict associate them with Christ's *spiritual* disciples: "Perico" and "Pedrico" (both forms of "Peter"); Martin (as in Saint Martin), and so on. The name "Manolin," of course, is a diminuitive of "Manuel," the Spanish form of "Emmanuel," the redeemer. And from the cadre of young adults, the one with this name will assume the secular and spiritual roles of the town's aged Christ-figure, Santiago, who lies dying at the end.

All of these young fishermen are thus identified with the fishers of men. And here Manolin's maturity intensifies the power of yet another set of allusions. There are several parallels to the Gospels of Saint Matthew and Saint Luke that can now be more fully glossed and appreciated as we recognize Manolin as a young man passing into full adulthood. Particularly revealing is the parallel between the novel and Matthew 4:21–22. James is in a boat with his father Zebedee and he and John "leave their father" to follow Christ. These are not children, but men, choosing—exactly as does Manolin at the end—to defy a biological parent and follow a surrogate father, in order to reject a utilitarian mode of fishing—and living—for one with spiritual dimensions.

We should not see a contradiction between Gospel and novel simply because in leaving their father for Christ the disciples seem to be exchanging "old" ways for "new," whereas in the novel the special young men abandon the new for the old. For both Christ and Santiago represent the *truly* "old thing" that informs Pedro Romero's craftmanship in *The Sun Also Rises*: the heightened awareness of participation in nature's mysteries that in *The Old Man and the Sea* is called the "great strangeness." In this regard, Santiago is to Manolin as Montoya (guardian and tutor of that "strangeness" in *The Sun Also Rises*) is to Pedro Romero (who is nineteen and called a "boy").

Had we space here, we could reexamine Manolin's total characterization, and observe that it is uniformly consistent with his maturity. We have, however, seen enough to appreciate some of the dimensions foregrounded by his adult status. And we should ask ourselves why—if those dimensions are important—Hemingway has portrayed Manolin's immediate person and personality so ambiguously that millions of us have been allowed to see him as an early adolescent and be profoundly moved by this restricted response to the novel. Singularly, none of his physical characteristics is described, as Santiago's are; and except for carrying the line, he does or says no one thing that in his culture defines—directly and by itself—either late childhood or early manhood. That is how Hemingway makes our response depend entirely on the way we read the larger contexts we have been observing in the narrative. And here Hemingway has offered different kinds of rewards for different levels of reading. On the one hand—hinting on the cultural ambiguities of "boy" and of Manolin's deference—there is the immediate warmth of some of the most appealing romantic archetypes: Santiago as ancient youth; Manolin as wise child—Wordsworth's "father of the man," another young lion sporting "upon the shore," yet (unlike Wordsworth's child) strange in his sober acceptance of "earthly freight." And against these seductive attractions, profound in themselves, Hemingway offers the darker complexities we have been noticing, appropriately accessible only through an arduous process of explication requiring something of the human qualities affirmed by the novel itself: resolution, tenacity, and an initiate's understanding of the varied communities of interest abounding in the practical world. Indeed, when we respond to the full implications of the narrative, we *become* initiates as we read—in the very process of deriving realities disclosed fragmentally, as they are in life—the process required of us by the works of James and Conrad, two of Hemingway's masters in this particular creation of form as content. Of course, this level of response is the "right" reading aesthetically, because it takes into account much data otherwise inconsistent within the novel. Hemingway's achievement does not support an interpretive indeterminacy valorizing whatever associations the work may prompt in us, nor could the notion be less applicable than it is to the works of this author.

In seeing Manolin as an early adolescent we have been deeply satisfied—but by what amounts to a paranovel, a closely related yet different aesthetic construct we have created out of the mythic content latent in the plot. And our response has screened out the refinement and complexity of the material's darker, more universal implications.

Yet such a restricted response is in no way unique to *The Old Man and the Sea*. In Hemingway's major works we are increasingly revising canonized interpretations that are qualified or radically corrected by newly recognized narrative facts glossed over for decades by readers distracted by his calculated ambiguity. In fact, this "trick," this tour de force of narrative ambiguity, allowing a work to speak with some validity to two or more readerships and to different levels of experience within individual readers, may well be Hemingway's artistic triumph—the best-kept secret of his celebrated iceberg theory. That would certainly explain his refusal to go beyond veiled hints to correct limited readings. And in this novel that ambiguity functions with precision. For social complexity, the very dimension most readily and widely agreed to be neglected in the work as we have usually read it, is exactly what comes to our attention as we recognize Manolin's adult conflict and the underlying opposition between the Virgin and the marketplace in his shore world.

For example, I had assumed, with Friedman, that when compared to *The Bear*, Faulkner's remarkably similar treatment of nature mysticism, *The Old Man and the Sea* failed to cope adequately with the social dimension of human life. In part 4 of *The Bear* social realities convincingly mitigate the glories of Ike's transcendent iconoclasm. Against this, Santiago's supposedly unmixed sublimity has seemed to beg questions about the real conflicts between individualism and human community. However, when we realize the central role of community division in the structure of *The Old Man and the Sea*, we see that the universe of this novel is far from the socially evasive, "cozy" cosmos some have labeled it. "I live in a good town," Santiago says, thinking of his supporters. But the struggle going on there between an old and new Cuba belies all charges of "sentimentality" in the novel's worldview or in Santiago's. The conflict between craft passion and materialism ashore matches the division between noble predators and opportunistic scavengers in the sea integrating the human community into the immemorial natural scheme.

Just as Santiago's opposition by the cowardly scavenger sharks is the additional ordeal he must bear at sea for going "far out" where the greatest marlin are found, so his human opposition—those whose passivity and greed are threatened by his stringent code—is the added burden he has borne on shore for his inflexible honor. Actually, the course of Santiago's recent life and of his impending death are even shown to be determined in part by the intense reaction of other *people* to the values he represents. Thinking Manolin a child, we have not noticed that without his aid the old man would have been unable to continue fishing and find his great marlin. Manolin's parents have not kept him from carrying the lines and arranging many of the charitable donations of food, bait, and services by the old man's other admirers. But it is because his parents' hostility has taken Manolin out of Santiago's boat that the old man undergoes, without the relief that might have saved him, the physical ordeal that ruptures his lungs. "If the boy were here. . . . Yes. If the boy were here. If the boy were here." The invocation has many implications. But one of them is a comment on the human community's discomfort with those rare individuals upon whom the survival of the many depends. In his boat, the taut line from the marlin snubbed over his shoulder, Santiago is "the towing bitt" between the human and the natural worlds. Yet he must bear with that weight the antipathy of the passive majority. Blinded by practical expediency, it fears those who go "beyond all people" to preserve civilization's identification with a world larger than society—the perspective crucial to the sense of wonder that gives human life its color.

Manolin is crying each time he withdraws from Santiago's bedside in the novel's closing scenes, until we leave him quietly watching the old man sleep once more. This time Santiago will dream again of the lions, as he could not upon his return—until reminded by his dialogue with Manolin that they most both act *as if* Santiago would be going out again. For the old man's approaching death, and a champion's commitment to "pull until he dies" as does the great fish, are the true subjects of this dialogue. Thus Manolin's tears are not a child's tears of grief and loss, but of those emotions compounded by adult remorse, as he sees the result of the suffering he has contributed to by accepting social and parental pressures and letting Santiago go out alone. They are also tears of wonder at the final price Santiago has paid for his choice to go out "too far." For it is the price Manolin will someday pay for the choice he now makes—the choice every "boy" makes when he becomes fully a man—to honor the values central to him, whatever the cost. And there is the immediate price. "What will your family say?" Santiago asks. "I do not care," Manolin answers, and with that forgoes his touching attempt to find a considerate compromise between his parents' conventional limitations and his commitment to his high vocation. Santiago's suffering has made him see, bitterly, that the time had already come to go with the old man again. Now it is too late, too late merely to serve; on this day Manolin himself becomes *El Campeón* of the values his parents most scorn. We need not overspecify his thoughts to know that his tears reflect all these considerations during the brief rite of passage into complete manhood we observe in the concluding dialogue with his dying mentor. His grief is part of the champion's burden the old man must at last leave entirely to the young man—as he had the weight of the fishing lines. Having carried those "heavy" lines now becomes symbolic as well as tangible evidence of "the boy's" readiness, as he waits reverently that afternoon tot take up the full burden of championship. He perpetuates a sacrifice older than the torero's, than Christ's, than the Inuit hunter's vow: "I who was born to die shall live that the world of men may touch the world of animals." And it is reenacted in Santiago's very real Cuban village in 1950—as always everywhere—by the few for the many, even the many who scorn their efforts.

Recognizing this human portion of nature's paradoxical scheme in *The Old Man and the Sea* is a good place to begin in combating our persistent tendency to reduce and distort Hemingway's complex portrayals of the human condition. His reliance throughout this novel on a subtly evoked Cuban consciousness so long overlooked should also caution those who proclaim that interpretive criticism of Hemingway's work has run its course. Contemplating the wealth of implication we are directed to construe from the quotidian topicalities of this short novel, we think of Keats's summation of the romantic aesthetic: "Pack every rift with ore." It is unlikely that we have sufficiently explicated any of Hemingway's narratives. He was "a strange old man." "And"—as Santiago reminds us in this work—"There are *many* tricks" (emphasis added).

We can expect new dimensions of Hemingway's artistry to keep surfacing, on and on, as we increasingly acknowledge his modernist method and turn more readily to the library and other sources of information clarifying the narrative facts that govern his metaphors and symbols. We have only to read his works with the attention to topical and historical specificity that he exercised as he wrote.

Chronology

1899   Ernest Miller Hemingway born July 21 in Oak Park, Illinois, the second of six children of Clarence Edmonds Hemingway, MD, and Grace Hall Hemingway, a singer and music teacher.

1900   Begins family visits to Windemere, their summer cottage in northern Michigan.

1905   Enters first grade.

1913   Attends Oak Park and River Forest High School; shows promise as a writer and journalist.

1917   Graduates from Oak Park High School; rejected by U.S. Army for service in World War I because of eye injured in boxing; works as cub reporter for *Kansas City Star.*

1918   Serves in Italy as Red Cross ambulance driver; suffers severe injury to legs under heavy machine gun fire on July 8, two weeks before his nineteenth birthday, near Fossalto di Piave; meets and falls in love with nurse Agnes von Kurowsky while recuperating in Milan. She rejects him as too young.

1919   Returns to United States.

1920–24   Reporter and foreign correspondent for *Toronto Star* and *Star Weekly*.

1921   Marries Hadley Richardson; moves to Paris with letters of introduction from Sherwood Anderson.

1922   Reports on Greek-Turkish war for *Toronto Star*; prose style begins to emerge. Meets Ezra Pound and Gertrude Stein. Hadley loses all Hemingway's unpublished manuscripts on a train.

1923   *Three Stories and Ten Poems*, which includes "Up in Michigan," "Out of Season," and "My Old Man," published in Paris. Goes to Spain for bullfights in Pamplona; returns to Toronto for birth of son, John Hadley (Bumby) in October.

1924   Helps Ford Madox Ford to edit the *transatlantic review*, which publishes "Indian Camp" and other early stories. *in our time*, thirty-two pages, published in Paris.

1925   *In Our Time*, American edition, published by Boni & Liveright; adds fourteen short stories to the earlier vignettes. Hemingway's first American book; introduces semiautobiographical character Nick Adams. Meets and becomes friends with F. Scott Fitzgerald.

1926   Fitzgerald sends him to Scribner's editor Maxwell Perkins. *Torrents of Spring* published in May; *The Sun Also Rises* published in October.

1927   *Men Without Women* published; contains fourteen short stories, including "Hills Like White Elephants" and "The Killers." Divorces Hadley Richardson; marries Pauline Pfeiffer.

1928   Moves to Key West, Florida; son Patrick born. Dr. Clarence Hemingway commits suicide with .32 revolver.

1929   *A Farewell to Arms* published; Hemingway's first commercial success; 80,000 copies sold in first four months.

1931   Son Gregory Hancock born.

1932   *Death in the Afternoon* published.

1933 *Winner Take Nothing*, a collection of fourteen short stories, published. Publishes first of thirty-one articles and stories to appear in *Esquire* during next six years. Goes on safari to Africa.

1935 *Green Hills of Africa* published.

1936–37 Writes, gives speeches, and raises money for Loyalists in Spanish civil war; works on propaganda film *The Spanish Earth*.

1937 *To Have and Have Not* published. Returns to Spain as war correspondent, on Loyalist side, for North American Newspaper Alliance.

1938 *The Fifth Column and the First Forty-Nine Stories* published; contains the play *The Spanish Earth*, the short stories in the three previous collections, and seven previously published stories.

1939 Separates from Pauline Pfeiffer and moves to Finca Vigia, a house near Havana, Cuba.

1940 *For Whom the Bell Tolls*, a best-seller, published. Divorced by Pauline Pfeiffer; marries Martha Gellhorn. Buys house in Cuba, where he lives throughout most of 1940s and 1950s.

1942 Edits and writes introduction for *Men at War*, a collection of war stories. In his boat *Pilar*, hunts for German submarines in Caribbean; finds none.

1942–45 War correspondent in Europe for newspapers and magazines.

1944 Observes D-Day; takes part in Allied liberation of Paris with partisan unit. Begins relationship with news correspondent Mary Welsh. Divorced by Martha Gellhorn in December.

1946 Marries Mary Welsh in March.

1950 *Across the River and Into the Trees* published.

1952 *The Old Man and the Sea* published in its entirety in *Life* magazine on September 1.

1953   Returns to Africa for safari with Mary.

1954   Receives Nobel Prize for Literature; cited for "forceful and style-making mastery of the art of modern narration." In January, severely injured in two separate plane crashes in Africa; reported dead.

1959   Health declining; follows bullfights in Spain where he observes sixtieth birthday.

1960   Returns to United States and settles in Ketchum, Idaho.

1961   Undergoes electroshock treatment for depression. Dies of self-inflicted gunshot wound July 2, in Ketchum home. Buried in Sun Valley, Idaho.

1964   *A Moveable Feast* published.

1970   *Islands in the Stream* published.

1972   *The Nick Adams Stories* collected in one volume; includes previously unpublished stories and fragments.

1981   *Ernest Hemingway: Selected Letters*, edited by Carlos Baker, published.

1985   *The Dangerous Summer* and *Dateline Toronto: The Complete Toronto Star Dispatches*, 1920–24, published.

1986   *The Garden of Eden*, Hemingway's last manuscript, heavily edited and rearranged, published.

1987   *The Complete Short Stories of Ernest Hemingway* published.

Contributors

HAROLD BLOOM is Sterling Professor of Humanities at Yale University and Professor of English at New York University. His works include *Shelley's Mythmaking* (1959), *The Visionary Company* (1961), *The Anxiety of Influence* (1973), *Agon: Towards a Theory of Revisionism* (1982), *The Book of J* (1990), *The American Religion* (1992), and *The Western Canon* (1994). His forthcoming books are a study of Shakespeare and *Freud, Transference and Authority*, which considers all of Freud's major writings. A MacArthur Prize Fellow, Professor Bloom is the editor of more than thirty anthologies and general editor of five series of literary criticism published by Chelsea House.

WILLIAM FAULKNER (1897–1962) was author of many novels and stories, including *The Sound and the Fury* (1929), *As I Lay Dying* (1930), *Light in August* (1932), *Absalom! Absalom!* (1936). He won the 1950 Nobel Prize for Literature.

CARLOS BAKER (1909–1987) was Professor of English at Princeton University and author of *Hemingway and His Critics* (1961), and *Hemingway, the Writer as Artist* (1956), a study of Shelley's poetry and two novels, and editor of *Ernest Hemingway, Selected Letters* (1981). *Emerson Among the Eccentrics* was published in 1996.

LEO GURKO is author of *Ernest Hemingway and the Pursuit of Heroism* (1968), *Joseph Conrad, Giant in Exile* (1962), and *Heroes, Highbrows, and the Popular Mind* (1953).

DELMORE SCHWARTZ (1913–1966) was a poet, critic, and short story writer whose works are collected in *Delmore Schwartz and James Laughlin: Selected Letters* (1993), *Last and Lost Poems of Delmore Schwartz* (1979), *In Dreams Begin Responsibilities and Other Stories* (1978), and *Selected Essays of Delmore Schwartz* (1970).

JOSEPH WALDMEIR has published many articles and essays on modern fiction. He is author of *Miss Tina Did It: and Other Fresh Looks at Modern Fiction* (1997), co-editor of *Hemingway: Up in Michigan Perspectives* (1995), and editor of *Critical Essays on John Barth* (1980).

NEMI D'AGOSTINO (1924–1992) was professor of English literature at the University of Trieste and author of critical volumes on Herman Melville, Ezra Pound, and William Shakespeare.

CLINTON S. BURHANS JR. is author of *The Would-Be Writer* (1966) and essays on Hemingway, Twain, Hawthorne, and Sidney.

ROBERT P. WEEKS was Professor of English at the College of Engineering, University of Michigan and is author of *Hemingway*, in the 20th Century Visions series (1962). His articles have appeared in scholarly journals, *Harper's*, and *The Nation*.

BICKFORD SYLVESTER is Associate Professor of English at the University of British Columbia. He has published essays on Shakespeare, Marvell, Wordsworth, and Hemingway.

PHILIP YOUNG is author of *Hawthorne's Secret* (1984), *Revolutionary Ladies* (1977), *Three Bags Full: Essays in American Fiction* (1972), and editor of *The Hemingway Manuscripts; an Inventory* (1969).

CLAIRE ROSENFIELD has taught at the Radcliffe Institute for Independent Studies, the University of Texas, and Rutgers University, and has been a Fellow at the Center for Advanced Study in the Behavioral Sciences. Her works include *Paradise of Snakes: An Archetypal Analysis of Conrad's Political Novels* (1967) and essays published in *Daedalus, Literature and Psychology*, and *Psychiatry and Social Science*.

SHELDON NORMAN GREBSTEIN is Professor of English and Director of Graduate English Studies at the State University of New York, Binghamton. The author of many articles and book reviews, his works include

Sinclair Lewis (1962) and *John O'Hara* (1968). He is editor of *Perspectives in Contemporary Criticism* (1968).

LINDA W. WAGNER is author of many books, articles and essays on American writers and poets. She is editor of *T.S. Eliot: A Collection of Criticism* (1974) and her published works include *The Poems of William Carlos Williams, a Critical Study* (1964), *Critical Essays on Joyce Carol Oates* (1979), *American Modern: Essays in Fiction and Poetry* (1980), and several volumes of poetry.

G.R. WILSON JR. is Professor of English and Associate Dean of Arts and Sciences at the University of South Alabama. He has published articles on Chaucer, Donne, Melville, and Faulkner, among others, in journals such as *Studies in English Literature.*

JAMES H. JUSTUS is Professor of English at Indiana University. He has written on American authors Charles Brockden Brown, Nathaniel Hawthorne, Kate Chopin, William Faulkner, and other writers of the American South. His works include *The Achievement of Robert Penn Warren* (1981).

GERRY BRENNER is author and editor of several books on the works of Ernest Hemingway, including *The Old Man and the Sea: Story of a Common Man* (1991).

DAVID TIMMS is Lecturer in English and American Literature at the University of Kent at Canterbury. He is editor of several critical volumes, including *Herman Melville: Reassessments* (1984), *Edgar Allan Poe: the Design of Order* (1986), *Scott Fitzgerald: The Promises of Life* (1989), *Writing and America* (1996), and he is author of *Black American Fiction Since Richard Wright* (1983).

Bibliography

Baker, Carlos. *Hemingway: The Writer as Artist*. 1952. 2nd edition. Princeton: Princeton University Press, 1956.

Barbour, James and Robert Sattelmeyer. "Baseball and Baseball Talk in *The Old Man and the Sea*," *Fitzgerald / Hemingway Annual 1975*, 281–87.

Benson, Jackson J. *Hemingway: The Writer's Art of Self-Defense*. Minneapolis: University of Minnesota Press, 1969.

Bradford, M. "On the Importance of Discovering God: Faulkner and Hemingway's *The Old Man and the Sea*," *Mississippi Quarterly* 20 (1967): 158–62.

Donaldson, Scott. *By Force of Will: The Life and Art of Ernest Hemingway*. New York: Viking, 1977.

———. "The Case of the Vanishing American and Other Puzzlements in Hemingway's Fiction," *Hemingway Notes* 6 (Spring 1981): 16–19.

Flora, Joseph M. "Biblical Allusion in *The Old Man and the Sea*," *Studies in Short Fiction* 10 (1973): 143–47.

Fuentes, Norberto. *Hemingway in Cuba*. New York: Carol, 1984.

Hemingway, Ernest. *The Old Man and the Sea*. New York: Scribner's, 1952.

Hurley, C. Harold. *Hemingway's Debt to Baseball in The Old Man and the Sea: A Collection of Critical Readings*. Lewiston, NY: Mellen, 1992.

Johnston, Kenneth. "The Star in Hemingway's *The Old Man and the Sea*," *American Literature* 42 (1970): 388–91.

Laurence, Frank M. *Hemingway and the Movies*. Jackson: University Press of Mississippi, 1981.

Mansell, Darrel. "Why Did Ernest Hemingway Write *The Old Man and the Sea*?" *Fitzgerald and Hemingway Annual* (1975): 311–24.

Monteiro, George. "Santiago, DiMaggio, and Hemingway: the Ageing Professionals of *The Old Man and the Sea*," *Fitzgerald / Hemingway Annual 1974*, 273–80.

———. "The Reds, The White Sox and *The Old Man and the Sea*," *Notes on Contemporary Literature* 4:3 (1974): 7–9.

Nagel, James, ed. *Ernest Hemingway: The Writer in Context*. Madison: University of Wisconsin Press, 1984.

Scafella, Frank, ed. *Hemingway: Essays of Reassessment*. New York: Oxford University Press, 1991.

O'Faolain, Sean. "Ernest Hemingway," *The Vanishing Hero*. Boston: Atlantic Monthly Press, 1957. 112–45.

Stoneback, H.R. "Hemingway's Extended Vision: *The Old Man and the Sea, PMLA* 81 (1966): 130–38.

———. "'They Went Through This Fiction Every Day': Informed Illusion in *The Old Man and the Sea*," *Modern Fiction Studies* 12 (1966–67): 473–76.

Sylvester, Bickford. "Hemingway's Extended Vision: *The Old Man and the Sea*," *PMLA* 81 (1966): 130–38.

Waldmeir, Joseph J. "And the Wench is Faith and Value," *Studies in Short Fiction* 24:4 (Fall 1987): 393–98.

Waldron, Edward. " 'The Pearl' and *The Old Man and the Sea*," *Steinbeck Quarterly* 13 (1980): 98–106.

Williams, Wirt. *The Tragic Art of Ernest Hemingway*. Baton Rouge: Louisiana State University Press, 1981.

Wilson, G.R. "Incarnation and Redemption in *The Old Man and the Sea*," *Studies in Short Fiction* 14:4 (Fall 1977): 369–73.

Acknowledgments

Review of *The Old Man and the Sea* by William Faulkner from *Shenandoah* 3 (Autumn 1952): 55, and from *Essays, Speeches and Public Letters* (1952) by William Faulkner, edited by James B. Meriwether, reprinted in *Ernest Hemingway: Six Decades of Criticism* by Linda W. Wagner. Copyright © 1987 by Linda W. Wagner.

"The Boy and the Lions" by Carlos Baker, section III of chapter XII, "The Ancient Mariner" in *Hemingway: The Writer as Artist*, 3rd edition, by Carlos Baker. Reprinted in *Twentieth Century Interpretations of The Old Man and the Sea*, edited by Katharine T. Jobes. Copyright © 1952 by Carlos Baker.

"The Heroic Impulse in *The Old Man and the Sea*" by Leo Gurko from *English Journal* XLIV (October 1955): 377–82, and *College English* XVII (October 1955): 11–15. Reprinted in *Twentieth Century Interpretations of The Old Man and the Sea*, edited by Katharine T. Jobes. Copyright © 1955 by the National Council of Teachers of English.

"*The Old Man and the Sea* and the American Dream" by Delmore Schwartz from "The Fiction of Ernest Hemingway: Moral Historian of the American Dream" in *Perspectives USA* 13 (Autumn 1955): 82–88. Titled and reprinted in *Twentieth Century Interpretations of The Old Man and the Sea*, edited by Katharine T. Jobes. Copyright © 1955 by Intercultural Publications, Inc.

"Confiteor Hominem: Ernest Hemingway's Religion of Man" by Joseph Waldmeir from *PMASAL* XLII (1956): 277–81. Reprinted in *Twentieth Century Views: Hemingway*, edited by Robert P. Weeks. Copyright © The University of Michigan Press.

"The Later Hemingway" by Nemi D'Agostino, translated by Barbara Arnett Melchiori, from *The Sewanee Review* LXVIII (Summer 1960): 482–93. Reprinted in *Twentieth Century Views: Hemingway*, edited by Robert P. Weeks. Copyright © 1960 by The University of the South.

"*The Old Man and the Sea*: Hemingway's Tragic Vision of Man" by Clinton S. Burhans Jr., from *American Literature* XXXI (January 1960): 446–55. Reprinted in *Twentieth Century Interpretations of The Old Man and the Sea*, edited by Katharine T. Jobes. Copyright © 1960 by Duke University Press.

"Fakery in *The Old Man and the Sea*" by Robert P. Weeks from *College English* 24 (1962): 188–92. Copyright © 1962 by the National Council of Teachers of English.

"Hemingway's Extended Vision: *The Old Man and the Sea*" by Bickford Sylvester from *PMLA* 81 (1966): 130–38. Copyright © 1966 by Modern Language Association.

"*The Old Man and the Sea*: Vision/Revision" by Philip Young from Chapter 3, "Death and Transfiguration," and II from the "Afterword" of *Ernest Hemingway: A Reconsideration* by Philip Young. Reprinted in *Twentieth Century Interpretations of The Old Man and the Sea*, edited by Katharine T. Jobes. Copyright © 1966 by Philip Young.

"New World, Old Myths" by Claire Rosenfield from *Twentieth Century Interpretations of The Old Man and the Sea*, edited by Katharine T. Jobes. Copyright © 1968 by Claire Rosenfield.

"Hemingway's Craft in *The Old Man and the Sea*" by Sheldon Norman Grebstein from *The Fifties: Fiction, Poetry, Drama*. edited by Warren French. Copyright © 1970 by Warren French.

"The Poem of Santiago and Manolin" by Linda W. Wagner from *Modern Fiction Studies* 19:4 (Winter 1973–74): 517–30, reprinted in *Ernest Hemingway: Six Decades of Criticism*, edited by Linda W. Wagner. Copyright © 1987 by Linda W. Wagner.

"Incarnation and Redemption in *The Old Man and the Sea*" by G.R. Wilson Jr. from *Studies in Short Fiction* 14:4 (Fall 1977): 369–73. Copyright © 1977 by Newberry College.

"The Later Fiction: Hemingway and the Aesthetics of Failure" by James H. Justus from *Ernest Hemingway: New Critical Essays*, edited by A. Robert Lee. Copyright © 1983 by Vision Press Ltd.

"A Not-So-Strange Old Man: *The Old Man and the Sea*" by Gerry Brenner from *Concealments in Hemingway's Works* by Gerry Brenner. Copyright © 1983 by the Ohio State University Press.

Index